New York

Megacities

Series Editor: H. V. Savitch

As drivers of economic growth, demographic change and consumption hyper-conurbations offer unique opportunities to their hinterlands and national economies, as well as huge challenges of governance, planning and provisioning. Each book in this series examines the political and economic development of a specific megacity and explores how and why they have evolved and how policy decisions, couched in geopolitics, have shaped their outcomes. The series covers both paradigmatic mature megacities of the developed world, as well as the fast-growing emerging megacities of South and East Asia, and Latin America.

Published

London
Mike Raco and Frances Brill

Mexico City
Martha Schteingart, Jaime Sobrino and Vicente Ugalde

New York
Jill S. Gross and H. V. Savitch

Paris
Christian Lefèvre

New York

Jill S. Gross and H. V. Savitch

agenda
publishing

Dedicated to our students, past, present and future.

© Jill S. Gross and H. V. Savitch 2023

First published in 2023 by Agenda Publishing

Agenda Publishing Limited
The Core
Bath Lane
Newcastle Helix
Newcastle upon Tyne
NE4 5TF
www.agendapub.com

ISBN 978-1-78821-203-8 (hardcover)
ISBN 978-1-78821-204-5 (paperback)

British Library Cataloguing-in-Publication Data
A catalogue record for this book is available from the British Library

Typeset by Newgen Publishing UK
Printed and bound in the UK by CPI Group (UK) Ltd, Croydon, CR0 4YY

Contents

Preface and acknowledgements

Alison Howson was first to broach the idea of doing a series on the world's megacities. We took to it immediately and with enthusiasm. Both of us had been familiar with the world's great cities from both scholarly and personal experience. The promise of doing original work on New York sparked our imaginations. It is, after all, an ideal example of a megacity. Its five counties (boroughs) cover a land mass of more than 200 square miles, and its population of more than eight million people and its high densities make for one of the largest and most packed cities on the planet. In reflecting further, we noted that New York was filled with seeming contradictions. Travelling each day along a vast web of highways, airports and rail can be either surprisingly easy or painfully slow. The New York megacity is immensely rich and deeply impoverished. Its culture and people are steeped in kindness, yet renowned to be rude. It is not the contradictions themselves that pose the issue, but New York's size and diversity that provide the space and opportunity for an immensity of contrasts.

From a strictly formal point of view New York City falls just short of the ten million residents needed to constitute a megacity. We are, however, saved from this criterion by the reality of a Greater New York, whose population reaches 15 million. The day-to-day routines of the larger metropolis cross political boundaries with hardly a thought about who is doing business where. Commuters freely travel throughout the region for commerce, to visit friends or to see the sights. For this reason we have set our focus on a reachable New York metropolis that stretches across 13 counties.[1] This is the New York in which most people work, play and fight over.

---

1. For this reason there are multiple definitions of the New York region that cover small urban settlements to much larger urban agglomerations. Some of these are categorized as metropolitan statistical areas (MSAs), consolidated metropolitan statistical areas (CMSAs) or primary metropolitan statistical areas (PMSAs).

Why might it be important to write about this megacity? Firstly, context counts and "the city" itself exists in a greater environment of suburbs, other municipalities, special districts and state governance. The policies of surrounding localities have a profound effect on the city, whether they are related to exclusionary zoning or enormous traffic; both of which respectively have driven up housing affordability and hurt quality of life. A major source of New York's water supply is located about 40 miles beyond its northern boundary. Only a view of the larger New York can capture essential variables and provide context.

Secondly, we might want to know whether size really matters. Once a city reaches gargantuan proportions, the city's functions reflexively enlarge, its conflicts become supercharged and its policies drift into greater complexity. Thus, we see a profusion of public authorities (public benefit corporations) trying to knit together different parts of the metropolis. We also witness the volatility of the region's politics and occasional outbursts of collective violence. It takes smart and practical policies to help the megacity manage growth, and we take note of how its many parts interact. We explore how the megacity deals with problems of this sort, either collectively or through its individual parts.

Lastly, the mere existence of the New York megacity gives all cities a glimpse of their future. Many cities around the world grow every day by increments, without knowing where they could wind up. If this is where New York is today, are other big cities likely to follow? Somehow institutions, practices and policies need to accommodate growth. Whether cities do this in the "New York" style by increments or by a grand, comprehensive design is for each metropolis to decide. New York has been especially good at managing some crises – issues that come to mind are its ability to cope with weather disasters and deal with epidemics. Over the years the New York megacity has enlarged its functions and this should stoke the curiosity of other growing regions.

We trust the experience of the New York megacity will put these issues into perspective. This book is a venture in exploring critical questions. It begins with an overview of megacity complexities and introduces a framework used to analyze why tensions and crises arise, how they are coped with and whether the megacity is effective in managing them. We use critical events to demonstrate our propositions, ranging from the megacity's corporate development to its expanded governance and down to its changing neighbourhoods. We also examine how it functions as a "global city" in a competitive world. Finally, we end with a series of findings about the New York megacity and offer a number of "axioms" about its long-term resilience.

It takes a lifetime to appreciate the complexities of a great city, and even then we scratch at surfaces. We are so very privileged to be able to thank colleagues, friends and family for nurturing that experience. Hank Savitch is greatly indebted to his colleagues at Urban and Public Affairs at the University of Louisville. Ron Vogel, Steve Bourassa, Dave Simpson and David Imbroscio were superb friends and critics. Herman Boschken (San Jose State University) and Ron Vogel (Ryerson University, Canada) were immensely helpful when it came to treating New York in a global context. A raft of former students, many of whom have distinguished themselves, provided a much-valued context. Among these were David Collins, Grigoriy Ardashev, Kevin Dupont, Jeff Osborne, Lin Ye, Anar Valiyev, Ismaila Odogba, Lynn Roche-Phillips, Eric Yankson and Doddy Iskandar.

Jill S. Gross has had a front row seat to the evolving New York megacity story, having had the great fortune to live and work there for most of her life. The politics and development of the megacity have served as inspiration and influence for her research, writing and teaching. She is grateful for the support she has received from her colleagues in the Department of Urban Policy and Planning at Hunter College of the City University of New York, whose combined historic knowledge, cutting-edge research and contemporary hands-on experience in policy and planning for this great city have been invaluable. Her extended academic community in the US and abroad and at the Urban Affairs Association have also proved critical for this project. Her students are a constant source of inspiration, experiential knowledge, and enthusiasm about where this megacity has come from and what the future holds. The direct contributions of research assistant Erica Saunders, and Charles Rudoy for his case study materials on the New Jersey Gateway region, are so appreciated.

Family means everything. Susan Savitch captured Hank's heart more than 60 years ago and holds it to this day. With patience and love she has encouraged this work. Adam and Jonathan Savitch frequently wondered whether their dad might be writing the same book more than a dozen times. They were assured this was not the case. Jennifer Savitch was always positive and so very generous. Adam Savitch and Steven Salzgeber were always there to help. They were indispensable in producing new illustrations and rescuing old ones. Grandsons Luke and Ethan always cast a presence with their love.

Jill has had the amazing support of her husband Michael Marks, whom she describes as her rock, providing practical, emotional and intellectual support. He has listened to each story, provided some of his own, and most importantly – made sure she ate, slept and occasionally left her computer during the extended writing process. Her mother Diane Merzon, father Jack Gross and siblings Andrew and Ari Gross have served as her cheering section, as has her extended family Hildy, Marty, Scott and Peter Krull, Elizabeth Disney and Debby Gross. Close friends cannot be discounted, and two have been critical to all, Karen Schwartz and Gallya Lahav, who have served as sounding boards to this story, offering sage advice and encouragement throughout. Most importantly, it has been a great honour for Jill to work with one of her academic inspirations,

Hank Savitch. Having the opportunity to collaborate with him on this project has been among the great joys of her professional life.

Finally, Hank extends his appreciation to colleagues at Urban and Regional Planning at Florida Atlantic University. John Renne, Serena Hoermann and Louis Merlin continue to be good friends and office mates – through and beyond the pandemic.

Last but hardly least, we thank the editors and publishers at Agenda Publishing. Alison Howson possesses the rare qualities of kindness, curiosity, diligence and skill. It was always a pleasure to work with her. Steven Gerrard was always a help and a stalwart professional. We are indebted to them.

1

Introduction: New York as a megacity

A megacity is a giant city whose urban core and surrounding localities hold ten million or more people. As a practical matter, megacities vary from country to country, but one common trait is its gigantism, stemming from its population, its economy, its governance, its geography and its social makeup. Megacities may be called metropolises (America), agglomerations (Europe) regions (China) or the "Greater" city (as in "Greater London"). This identification touches only the surface of what a megacity is about. The megacity's gargantuan dimensions include the magnitude of its society and its built environment, the extensiveness of its commerce, the scope of its policies and the complexity of its operations. Added up, the sheer weight of the megacity exerts a prodigious influence on the nation and sometimes on the world.

Not all megacities are able to merge these qualities into a synergistic whole, but New York amply succeeds. New York's City's population alone holds 8.3 million – add more than 7 million in its near suburbs and we have a composite of 15 million people, sitting on more than 4,000 square miles of land (Statista 2019; US Census Bureau 2020b). The New York megacity holds more people than modestly sized but important nations such as Belgium, Israel, Sweden or Greece. Its land mass is about the same size as South Korea or the Netherlands. Its gross metropolitan product (GMP) of more than $1.53 trillion surpasses the gross national product of most nations of the world, and its economic influence reverberates across continents. Much as New York's prosperity continues to buoy markets abroad, its fiscal collapse in 1975 and later in 2008, sent shock waves through the most advanced economies of Europe, Asia and the Americas. Clearly, New York's fate goes well beyond its region. Although it is too much to claim that where New York goes others are sure to follow, this particular megacity has a global reach.

Change and its cycles

The history of the New York megacity is laced with threats to its viability, but remarkably and strongly it has always come back. As we see it, the core questions rest on how does a megacity, like New York, manage that comeback? What are the strengths and weaknesses that support or hinder its recovery? A corollary question pertains to what best explains the megacity's adaptation to its gravest predicaments and what does that adaptation look like? New York has always faced threats of one sort or another, so much so that we have come to view crises as endemic to its very nature. After all, crises are an integral part of the megacity's hyper-capitalism, and they continually shape its economy, its social structure and its direction of change. Finally, we add that the processes by which the megacity manages change are slow, incremental and take place among a swirl of competing politics. This too is part of megacity pluralism and democratic politics.

Towards examining these issues, we offer a framework based on cycles of change that is driven by key factors of: (1) *growth*, largely, although not exclusively, economic; (2) *tensions or crises* that stem from that growth; and (3) *adaptation* to manage those tensions in the form of policy initiatives. By the term "growth", we refer to the megacity's own capacity to leverage enormous investments and snowball them into multiple permutations. Megacity growth is based upon "economies of agglomeration", in which the clustering of business, people and infrastructure can create advantages that feed into and build upon one another in circular patterns of causation. Growth can create wealth, but it also can produce profound social tensions and, sometimes, much deeper endemic crises. Growth occurs within a structural context and is layered upon a deep institutional history, which shapes the course and content of events.

Tensions can best be defined as deeply seated pressures either between social classes or between social classes and political elites. Most of the time these tensions are limited or contained within specific communities. There are times, however, when existing conditions worsen and spread through the larger order. The upshot: crises that can morph into system-wide breakdown.[1] Before that breakdown occurs, successful cities will go through a process of political *adaptation*, which seeks to ameliorate or in some way dispose of those tensions. Governmental policies, programmes, plans or bureaucratic practices are typically designed to do this. We lay out this picture in broad brushstrokes, but then dig into these cycles of growth, leadership and socio-spatial change

---

1. As we shall see, there is more than one path to a crisis. Some crises arrive abruptly and can come as a complete surprise. Often, abrupt crises are externally imposed as in a terrorist attack (9/11) or as part of a severe weather event (superstorm Sandy).

in more detail in the chapters to follow. Figure 1.1 below shows the New York megacity as going through cycles of growth, tensions/crises and adaptation.

Several caveats are in order when analysing this figure. First, the examples are not meant to be exhaustive, but to illustrate some basic points. Second, descriptions within each of the cycles are generalized and do not always match one another in a one-to-one correspondence. And third, illustrations within the cycle of adaptation may or may not be successful nor even necessarily desirable. They are simply descriptions of events and efforts at adaptation.

In the chapters that follow we employ the megacity cycle to elucidate the "boom and bust" features of the economy, property markets, housing, neighbourhoods and government. We see this as a useful framework for both describing the New York megacity and explaining fundamental aspects (see Mapping the Book at the end of this chapter).

The simplest illustration of growth, crises and adaptation can be found in New York's real estate market. The boom and busts of land-use markets lie at the core megacity politics. New York's property boom began at the turn of the millennium and gathered steam through its second decade. Massive investment, rehabilitation and new construction brought a burgeoning middle class into once blue collar, industrial neighbourhoods. In Manhattan, the Lower East Side and SoHo saw the conversion of old tenements and warehouses initially into affordable working spaces for artists, then into fancy studios and loft apartments. In Brooklyn, old neighbourhoods such as Vinegar Hill, Red Hook

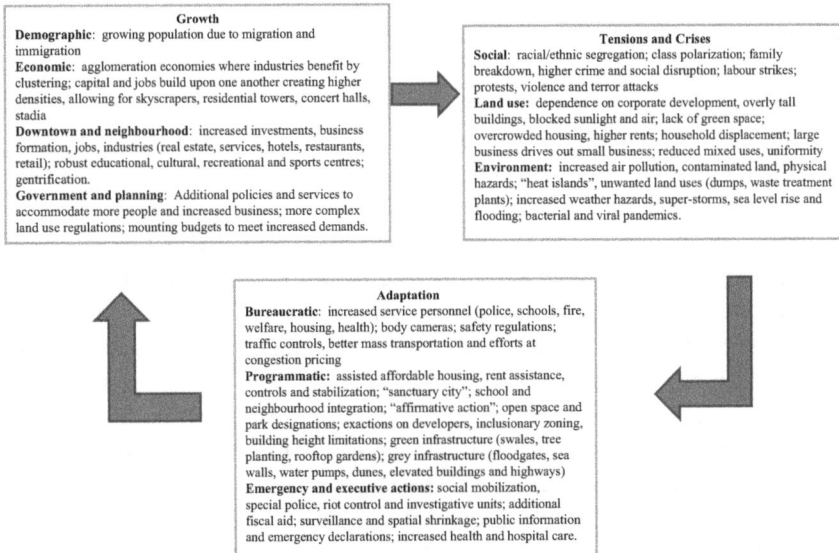

Growth
Demographic: growing population due to migration and immigration
Economic: agglomeration economies where industries benefit by clustering; capital and jobs build upon one another creating higher densities, allowing for skyscrapers, residential towers, concert halls, stadia
Downtown and neighbourhood: increased investments, business formation, jobs, industries (real estate, services, hotels, restaurants, retail); robust educational, cultural, recreational and sports centres; gentrification.
Government and planning: Additional policies and services to accommodate more people and increased business; more complex land use regulations; mounting budgets to meet increased demands.

Tensions and Crises
Social: racial/ethnic segregation; class polarization; family breakdown, higher crime and social disruption; labour strikes; protests, violence and terror attacks
Land use: dependence on corporate development, overly tall buildings, blocked sunlight and air; lack of green space; overcrowded housing, higher rents; household displacement; large business drives out small business; reduced mixed uses, uniformity
Environment: increased air pollution, contaminated land, physical hazards; "heat islands", unwanted land uses (dumps, waste treatment plants); increased weather hazards, super-storms, sea level rise and flooding; bacterial and viral pandemics.

Adaptation
Bureaucratic: increased service personnel (police, schools, fire, welfare, housing, health); body cameras; safety regulations; traffic controls, better mass transportation and efforts at congestion pricing
Programmatic: assisted affordable housing, rent assistance, controls and stabilization; "sanctuary city"; school and neighbourhood integration; "affirmative action"; open space and park designations; exactions on developers, inclusionary zoning, building height limitations; green infrastructure (swales, tree planting, rooftop gardens); grey infrastructure (floodgates, sea walls, water pumps, dunes, elevated buildings and highways)
Emergency and executive actions: social mobilization, special police, riot control and investigative units; additional fiscal aid; surveillance and spatial shrinkage; public information and emergency declarations; increased health and hospital care.

Figure 1.1 The New York megacity's cycles of change: growth, tension/crises and adaptation.

and Williamsburg followed a similar process and became rapidly gentrified. In the Bronx, Fordham Road renewed itself with new businesses. Even well-settled middle-class areas in Flushing, Queens and Staten Island have experienced waves of investment and increased population. Moving outwards to nearby communities across the Hudson River in New Jersey, areas such as Jersey City, Hoboken and, to a lesser extent, Newark have benefitted from the talents of new immigration, increased investment and proximity to the urban core. To the north, Westchester and its affluent towns such as New Rochelle, Scarsdale and Tarrytown have swelled their already steep housing prices and today face pressures to accommodate new populations. Much the same dynamic has occurred in Nassau and Suffolk counties, whose towns typify the Levittown image of suburban prosperity, although with an increasingly diverse ethnic population once prevented from settling here through exclusionary zoning and steering. Only time will tell whether the Covid-19 pandemic will put a deathly clamp on this dynamic and change the megacity paradigm.

Even without the Covid-19 pandemic, growth engenders problems and consequent tensions. Housing has become less affordable for the low income and middle classes, with rental and purchasing costs mounting every year. Maintaining a home is the most significant expense incurred by New Yorkers and by 2019 it consumed over 32 per cent of a typical household's income (Stringer 2019). More than half of New Yorkers are considered "rent burdened", spending more than 32 per cent of their income on housing. Another quarter of the city's population are "severely rent burdened", obliged to spend more than half of its income on housing (City of New York 2019: 25). The pattern is mirrored across the metropolis, with 45–50 per cent of renters in the counties surrounding the core spending between 30 and 50 per cent of their income on housing (US Census Bureau 2018b).

Growth has brought the positive effects of gentrification, enabling new households and businesses to settle in old neighbourhoods, increasing opportunities for consumers and brightening once grey streets with fresh investment. Nevertheless, there are also negatives in the form of displacement for those who can no longer afford to live in improved neighbourhoods and boosting rents for hard-pressed tenants determined to stay in the "old neighbourhood". Moreover, the necessity of accommodating a better-educated labour force to fuel the economy of the megacity requires a host of different and high-quality social amenities such as running tracks, bicycle paths, scenic sites and street festivals – all of which weigh on local budgets. At a different end of the cost scale, areas where immigrants have settled necessitate bilingual education, health, economic development and social services. Altogether, costs climb for the region's localities, with the highest expenditures made for human-intensive services such as education, public safety (police, fire) and social services (DiNapoli 2018: 11).

More deeply, social divisions intensified both within and immediately outside the city. These settlement patterns have meant that, although the megacity may be among the most diverse, by any number of indices it is also among the most socially and economically segregated in the nation. Thus, black and Hispanic residents are not only clustered in their respective neighbourhood spaces but they experience less exposure to other groups and their daily activities are carried out in greater isolation from other groups (Brown University 2010; Kucsera & Orfield 2014).

On top of this, the relationship between New York City and its suburbs has become more complicated, especially as congestion and traffic grow in what seems to be exponential proportions. Indeed, although the megacity region, in principle, represents a shared-commons, its diverse stakeholders often find themselves engaged in a complex political dance, at times leading to conflict and at other times entailing cooperative governance (Gross & Nelles 2018).

There is another side to megacity power, and that is its structural vulnerability to different kinds of externally generated perils. The spread of Covid-19 in early spring 2020 is only one in a series of sporadic but severe attacks, each of which has had profound long-term consequences. In the last 20 years, the terror attacks of 9/11 in 2001, the fiscal crisis of 2008 and superstorm Sandy of 2012 have struck the city – all of which were driven by what was commonly thought to be megacity strengths, namely its high population, its elevated density, its concentrated financial infrastructure and its thorough internationalization. Although these have always been regarded as positive factors to be emulated by other cities, events have shown they can also become serious negatives – at times used against the city to bring about its collapse or paralysis. It falls to politics and policy outputs to attempt to ameliorate, if not partially resolve mounting tensions and crises.

Every stride towards growth or change produces its own challenges of change. Rent control and rent stabilization have always been a city mandate but are now more pressing than ever as real-estate values continue to rise. Expensive housing for blue collar families and a rising middle class have led to demands for "inclusionary zoning" and more "affordable housing", often putting needy populations (and city officials) into conflict with other residents and developers. Drug-induced crime, such as the crack cocaine epidemic of the late 1980s, led to a demand for safe streets, which, in turn, gave birth to more aggressive policing, often putting minority populations in conflict with police.

Education has always been an important public responsibility, and control in this policy sector has a long and contested history across the megacity. School decentralization was implemented in New York City during the tumultuous days of 1969 with the creation of community-based school boards. Ocean Hill-Brownsville became the focal point of intense conflict between the teachers' union and community activists and has had a lasting impact. Moving outwards into the surrounding communities across the region, local control was largely preserved until the late 1990s. Given the scale and size of the public education system across the region, one should not be at all surprised by its political significance for the megacity.

As labour force demands exceeded the capacity of schools to educate, local leadership yet again adapted by creating "charter schools" and "magnet schools".[2] In 1989 the state of New Jersey took control of the schools in Jersey City, and in 1995 it took control in Newark, in an effort to improve outcomes. In 2002 New York City Mayor Michael Bloomberg assumed control of education in an effort to inject his style of corporate management into the system, with a promise of improved outcomes. Innovations in education, in turn, have led to new controversies over control, and whether funding charter schools detracted from public schools, as well as whether entrance into magnet schools should be based on merit or reflect the larger population. Education itself is a multifaceted problem, where broken families, lack of opportunity and increased delinquency put enormous pressures on the schools to deliver what may not really be deliverable.

The message here is that growth has produced massive change, nor is that change a complete or pure benefit. It has both anticipated and unanticipated consequences. Growth also takes place within certain geographic dimensions that describe the New York megacity. Other features through which growth occurs are embedded, relatively permanent features of the megacity, such as the infrastructure that knits its "island" geography together, its diverse and unequal social classes, its regional coherence and its extraordinary density. It is to these features we now turn.

Territorial dimensions of demography and diversity

The New York megacity sprawls across 13 counties covering New York and New Jersey and is home to more than 15 million people. This includes the five boroughs of New York City (Manhattan, the Bronx, Brooklyn, Queens and Staten Island) plus Westchester, Nassau and Suffolk in New York State; and

---

2. A charter school is a tax-supported institution established by an agreement between the public school system and an outside group (parents, teachers, nonprofit organizations), which operates the school, free of many local and state educational regulations, so as to achieve set goals. Magnet schools are a small category of public school that emphasize specific areas of study or a particular teaching method that draw students from across the city. They are subject to regulation by the public school system that operates them, differentiating them from charter schools, which work under charters that provide more autonomy.

Bergen, Hudson, Essex, Union and Passaic counties in New Jersey.[3] Through the decades its geography accommodated the clustering of a huge population built around an intricate pattern of waterways that made possible the movement of people and goods. With each increment of bridges, tunnels, roadways and airports that laced its coastlines, the region rippled with unprecedented growth. Its economic entanglement led to a unique interdependence among the region's localities. Figure 1.2 presents a picture of the megacity's contours and connectors.

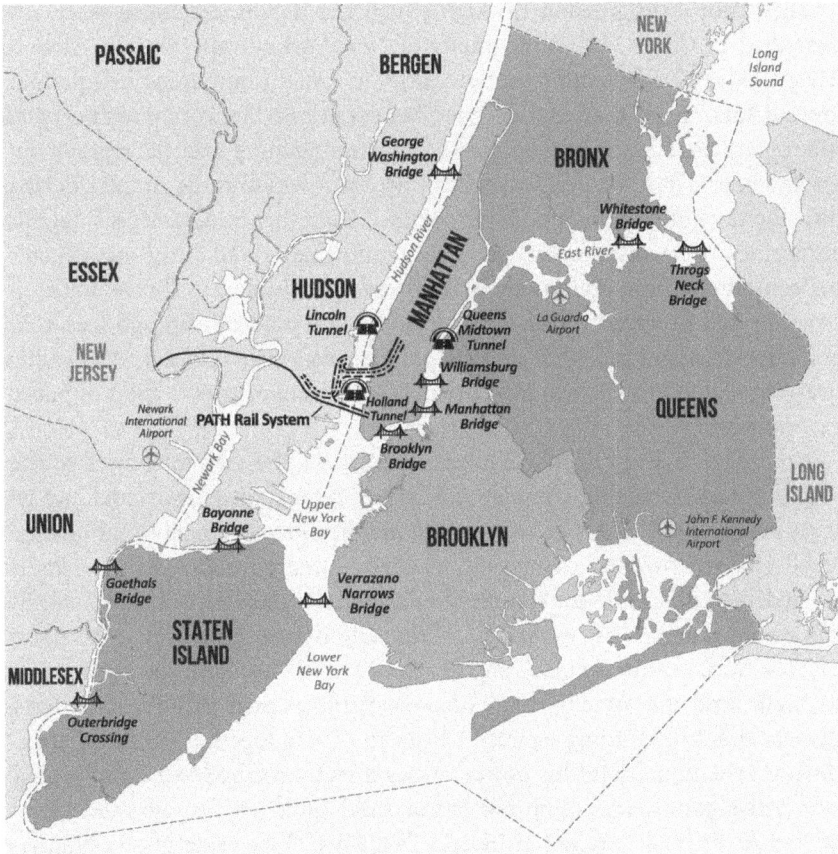

Figure 1.2 Map of the New York megacity and connectors.

_____

3. In 1898 New York City amalgamated five adjacent counties, designated henceforth as "boroughs". The counties and boroughs are respectively known as New York County (Manhattan), Kings County (Brooklyn) Bronx County (the Bronx); Queens County (Queens) and Richmond County (Staten Island). We adopt the more commonly used borough names.

At the heart of the region are the Upper New York and Newark Bays, around which Lower Manhattan, Kings County (Brooklyn) and Hudson, Essex and Passaic counties formed a commercial nucleus that radiates in all directions. The East River and Hudson Rivers serve as crucial passageways, through which shipping passes and along which docks, warehouses and factories have sprung up. A half-dozen crossings, overpasses, underpasses and railway connectors knit together the many swatches of land along those waterways. During the latter part of the twentieth century that nucleus burst eastward onto Long Island, northward into Westchester and westward into the rest of New Jersey.

The historic progression through which the region developed is vividly described in Caro's (1975) biography of New York's master builder, Robert Moses. Moses fixed his sights on New York City and the numerous jurisdictions around it. For more than four decades Moses outlasted mayors, governors and other politicians, while building a vast empire stretching over the region's rivers and bays. His great political accomplishment was to forge an interlocking directorate of numerous "public authorities" and other bodies. Moses' "public authorities" were autonomous governing units that served as the instruments for constructing the region's tunnels, bridges and highways. Public authorities were self-financed through bonds and loans; paid off through fees, tolls and other user charges. That singular ability gave Moses unchecked rulership over the region's transportation corridors (entailing over 600 miles of paved expressways).

Control over the region's thoroughfares paved the way for Moses to put together parks, housing complexes, beaches, recreation halls, stadia and an array public works. Much of his work ran roughshod over neighbourhoods and small property owners. Then again, he gave a hungry public what it so badly needed – a respite from the tumult of a clogged city that was only reachable by private automobile. The exclusivity of the automobile ensured that the poorest New Yorkers, mostly black and Hispanic, would not have the same access to public amenities or suburban homeownership as their white counterparts. The sheer act of building enabled Moses to cobble together powerful coalitions. At the pinnacle of his power Moses directly controlled a dozen public authorities, councils or commissions and could influence the wages and profits of over 80,000 people (Caro 1975: 362, 764, 1194). Like other master builders he traded on the favour of developers, bankers, labour unions and most of all won over a grateful, largely white, blue collar and middle-class public, while satiating the poorest neighbourhoods with public parks and swimming pools.

In his later years Moses liked to remind audiences that he was the man who cleared one of the biggest slums in Manhattan and replaced it with the famed Lincoln Center. But by the 1960s Moses' power had begun to wane. His most ambitious project at the time was to build a major expressway through

Lower Manhattan designed to connect the city's bridges and tunnels for easier vehicular travel into New Jersey. The expressway project would have torn up neighbourhoods, especially parts of historic Greenwich Village. Years earlier that kind of radical surgery might have even passed, but after mid-century it was seen as destructive. New York's political leadership, its high society and the media had become disenchanted with monumental highways and Moses' pet project was shelved. New local leaders, such as Jane Jacobs, also emerged to support neighbourhoods and preserve local economies (Jacobs 1961).

All the same, Robert Moses established himself as the progenitor of the modern megacity – big in every way and designed for fast-paced capitalism. In the course of his decades-long tenure, Moses envisioned a metropolis that extended in a giant radius around Manhattan for many miles. He demonstrated that controlling a built environment could also shape how people lived and how they engaged in politics. During Moses' reign and since his departure the New York megacity has taken an increasingly complex form. In the near and distant suburbs, numerous new "edge cities" have sprung up. Office parks, retail malls and housing subdivisions cover once open fields

Ribbons of fast-food eateries and gas stations filled the remaining spaces. Today the megacity is a composite of heavily urbanized neighbourhoods within New York City's five boroughs and older cities across the Hudson in New Jersey (Newark, Jersey City, Elizabeth, Paterson), well-settled townships in near suburbs (Nassau, Lower Westchester, Bergen) and pastoral surroundings in distant suburbs (Suffolk, Upper Westchester and Northern Bergen Counties). Table 1.1 displays 13 counties of the megacity by population growth during nearly 20 years.

All of the megacity's counties increased in population since the last decade. Some key increases were recorded in Hudson County (11 per cent), which contains gentrifying older cities of Hoboken and Jersey City as well as Manhattan (6 per cent) and Brooklyn (4.8 per cent), whose older neighbourhoods became "hot places" for artists and young professionals. And today, as housing affordability continues to be a challenge across the metropolis, lower income communities in areas such as the Bronx are growing even more rapidly (9.2 per cent), where some 51 per cent of borough residents are rent burdened.

What makes all of this unusual is that the New York megacity has been a mature region for over a half century, and growth tends to slow in mature metropolises. With a base of more than 15 million people, we might have expected that New York would follow a pattern of slow growth. Instead, it added over 681,000 residents amounting to a total increase of 5 per cent. Doing this on a small demographic base is one matter, but adding to an already huge megacity base is quite another. Thus, a young sunbelt metropolis such as Phoenix, with a population of 1.3 million, added 300,000 residents during the

Table 1.1 Population in 13 counties of the New York megacity, 2000–18

County	Total Population 2000	Total Population 2018	Percentage change
New York (Manhattan)	1,537,195	1,628,701	6.0
Kings (Brooklyn)	2,465,326	2,582,830	4.8
Queens	2,229,379	2,278,906	2.2
Richmond (Staten Island)	443,728	476,179	7.3
Bronx	1,332,650	1,432,132	7.5
Nassau	1,334,544	1,358,343	1.8
Suffolk	1,419,369	1,481,093	4.3
Westchester	923,459	967,612	4.8
Bergen	884,118	936,692	5.9
Hudson	608,975	676,061	11.0
Essex	793,633	799,767	0.8
Union	522,541	558,067	6.8
Passaic	501,226	501,826	0.0
Total	14,996,143	15,678,820	4.7

Source: US Bureau of the Census, ACS 2000 and 2018.

same period, and it could boast a resounding 23 per cent increase. As a percentage this sounds high, but in absolute numbers and by megacity standards it is a mere drop in the ocean.

Where did the increased megacity population come from? Megacities often attract immigrants because they are big, diverse and offer opportunities. At last count, some 4.87 million immigrants lived in the New York megacity (US Census Bureau 2018a). New York's immigrant community alone is larger than the city of Chicago (NYC Planning 2017). Approximately 800 languages are spoken on the streets of New York (Roberts 2010).

Immigrants often gravitate to where they are likely to find fellow nationals. The New York region has an abundance of ethnic communities and has always welcomed immigrants. In the late nineteenth century thousands of immigrants from Ireland poured into the region. Succeeding the Irish were Italians and Jews from Eastern and Central Europe. By the 1950s African-Americans and Puerto Ricans moved into various parts of the metropolis. In similar fashion, the twenty-first century ushered in an influx of "new immigrants" from Latin America, the Caribbean, East Asia and South Asia. Naturally, the region's population is renewed through births and migration from other states, but it is the foreign-born residents that give the New York megacity a demographic edge. Figure 1.3 shows the extent of that edge.

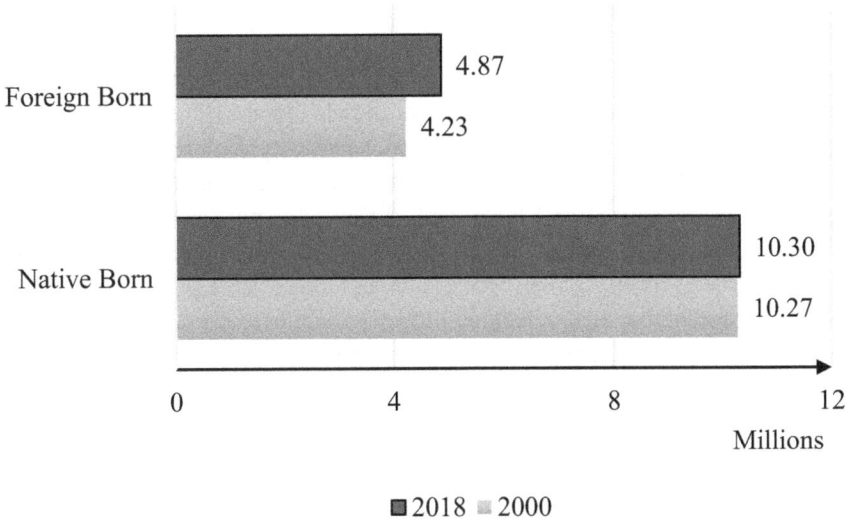

Figure 1.3 Foreign and native-born population in the New York megacity in millions, 2000 and 2018.
Source: American Factfinder 2018.

Foreign-born residents make up a significant portion of the region's population – nearly five million or one-third of the population and they constitute 46 per cent of the formal workforce (NYC Planning 2017). Although authorities in Washington DC have recently endeavoured to curtail immigration, the number of foreign residents here grew by 2.2 million from 2000 up through 2018 (US Census Bureau 2018a). Immigrants account for almost one-half of small businesses in the city, roughly half of its workforce (*Economist* 2020a: 16). Nevertheless, Trump administration policies have led to a decrease of nearly 45 per cent in the rate of immigrant growth. In 2019, 34,000 immigrants chose to live in the city as opposed to nearly twice that number a year earlier (King 2020).[4]

There was a time when, like their predecessors, these immigrants might have settled in Manhattan and parts of Brooklyn. Whereas some of the "new immigrants" followed that path, most did not. For one, many of the "old immigrant" neighbourhoods such as "Hell's Kitchen" on Manhattan's Upper West Side or on the Lower East Side were already gentrified and priced out of reach. For another, the rest of the region has grown and offers greater opportunities for recent immigrants, including already settled neighbourhoods by co-nationals. Finally, jobs and businesses have also dispersed throughout the region, mostly due to increased capacity of roads, bridges, tunnels, rail and buses.

---

4. As will be discussed in Chapters 3 and 4, immigration has tended to generate pressures for policies and programmes supporting immigrant rights to the city.

Local development policy has usually accommodated infrastructure growth. Like most social classes, immigrants too have settled in the expanded region. Today we see a sizeable South Asian community in Queens (Flushing) and large Hispanic populations in Hudson (Hoboken, Jersey City) Union (Elizabeth) and Essex (Newark). New Jersey has the highest proportion of South Asian Indians in the nation, estimated at 4.1 per cent of the state's population (US Census Bureau 2020a). Although many South Asians have settled in small, modest municipalities within the metropolis such as Jersey City, a good many other Asian immigrants have gained higher incomes and moved into affluent suburbs. As we will see in Chapter 5, ethnic distinctions layer onto many of the tensions that underlie this complex megacity (City of New York 2011). Figure 1.4 displays select localities and neighbourhoods within the city and the larger region.

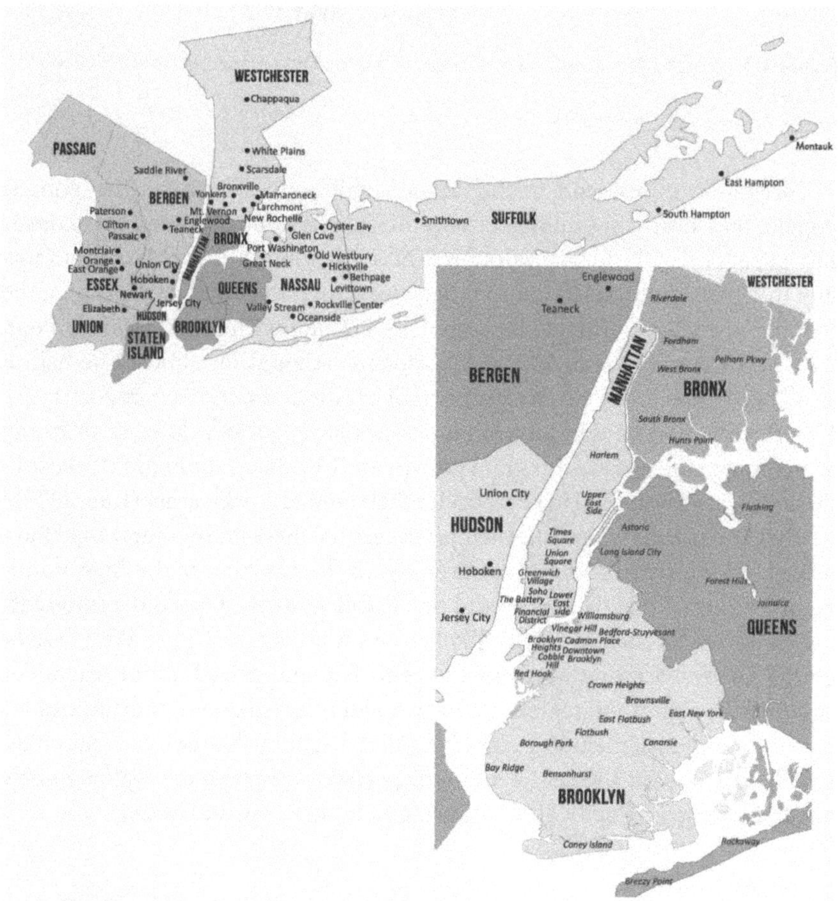

Figure 1.4 Map of neighbourhoods and localities within the New York megacity.

New York is the nation's and perhaps the world's greatest exemplar of a cosmopolitan, polyglot megacity. Turning to the city proper, the last three censuses showed it becoming still more multinational and multiethnic. Although white inhabitants of European origin still constitute the largest single group, its share of the city's population has declined. African-American populations remained stable, whereas Hispanic (Latinos) and Asian populations rose substantially. Looked at in greater detail, in 1980 white residents constituted a majority of 51 per cent of New York City's population, but by 2019 its proportion had shrunk to a plurality of 43 per cent. The black population remained steady at 24 per cent, with Hispanics and Asians increasing in proportion. In 1980 Latinos had become the second-largest ethnic group at 20 per cent, and by 2019 this had grown to 29 per cent. Likewise, in 1980, East and South Asians constituted just 3.2 per cent of the city's population but by 2019 had risen to 14 per cent of the population (Brown University 2010; US Census Bureau 2020a).

Social polarization and its nasty spillover

The larger New York region refracted these tendencies, although with some time lag and to a lesser extent. White populations still constituted a majority of the larger region at nearly 53 per cent, followed by Latino residents at 26 per cent, the black population stabilized at 20 per cent and Asians rose considerably to almost 12 per cent. Figure 1.5 gives us a glimpse of regional changes during the last two decades.

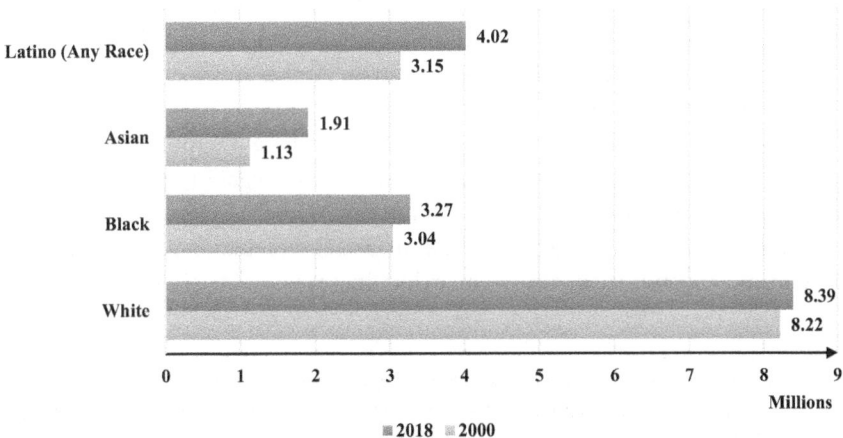

Figure 1.5 New York megacity by race and ethnic makeup, 2000–18.
Source: US Bureau of the Census, 2000 and 2018.

Although racial diversity enriches the area in countless ways, it also carries tensions and sometimes severe conflicts. The discord in the region rides on waves emanating from poor racially and ethnically segregated enclaves that are in sharp contrast to white middle-class communities. Variations in income, family structure, education, health, housing, jobs and the culture of a group can shape the fortunes of the megacity. Above all, New York is a city of neighbourhoods and the rest of the megacity is a region of small municipalities and towns. The wealthiest white populations cluster on Manhattan's Upper East Side and Midtown and in trendy parts of Brooklyn; middle-class and blue-collar neighbourhoods are located in Brooklyn's Bensonhurst, Borough Park and Bay Ridge, and in the "outer boroughs" of Queens and Staten Island. Hispanic and especially Puerto Rican populations have a strong presence in South Bronx and East Harlem. African-Americans and Caribbean islanders locate in Harlem and in Brooklyn's Bedford Stuyvesant, East Flatbush, Brownsville, Fort Greene and East New York. There are now four "Chinatowns" in New York (three in Brooklyn and one in Manhattan) and a "little Pakistan" has become established in Brooklyn. At last count there were three "little Indias" in parts of New Jersey. In the rest of the region, wealthy upper middle-class white populations largely inhabit the suburbs stretching out on Long Island and in New Jersey's Bergen County. Newark (Essex) is well known for its black population, while Hoboken, Paterson and Jersey City (Hudson) have large Hispanic populations and growing South Asian communities.

Place of residence is important. It can predict how the children of different social classes grow up, what level of education they are likely to reach, whom they befriend and whether they can pursue successful careers. A commonly used measure of social segregation is the Index of Dissimilarity. Known also as the "segregation index", the Index of Dissimilarity measures the degree of ethnic/racial concentration within a given area. It measures the range between "complete integration" at zero to "complete segregation" at 100.[5] The New York megacity holds the dubious distinction of being among the more racially segregated metropolises in the country, with a black segregation index above 74 and a Hispanic index at 47.7 (Brown University 2010; City Observatory 2020).

We should also acknowledge that ethnic/racial segregation is compounded by chronic income inequality, which has increased over time. Manhattan

---

5. The dissimilarity index measures whether one particular group is distributed across census tracts in the metropolitan area in the same way as another group. A high value indicates that the two groups tend to live in different tracts. A value of 60 (or above) is considered very high. It means that 60 per cent (or more) of the members of one group would need to move to a different tract in order for the two groups to be equally distributed. Values of 40 or 50 are usually considered a moderate level of segregation, and values of 30 or below are considered to be fairly low.

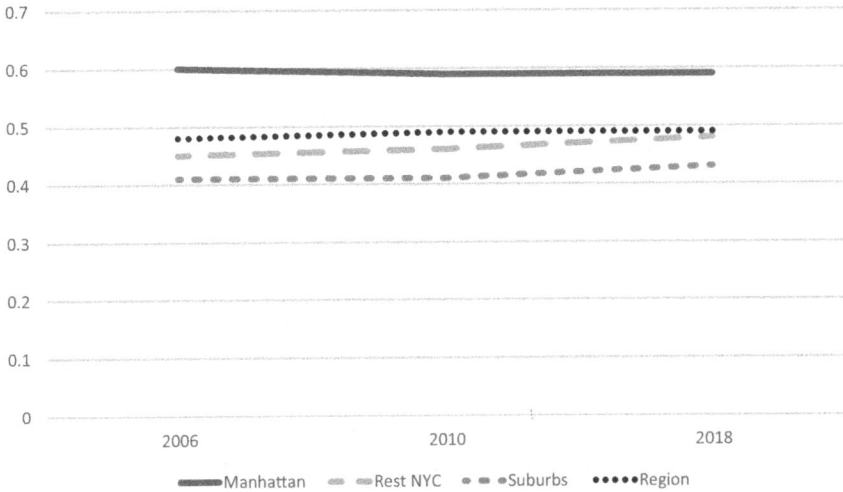

Figure 1.6 The New York megacity: Gini coefficients 2006, 2010 and 2018.
Source: Social Explorer, ACS 2006, one year estimates, SE, US Census, US Bureau of the Census, Gini Index of Income Inequality American Community Survey 2010 and 2018 B19083.

by far is the wealthiest borough with most of its affluence concentrated in white neighbourhoods south of Harlem. The megacity also has an abundance of wealthy suburban towns in Westchester (Scarsdale, Chappaqua), Nassau County (Old Westbury, Great Neck) and Suffolk County (the Hamptons). The poorest areas of the city are to be found in Harlem, South Bronx, parts of east Brooklyn (Brownsville, East New York) and in Newark.

Like disparities in racial integration, household income can also be measured. The applicable index here is the Gini Index, or coefficient, which can also be applied to different territorial jurisdictions. A Gini coefficient ranges from zero (0.00) as complete equality to 1.00 (complete inequality).[6] We emphasize that Gini coefficients are all about the evenness of a given jurisdiction. Areas that are evenly affluent or evenly poor can have low Gini coefficients. It also means that rich and poor areas can increase or decrease their unevenness, with little or no impact on per capita or household income. Thus, Manhattan with an impressive per capita income of $70,000 (2017) did slightly reduce its Gini coefficient by gentrifying more neighbourhoods. By comparison, the other boroughs with a per capita income in 2017 of $28,000 (less than half as much as Manhattan) actually saw an increase in their Gini Index, when some neighbourhoods heavily gentrified while others remained poor

---

6. Gini coefficients are geared to household income. A Gini index of less than 0.20 represents perfect income equality, 0.20–0.30 relative equality, 0.30–0.40 adequate equality, 0.4–0.5 big income gap, and above 0.5 represents severe income gap. The income distance is especially large between Manhattan and the other boroughs as well as rest of the region.

(US Bureau of Labor Statistics 2017). The figure below shows the trends within each of the megacity's territorial jurisdiction over nearly a period of 20 years.

Inequality in most of the New York megacity has tended upwards – even over a relatively short span of 20 years. Manhattan experienced a slight decrease in its Gini Index from 0.60 to 0.59. The biggest change occurred in the rest of New York City, which rose by 0.4. Apparently, some neighbourhoods in the boroughs attracted more affluent households, sharpening differences between neighbourhoods. New York City has gradually begun to resemble its European counterparts where wealthy households concentrate in the centre, whereas poorer households seek inexpensive housing further away.

The Gini Index puts income inequality in perspective. Consider that an interpretation of the Index describes 0.40 to 0.50 as a "big income gap" and anything above that represents a "severe income gap" (Research Gate 2019). Manhattan's 0.59 is above "severity" and both the borough's and region's 0.49 score hovers near "severity". The suburbs with a comparatively lower 0.43 are already classified as having a "big gap". All this weighs heavily on the megacity.

Another measure of well-being and disparity in the megacity can be found using the United Nation's Human Development Index (a composite score of life expectancy, education and income that ranges from 1 to 10). Researchers have found that the score for the megacity itself is relatively high at 6.32 (as compared with the national score of 5.17). However, within the region there is significant disparity. The Upper East Side, for example, scored a whopping 9.36, as contrasted with a score of 3.10 in Southwest Newark. Translated into day-to-day reality, "a baby born today to a family living on the Upper East Side can expect to live nearly fourteen years longer than a baby born today to a family living in Southwest Newark" (Lewis & Burd-Sharps 2018: 37).

Clearly, racial and income disparities manifest themselves, quite starkly, in the lived-in spaces of a given social class. One can experience different worlds that are only minutes apart by taking a subway ride from Manhattan's Turtle Bay into East Harlem or from Brooklyn's Park Slope into Brownsville. In the rest the region one can stroll through Upper Montclair and see smart, spacious houses and then take a 15-minute ride and see the crumbling, high-crime neighbourhoods of South Newark. Even so, the New York megacity still constates a recognizable, intercommunal metropolis. Notwithstanding the social and physical discrepancies, the megacity hangs together quite well. The reasons for this are somewhat enigmatic, and we now turn to what lies behind regional coherence.

The strange case of New York's regional cohesion

The New York megacity coheres in its own seemingly contradictory way. "The city", as Manhattan and sometimes the other boroughs are called, are regarded by the rest of the region with ambivalence.[7] In a study conducted in 1978, nearly half of suburban residents told survey interviewers that they strongly identified with the broader New York region. Little has changed over time. In a 2013 study of the "lived" region, researchers found that the majority of those interviewed (n=173), perceived themselves to be a part of much larger region – including the urban core and periphery, but extending beyond (Gross & Nelles 2014). In 1978 about three-quarters of those living in the suburbs expressed sympathy with "the city" in its time of fiscal travail and favoured federal aid to ease its indebtedness. Suburban dwellers also recognized the advantage of proximity to "the city" with 60 per cent of suburbanites saying they preferred to travel a longer distance to see its sports or attend cultural events. Yet, in that very same survey, a majority of suburbanites told interviewers they infrequently visited New York City and "cared very little" about it (Feron 1978; Kolbert 1991). The paradox of regional change signifies that the more people who leave the central city, the greater becomes the region's allegiance to it

How do we explain this paradox? "The city" is a place that suburbanites were glad to flee yet never forgot. Most were glad to have traded in crowded streets and small apartments for leafy suburbs and spacious houses. Nevertheless, many have brought their old values with them, especially political, so that formerly Republican suburbs flipped to the Democrats. These same migrants retain a powerful nostalgia for their old neighbourhoods and feel a refreshing energy when they visit. More recently, as the boomer population ages, many have begun to return to the core where the ability to age in place is more easily achieved. Since 2010, 21 per cent of the migrants to the urban core of the megacity came from the surrounding suburbs (Elstein 2018). With all of its plusses and minuses, "the city" is a place that suburbanites "love to hate", but which they could not do without.

The necessity to manage that "common fate" has enabled the megacity to muddle through and develop irregular instruments of governance. Save for New York City, the region does not have anything that resembles a comprehensive regional government. Some traditional scholars have characterized this as a serious void and described the region as a chaotic "crazy quilt" of ineffectual localities (Wood 1961; Danielson & Doig 1982; Miller & Cox 2014). Other scholars view the region in a different light. Rather than a "crazy quilt", the region could be seen as a tapestry of different localities performing highly varied services to suit very different local needs.

The New York region could be explained as a "complexly organized" system of overlapping, functional oriented governments (Parks & Oakerson 1989;

---

7. Manhattan is also called "the city" by New Yorkers living in the other four boroughs.

Ostrom 1990). Counties largely deal with transportation and social services; townships and cities manage land use; and special districts largely undertake specific functions such as education, water and sewage. When localities do find reason to cooperate, they rely on voluntary, interlocal agreements to share recreational facilities or collect trash. Also holding the regional tapestry together are regional bodies – the largest of which is the New York-New Jersey Port Authority. The states of New York and New Jersey also bring about coherence via state laws, mandates, budget controls and the imposition of their authority during emergencies. During the region's most severe crises, such as superstorm Sandy and the Covid-19 pandemic, state governments were on the ground with workers, facilities and special assistance.

There are, too, daily and frequent ways the megacity coheres. Jobs, commerce and money play an indispensable role in making sense of the larger region. Packed subways, congested highways and queues at bus stops and railway stations tell us that New Yorkers are decidedly peripatetic and willing to endure hours of commuting for their livelihoods. During an average day more than seven million New Yorkers have endured a tough intra-regional commute. It includes a variety of modes of transportation such as automobile, bus subway, rail, bicycling and walking.

As Figure 1.7 indicates, commutation hardly consists of residents moving in a simple direction amounting to a departure from a dormitory suburb and return from a central business district. Rather, everyday travel criss-crosses the region in a complex matrix of within county, out of county and across multiple counties commutes. The highest number of commutations actually takes place among the suburbs (34 per cent) and the second largest occurs among those travelling within the five boroughs of New York City (24.7 per cent). Coming in at a distant third, is commutation from other parts of New York City into Manhattan (15.8 per cent). Curiously, the stereotypical commute from suburbs to Manhattan accounts for just 6.5 per cent of total travel within the region. We should not underestimate this commute, however, because it consists of investors, opinion makers, managers and high-income social classes who influence regional politics.

Overall, we can say that the megacity region is dynamic, with jobs and people spread in all directions. Paradoxically, this makes for a greater semblance of cohesion rather than dispersal because the very act of travel requires that commuters from all parts of the region socialize with one another. That socialization takes place at railways, bus depots, restaurants, diners, theatres, sports stadia, gyms and many venues for meeting.

Lubricating the region's interactions are its revenue flows. Key to understanding these flows is where income is earned and where it is spent. "Following the money" is by now a landmark of political inquiry, and to do this we turn to the task of what the statisticians classify as "adjusting for residence". Here we

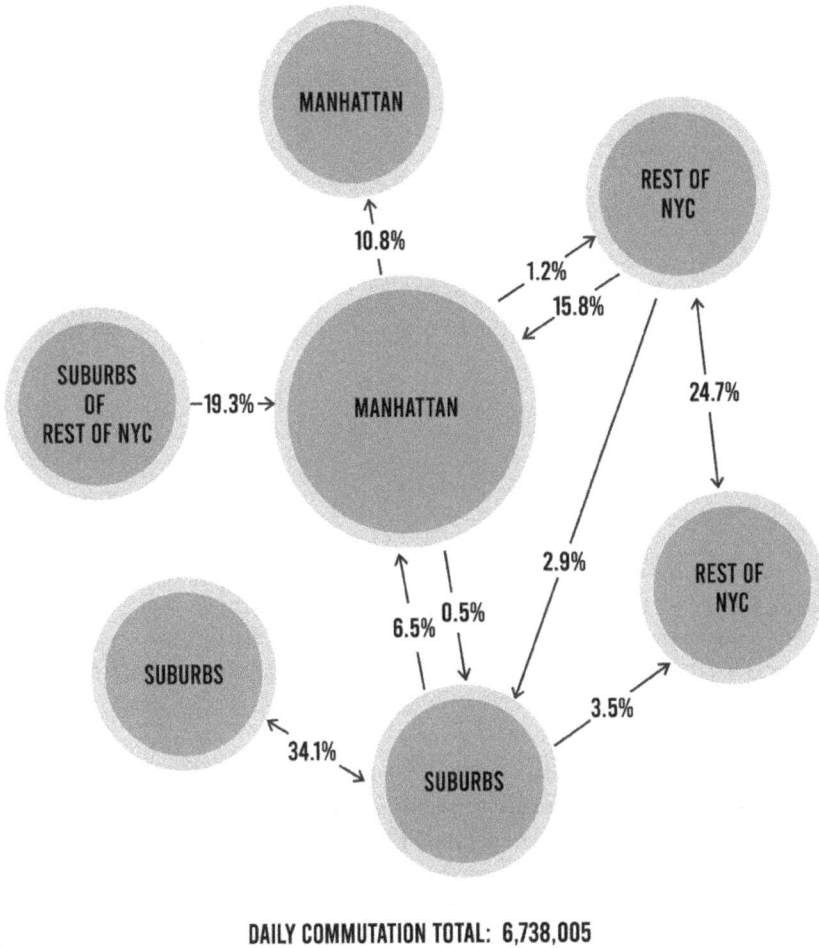

Figure 1.7 Commuting within the New York megacity: average day between 2009–13. *Source*: 2009–13 5-year ACS commuting flows.

employ the shorter version of that term, "residential adjustment", defined as the net inflow (positive) or outflow (negative) of net earnings by commuters. For example, if "x" earns a net income of $50,000 after taxes working in a factory in Brooklyn and lives in Nassau County, that sum would count as a negative residential adjustment for Brooklyn and a positive for Nassau County. We should understand that these earnings are mostly spent in the place of residence; in this example Nassau County rather than place of work, Brooklyn. Spending at a place of residence is normally used to pay for mortgage or rental expenses, transportation costs, food, clothing and other living costs. Figure 1.8 aggregates residential adjustment for all 13 counties in the New York megacity.

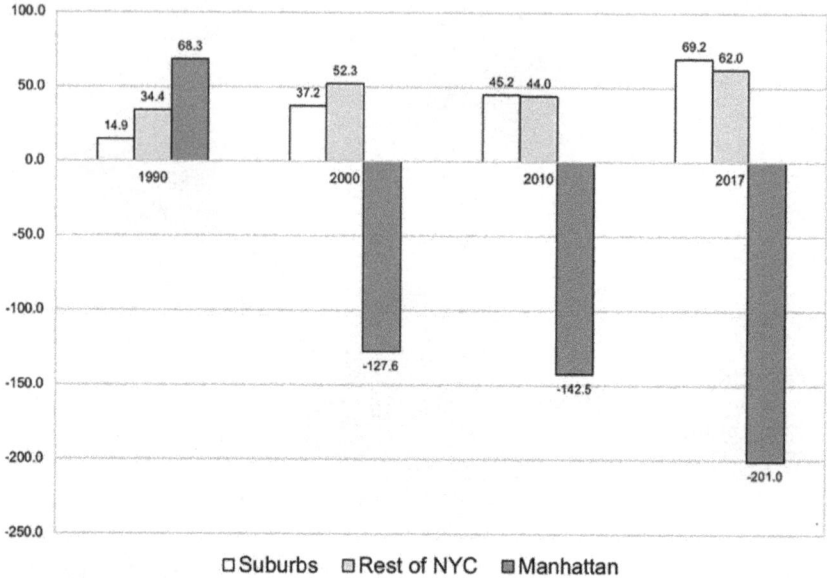

Figure 1.8 Residential adjustment in the New York megacity, 1990–2017 (in billions of dollars). *Source*: Bureau of Economic Analysis Table CAINC91 Gross Flow of Earnings: Adjustment for Residence for New York, Queens, Richmond, Kings, Bronx, Bergen, Essex, Union, Hudson, Westchester, Nassau, and Suffolk Counties (1990, 2000, 2010, 2017).

For the moment we focus on Manhattan between the years 1990 and 2017, by the category of earnings received and spent either in a place of residence or elsewhere. In 1990 Manhattan actually received more revenue ($68.3 billion) from its residents than was taken out. Most likely, Manhattanites worked in New York's other boroughs and commuted across its numerous bridges and tunnels to New Jersey. Meanwhile the rest of New York City received $34.4 billion and the suburbs gained $14.9 billion from outside earnings. All told the region was pretty much in balance. By the year 2000 that picture had changed and Manhattan became a net exporter of revenue in the amount of $127.6 billion. That amount climbed to $142.5 billion by 2010 and to more than $200 billion by 2017. In this instance we can see that from 2000 onward the rest of New York City and the suburbs received increasing income from other parts of the megacity or elsewhere.

We might understand why the rest of the region could "love to hate the city". For those outside of "the city", this small strip of granite called Manhattan is a moneyed power, possessing a nervous energy and a super-scaled built environment that is both awe-inspiring and worrying. "The city" is seen as a well-endowed beneficiary with a capacity to feed its workers, but it can also fail through fiscal recklessness, vulnerability to crises or the vicissitudes of the marketplace.

Density as a defining feature

Density defines the megacity. Density allows for a city to grow on limited land. Density enables economies of scale to nurture a multiplicity of industries. Density allows for as much as 50 per cent higher productivity as non-dense areas (*Economist* 2020b: 14). Density provides opportunities for different businesses to learn from one another and innovate. Density permits face-to-face meetings and can make all the difference about whether an agreement is concluded, a contract is signed, a product reaches the market or a small business can compete. Density makes supply chains possible and provides savings to consumers. Density magnifies the chances that a serendipitous encounter will revolutionize an entire industry. Finally, density enables locals and tourists to have Broadway theatres, major league sports, great libraries and cultural centres.

For density to be truly effective it needs to be mobilized and deployed. This means facilitating the travel of New Yorkers from one place to another, whether from home to workplace or workplace to a restaurant or a restaurant to the theatre. Only with mass can we have feasible mass transportation. Few megacities equal New York's subway, bus and regional rail operations in capacity and movability. Within the city, the subway system moves 5.5 million people daily, with its buses carrying more than 2.2 million and rail system carrying over 2.6 million (MTA Info 2018).[8] Considering the entire megacity, more than 10.3 million people are moved around each weekday (MTA Network 2019). The number of people moved throughout the New York megacity on any given weekday is two-and-a-half times the population of Los Angeles.

There are also social and environmental gains from density. In a megacity like New York, allowing greater densities (up-zoning) is sometimes used to incorporate affordable housing into new construction. This may or may not do much to enhance social integration, but it certainly improves the chance of diversifying daily encounters. We do know that density reduces automobile usage and gas consumption and that higher density census tracts consume nearly half the amount of gasoline as lower density tracts (Glaeser 2011: 207). Dense development cuts down on long-distance trips to work and social visits. This goes hand in hand with pedestrian-bicycle oriented street

---

8. The difference in commuter totals between this section and those presented in Figure 1.7 are due to differences in counting actual trips versus persons making those trips as well as differences in time periods.

designs, which has now taken over Times Square and is spreading into many neighbourhoods.

A tighter, clustered urban form is also more adaptable to reshaping cities as a low carbon environment (Palermo *et al.* 2020). Multiple-unit housing consumes less electricity than single-family houses and emits fewer greenhouse gases (GHGs). As New York City struggled to find ways to reduce GHGs its mayor at the time, Michael Bloomberg, took up the idea of planting one million new trees onto city streets in order to consume carbon dioxide and release more oxygen. By 2015 two mayors, Michael Bloomberg and Bill de Blasio, celebrated the planting of the city's millionth tree. Beginning in 2019 the first phase of a new skyscraper complex was underway on top of an old railyard at Hudson Yards. A second phase is scheduled for 2022. Among its many environment-saving features is a highly efficient "trigeneration microgrid technology" that produces on site, clean energy. Nothing like this could be built in a low-density environment.

Density falls off as one moves out from the epicentre of New York City. The fall-off is captured by the concept of a "density gradient". The steepness of a density gradient is measured by the percentage change in density for every one mile outside of a central business district. Density gradients present a picture of the relative concentration of human activity within different areas. New York City has the steepest density gradient in the United States, measured at -7.3 per cent. This means that for each mile of distance from Times Square the population drops by -7.3 per cent. By comparison, San Francisco has the second-steepest density gradient at -5.30 per cent, while Chicago comes in at a distant -2.40 (Bertaud & Malpezzi 2003: 20).

The most common and simplest way to understand density is by examining it as the average number of residents per square mile. Although this does pose the disadvantage of mixing high and low extremes of a population to obtain an average, it does provide an overview of what density looks like within the megacity's counties. Table 1.2 displays each of these counties between 2000 and 2017.[9] Interestingly, every county in the region increased

---

9. Density is more complicated and can be understood as related to a number of other components. In an article on "sprawl", Galster *et al.* (2001) shed a good deal of light on the companion concept of density. They outline a number of useful components such as: (1) continuity, the degree to which development is unbroken; (2) concentration, the degree to which development is disproportionately located; (3) clustering, the degree to which development is tightly bunched; (4) centrality, the degree to which development is located relative to a central business district; (5) nuclearity, the degree to which development is clustered at a singular versus a multi-nodal location; (6) mixed land uses, the degree to which different land uses commonly exist within the same small area; and (7) proximity, the degree to which different land uses are close to one another.

Table 1.2 Density in 13 counties of the New York megacity, 2000 and 2018

County	Population density per square mile		
	2000 population	2018 population	Percentage change
New York (Manhattan)	66,940.1	72,443.1	8.2
Kings (Brooklyn)	34,916.6	37,208.7	6.6
Queens	20,409.0	21,554.2	5.6
Richmond (Staten Island)	7,587.9	8,154.0	7.5
Bronx	31,709.3	34,580.7	9.1
Nassau	4,655.0	4,787.4	2.8
Suffolk	1,556.0	1,642.0	5.5
Westchester	2,133.6	2,265.6	6.2
Bergen	3,775.5	4,025.2	6.6
Hudson	13,043.6	14,716.5	12.8
Essex	6,285.4	6,341.8	0.9
Union	5,059.0	5,418.8	7.1
Passaic	2,543.0	2,546.0	0.0
TOTAL	5,927.3	6,304.48	6.4

Source: US Census Bureau, American Community Survey. Density for 2017 is calculated on the basis of the 2010 Census Area, but using 2018 population counts.

its density. Densification of the entire region rose by 6.4 per cent during this period. Hudson County led the pack with a 12.8 per cent rise, much of it due to the resettlement and gentrification of key cities such as Hoboken and Jersey City. Manhattan saw the second-highest increase with an 8.2 per cent increase in density.

All of this portends an enriched and prosperous region. The generator of regional vitality is at the core of the megacity in Manhattan. This 23-square-mile slab of granite houses the megacity's knowledge industry, which builds upon the proximity of daily encounters. The greater the incidence of knowledge-based industry, the greater the need for the cross fertilization of ideas and the more necessary the density. We should appreciate that Manhattan's density of more than 72,000 people per square mile is among the eight highest in the world, behind some extraordinarily concentrated places like Mumbai. The difference is that Manhattan builds very high, leaving relatively more space at street level. Manhattan also remains as the highest-density locale among the world's most affluent cities. Paris is well behind it at 55,000 people per square mile and Greater London is further behind at a mere 7,000 people per square mile. Paris and London may seem denser to the eye, because Paris' development is continuous and closer to human scale. Greater London's density is spread on a land area (606 square miles) that is almost twice the size of New York's 319 square miles.

Another demographic attribute of importance is household size. The megacity's trend towards smaller household size tells us something about the content of the region's density. Manhattan has the highest land values and this often discourages middle-income families from settling there. Since 2000 the number of four-person households fell by 9.5 per cent, leaving the conventional family as a distinct minority. More common for Manhattan are single-person households. This tells us something about the temper of life in Manhattan – often geared towards career professionals and executives and catering to a "creative class" of artists, writers, high tech and professionals. The other four boroughs of New York City also hold a substantial number of single-person households, although the decline of the four-person household is considerably less at 3.9 per cent. Here too, single- or two-person households are prevalent in parts of Brooklyn (Brooklyn Heights, Cobble Hill) and Queens (Astoria, Long Island City). The rest of the region also shows a drop of four-person households, although these are still abundant at more than 691,048. Established suburbs in New Jersey's Bergen County as well as Westchester, Nassau and Suffolk counties still count numerous four or more person households. Table 1.3 displays these tendencies in detail.

Conclusions

The New York megacity deserves its title. Its enormous agglomeration sprawls in every direction. Its physical, economic and public infrastructure has grown to match its dimensions. Any entity of this magnitude and energy can claim impressive accomplishments but is also saddled with protracted problems. The megacity thrives, not by cleanly meeting one challenge after another, but by managing them, as it has been by muddling through from one phase to the next. Our schema describes these phases as *growth, tensions/crises* and *adaptation*. Each one provides a window for examining what the megacity does and how it works.

Above all, the megacity is complicated and best understood as a bundle of contradictions. It has great wealth amidst great poverty. It sprawls greatly in some places and clusters greatly in others. Its governance is at once non-existent, yet governments of one kind or another function every day and are remarkably nimble. The region is at once a profusion of hundreds of self-identifying localities and a unifying geographic symbol. Identity is a multifocal

Table 1.3 Household size in the New York megacity, 2000 and 2017

Household size	Manhattan 2000	Manhattan 2017	Percentage change	Rest of NYC 2000	Rest of NYC 2017	Percentage change	Suburbs 2000	Suburbs 2017	Percentage change
1	354,336	350,865	−1.0	608,288	666,503	9.6	526,277	570,322	8.4
2	209,290	232,849	11.3	599,645	652,534	8.8	664,121	679,620	2.3
3	79,955	88,602	10.8	406,047	421,972	3.9	403,605	420,076	4.1
4+	95,063	86,029	−9.5	668,964	643,051	−3.9	691,048	667,745	−3.4

Source: American Factfinder 2017. Col. 2: 2000 Census household size data for New York County; col 3: 2017 American Community Survey household size data; cols 4, 7 and 10: authors' calculations; col 5: 2000 Census household size data for Kings, Queens, Richmond, and Bronx counties; col 6: 2017 American Community Survey household size data for Kings, Queens, Richmond, and Bronx counties; col 8: 2000 Census household size data for Bergen, Essex, Union, Hudson, Westchester, Nassau, and Suffolk counties.

and multiplex exercise. Ask most people in the region where they are from and most will proclaim they are "New Yorkers" and then follow up in the next sentence that they are from Brooklyn, Queens, Long Island, Westchester or New Jersey.

Among all of the megacity's enigmatic qualities are its Janus-like strength and weakness. One face, turned towards great strength, lies in the ability of a densely packed city, to facilitate economic growth, create an extraordinary transportation network and produce one of the world's most extraordinary civilizations. The other face, turned towards weakness, exposes the megacity's vulnerability to external attacks – from a terror attack or due to financial miscalculation or a result of storms and pandemics. The World Trade Center was targeted by terrorists because it was one of the most densely packed areas of the nation; the 2008 fiscal crisis was a product of massive agglomerations and transfers of capital, and Covid-19 could only be effectively transmitted in a densely packed global environment. These are only some of the idiosyncrasies of the New York megacity.

2

Crises, breakdowns and New York's endurance

Understanding crises and breakdowns

Sooner or later megacities face a crisis that threatens their well-being or even their survival – either through natural or human-made dangers. By crisis we mean a major problem or challenge to the core principles of a system. Crises derive from different sources and come in different forms. Like most "emergencies" they are unexpected, creeping up on a city by an uncommon, gradual intersection of events or by an abrupt, shocking strike. We categorize these crisis as: (1) natural (2) politico/violent (3) eco/fiscal and (4) techno/infrastructures. Examples of natural crises include weather disasters and widespread diseases. Politico/violent crises include serious challenges to the existing structure of power. Political crises need not necessarily be violent, but merely serve to threaten existing power. In 1971 the state of New York interposed its authority over the city because of endemic police corruption and conducted the Knapp Hearings, which questioned the legitimacy of existing local government. Other political/violent crises did end in violence, such as the Newark riot of 1967 and civil disruptions in northern New Jersey and New York City in the wake of Martin Luther King's assassination during 1968. Eco/fiscal crises pertain to commercial upheavals and revenue breakdowns, the most notorious occurring in 1975–76 and 2007–08. Finally, techno/infrastructure crises pertain to the physical breakdown of the region's electric grid, transportation corridors or water resources. A prime example of the latter includes the region's largest electric blackout during the summer of 1977, which left nine million people without power and another more limited blackout at its 42nd-year anniversary.

Crises yield political consequences. They can create conditions for realigning the electorate and bring new political coalitions into power. The politics of crises also produces a "crisis manager". Success or failure can make or break the career of public figures. Politicians assign blame for their cause and take credit for their resolution. Chances are the more politicians urge that we keep "politics out of a crisis" the greater the chance that politics will enter the fray, especially as the crisis is resolved. Few stratagems have been as worthy of repeating as Winston Churchill's advice in the Second World War: "Never let a good crisis go to waste" (Mutter 2016).

Frequently the core of a crisis takes place at the epicentre of the megacity, namely its largest principal city or commercial core. For the New York region that would be the island of Manhattan. This should not, however, detract from the rest of the region's experience with crisis, where shock waves originating in the centre often spread in a pattern of concentric-like circles. The outward flow of shocks has become more intense in recent decades as metropolitan regions urbanize and become more integrated. One of New York's earlier politico/violent crises was the raft riots of 1863, most of which were contained within Manhattan Island. A century later, in 1975, that containment had evaporated as an eco/fiscal crisis gripped the entire region. We present a thumbnail sketch of these two crises before going on to discuss contemporary, twenty-first-century crises.

The Draft Riots of 1863

Prior to the outbreak of the Civil War, New York's commercial class enjoyed strong ties with the cotton economy of the South and many of its luminaries sympathized with the Confederacy. The ties were strong enough to bring Mayor Fernando Wood onto the side of the South and urge the city to "declare (its) independence from Albany and Washington" (Roberts 2010). The mayor's entreaties came to nothing, but years later the same sympathy for the South became coupled to anxiety over military conscription that prompted talk about rebellion. At the outbreak of Civil War that talk materialized as large numbers of young men were drafted into the Union Army. At the time, potential draftees could buy their way out of army duty by paying $300 for a substitute. The burden of military service fell onto working-class Irish immigrants.

The tinder of discontent against wealthier citizens sparked massive demonstrations, not only against the privileged, but against the existing political order. Throngs of rioters destroyed public buildings, churches and fire stations, and mobs crashed onto the threshold of the New York Times Building before being stopped. The violence was soon directed towards the city's recently freed black population, who were accused of taking jobs from the white population. As the riots boiled over, black residents were seized and lynched, the sight of which caused that population to flee into Brooklyn.

By rough and disputed count, the draft riots took the lives of 120 persons. One source put fatalities at 2,000 and injuries over 8,000 (Bernstein 1990).

The collective violence was severe enough to call in the New York State militia. President Lincoln also found it necessary to divert troops that had just fought in the Battle of Gettysburg to deploy to New York. By this time the city had been brought to its knees and one general called for the imposition of martial law. Eventually the mayhem was quelled and the city saved by the imposition of military force.

Fiscal breakdown of 1975

The fiscal crisis of the mid-1970s was altogether different. Its origin lay not in violence but in political mismanagement. Mayor John Lindsay (1966–73) presided over the city's drift towards economic collapse. Mayor Abe Beame (1974–77), who had previously served as the city's comptroller, tried to weather the storm without success. The route towards economic calamity was paved by both men, who sought political support from the city's most powerful interest groups. Lindsay granted key labour unions excessive pay and benefits, and even found himself in the middle of a "parity war" between the city's unions – agreeing to fund one union's demands only to find himself in a vicious legal cycle of funding another's higher wage demands. The city's municipal colleges were among the few in the country that were tuition-free and the city's municipal hospitals offered services at low or no cost. The city also raised welfare payments, only to find that an increased number of recipients had moved into the city to reap the benefits. By the end of the early 1970s, the welfare rolls contained over one million recipients – or about 12.5 per cent of the population (Ferretti 1976; Morris 1980).

On top of this, the New York region had begun to feel the effects of deindustrialization. Manufacturing and assembly were fleeing the city in a quest for cheaper labour. Inflation had begun to take its toll. By the time Abe Beame strode into the mayoralty, he found that spending had risen 30 per cent in real dollars, the city's tax base was eroding and the larger economy was about to descend into shambles (Freudenberg *et al.* 2006; Stein 1976).

Both Lindsay and Beame answered the call for increased expenditure by borrowing. For a time, municipal bonds, backed by promised revenue streams, filled the city's coffers. Investment bankers enjoyed selling discounted bonds because they yielded handsome profits, pension fund managers were enthusiastic about them because they offered tax-free income and taxpayers supported them because they spurred the economy with no direct costs. Municipal bonds seemed like a perfect "fiscal fix" but like any addiction they were difficult to keep in check. By 1974 the New York City debt accounted for nearly half of the nation's bond flow (Morris 1980; Shefter 1992). Debt service had soared by 56 per cent and interest rates had climbed by more than 8.5 per cent. After city borrowing hit a saturation point, city and state money managers tried issuing "moral obligation bonds". By 1975 that too fell upon the shoals of default along with the entire package of city debt (Reagan 2017).

Effectively, the banks had shut their teller windows. As if to demonstrate the city could still hit a lower point, President Gerald Ford refused Mayor Beam's request for federal aid. The ominous headline in one newspaper read: "Ford to City: Drop Dead" (Van Riper 1975). Clearly, New York City had run itself into the fiscal ground. New York's governor, Hugh Carey, and the mayor, Abe Beame, warned that without federal aid the city could face massive protest. Their predictions proved accurate. Across the city, strikers blocked bridges and highways and students from the City University ringed the mayor's residence at Gracie Mansion.

The state of New York was obliged to step in and effectively take over the city's governance. Decisions of any import were placed under the jurisdictions of two state agencies (Bailey 1984). Not until 1982, seven years after the fiscal catastrophe, was the city able to return to the bond markets and begin to take charge of its own affairs. These episodes of politico/violent and eco/fiscal crisis illustrate that most crises can be overcome. James Q. Wilson (1967) famously quipped: "If enough people do not like something it becomes a problem; if the intellectuals agree with them, it becomes a crisis."

True, the word "crisis" has been overused and exaggerated, but there have been real crises that contain within them the seeds of breakdown. A crisis also reflects a turning point in a situation. Recovery comes either by restoring an earlier condition and reinstating the former balance of forces or by transforming the situation into a new state of affairs. Anything else leads to breakdown or a total collapse of a system, personified by chaos and instability. Or it may be that restoration is followed by an actual transformation into a new state of affairs. Most anything else leads to breakdown or a total collapse of a system, personified by chaos and instability.[1]

Twenty-first-century crises

In this chapter we ask: What was the content and cost of the crisis? How did the city and region around it respond? How resilient is the megacity in coping with crises? Most important, what do crises tell us about change and what have been their enduring effects? The answers to these questions can also be found in how the public remembers a crisis and formulates future policies. Crises

---

1. For a theoretical and applied analyses of crisis government see Clinton Rossiter's (1948) classic, *Constitutional Dictatorship*.

become part of a region's institutional memory. The 9/11 attack was an act of politico/violence that deeply unsettled New Yorkers. Fully 59 per cent of them reported knowing someone who was killed or hurt in the attacks. A majority of residents living close to the area of attack reported frequent sleepless nights and many showed an inclination to move from the city (Pew Research Center 2002). Superstorm Sandy also caused quite a bit of public trauma. A Gallup poll conducted soon after Sandy showed higher levels of worry and stress throughout the region. Logically, the highest stress was found among residents who lived in the most severely damaged areas (Gallup 2019; Schwartz *et al.* 2016a). The Covid-19 pandemic also hit New Yorkers harder than residents in other parts of the country – perhaps because New York was one of the earliest sites for the outbreak of the disease (Centers for Disease Control 2020).[2]

The megacity's twenty-first-century crises had a character of their own. One of the crises, the 9/11 attack, was a case of pure politico/violence. The two remaining crises, superstorm Sandy and the Covid-19 pandemic, were natural crises. All three events were highly unusual, entirely unexpected and ridden with trauma. The 9/11 attack took place at the dawn of the new millennium as a massive, first of its kind terror attack on the World Trade Center. Superstorm Sandy was a freak natural crisis, producing a weather hazard that astounded meteorologists. It made landfall on the Jersey Shore in October 2012. The Covid-19 pandemic is believed to have originated in the New York area during March 2020, through individuals who had recently travelled from Europe or elsewhere in the United States.

9/11 and the World Trade Center

The attack

It was early autumn and a bright, sunny morning in New York City, the kind of day that locals call, "Indian Summer". The air was crisp and the only thing interrupting a brilliantly blue sky were a few puffy white clouds. And then

---

2. Trauma has a way of searing into peoples' thoughts and shaping their reaction. Almost immediately after the onset of a crisis, the region's institutional memory kicks in to shape the content of public response. In each of these crises New Yorkers responded with distinct, very stringent policies. Thus, 9/11 was followed by an umbrella of surveillance cameras, the installation of physical barriers around public buildings and a virtual "shrinkage" of public space. Superstorm Sandy resulted in massive plans and projects to insulate Lower Manhattan from disastrous flooding. The Covid-19 pandemic brought on massive closures of business, mandatory wearing of masks and large-scale plans to vaccinate.

the world changed. Quite literally out of the blue, two large passenger planes flew low and headed towards a strike on Lower Manhattan. American Airlines Flight 11 and United Airlines Flight 175 had been hijacked by radical Islamists, belonging to a little-known terrorist group called al Qaeda. From a distance of halfway around the world, its leader, Osama Bin Laden, had planned the assault. At 8.46am the first hijacked aircraft struck the North Tower of the World Trade Center. Another pirated plane hit the South Tower just 16 minutes later at 9.02am. Both Towers collapsed within an hour of being struck, enveloping the streets below in a horrid blizzard of ash. The seismic vibration of the cataclysm measured between 2.1 and 2.3 on the Richter scale.

The sudden disintegration of these buildings produced pressure waves that spread more than a million tons of pulverized glass, asbestos and concrete in all directions. Enormous billows of wreckage rumbled through the narrow downtown streets. Their density and pressure lifted small vehicles, broke water and gas lines and smashed windows. Because rescue workers were taken up with trying to save lives, most of the damage was left to simmer. Buildings continued to burn and sprouting water mains were left unattended for hours afterwards.

At and above ground, chaos reigned. Office workers caught on the upper floors of the North and South Towers made their way to higher levels because they mistakenly believed they could be saved by helicopters. On the ground, crowds fled from the site, blocking police and firefighters. The command structure for "first responders", from those in the uniformed services to emergency medical technicians and ambulance drivers, fell apart. Emergency phone operators were left helpless, unable to provide escape routes or give sound advice to those trapped inside the towers. Amidst the tumult, communications were plagued by mechanical failures. Phone lines failed to operate and computers did "crazy things".

The selection of Lower Manhattan was an act of quintessential urban terrorism. The attackers turned the megacity's own might against itself. "Ground zero", as the site of the World Trade Center came to be known, was one of the world's richest strategic targets. Its geographic morphology consisted of a highly clustered, intricately woven bevy of skyscrapers and a business district that held the tiller of world finance.

It was as if the entire neighbourhood had been designed for urban terrorism. During the day the neighbourhood population swelled to 58,000 workers. Its thousands of incoming commuters would be the fodder for mass pandemonium. The pre-eminence of the Twin Towers, coupled to clusters of satellites, made the site vulnerable to a contagion of firestorms. Bin Laden, who had been in the construction business, correctly calculated that, once struck, the skyscrapers would tumble upon one another, magnify the physical destruction and amplify human shock (Savitch 2008). The impact of an explosion could be telegraphed through streets and underground subways, contaminating the air with a swill of fumes and fragments for miles around.

From a schematic point of view the site was a large complex of seven buildings, with the Twin Towers serving as its flagship. The complex was ringed by four buildings of the World Financial Center (home to American Express and Merrill Lynch) and a bevy of banks, insurance companies, hotels, a post office and a cultural centre (the Winter Garden). The New York Stock Exchange is just three short blocks to the southeast. Some commuters travel by bus, automobile, or foot while the largest number are funnelled to their offices by a network of underground mass transit. Figure 2.1 presents a visual rendition of the area. Seven buildings of the World Trade Center (WTC) are designated. To the west are four buildings of the World Financial Center (WFC), the Winter Garden and North Bridge.

The attack had its intended effect. The megacity was caught in panic and confusion. The numbers of dead and injured continually changed and at one-point estimates went as high as 5,000 dead and more than twice that number injured. Trying to locate missing victims was especially disheartening. Relatives and friends of the missing were forced to take matters into their own hands and walked around the site for days with photographs in hand. When

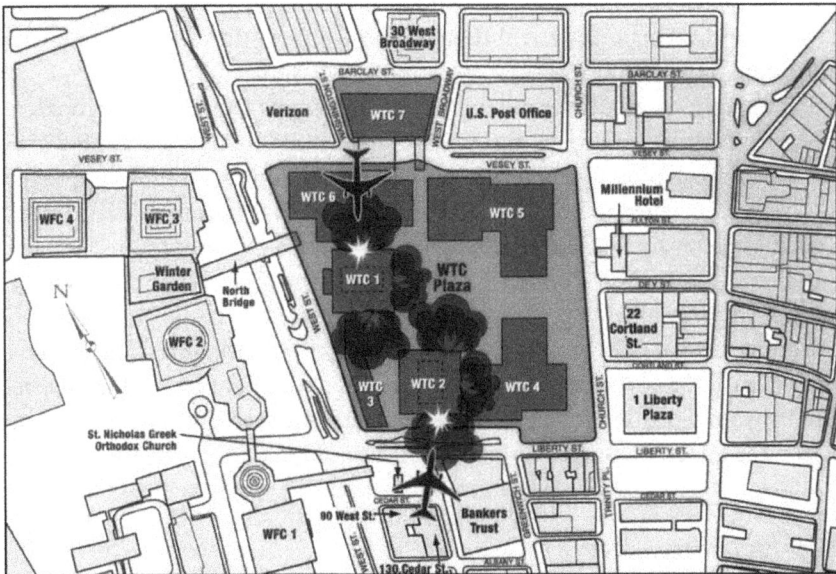

Figure 2.1 Attack on the World Trade Center, 11 September 2001.
Source: Federal Emergency Management Agency. World Trade Center Building Performance Study, FEMA, Region II, New York.

the dust had settled, 9/11 left 2,977 civilians dead, and injured another 25,000 people. It was the deadliest attack ever on American soil.

The propaganda value of striking at the heart of western capitalism was immense. The advantages of attacking it were apparent for any terrorist, yet absolutely unfathomable for most citizens. History informs us that Bin Laden had not been the first to see that value. Over the course of time, a few square miles within New York City's had been either the intended or the actual target of a dozen terrorist attacks. The most memorable of these occurred just eight years before 9/11 when terrorists offered a preview of what was in store for the World Trade Center. In 1993 terrorists exploded a truck loaded with explosives in one of the skyscraper's underground parking lots. The blast, inspired by a blind Muslim cleric, carved a 100-foot crater several stories deep into the World Trade Center and killed six people, but it failed to arouse national alarm.

The first bombing in Lower Manhattan did not occur on 9/11 but more than 80 years earlier. On 16 September 1920 a horse-drawn cart, laden with explosives, pulled up to the front of Wall and Broad Streets. The cart was set alight just as swarms of pedestrians had poured out of the surrounding buildings to enjoy lunch. The blast caused the deaths of 40 people and scores injured. This time it was not Islamic Jihadists but secular anarchists who invoked the violence. The attackers left behind pink leaflets as a warning to capitalists, which read: "There will have to be bloodshed; we will not dodge; there will have to be murder; we will kill because it is necessary; there will have to be destruction; we will destroy to rid the world of your tyrannical institutions" (Susskind 2006).

9/11 became a model for other attacks. The targets included the Brooklyn Bridge, the Holland Tunnel, the Empire State Building and Herald Square. The most frightening prospect was centred on the New York subway system. Al Qaeda threatened to bring about a sequel to 9/11, this time modelled after a Japanese terrorist release of Sarin gas into a Tokyo subway train. The idea was to construct a bulky device capable of releasing a deadly combination of sodium chloride and hydrogen into a bus or subway coach. The gas works by poisoning human cells, stopping the flow of oxygen and bringing about an agonizing death (Susskind 2006). Cell members were thought to have arrived in the city from North Africa and were readying themselves. For some unknown reason the attack was either thwarted or called off.

Response and recovery

Many Americans can remember the iconic photo of George W. Bush, standing upon the wreckage of the World Trade Center, one arm around a fire fighter and the other holding a bull horn. Speaking to the crowd of first responders, Bush assured them:

> I want you all to know that America today, America today is on bended knee, in prayer for the people whose lives were lost here, for the workers who work here, for the families who mourn. This nation stands with the good people of New York City and New Jersey and Connecticut as we mourn the loss of thousands of our citizens.
>
> (Bush 2001)

As Bush continued his speech in the throes of pandemonium, rescue workers yelled back, "We can't hear you!" To which Bush replied, "I can hear you! I can hear you! The rest of the world hears you. And the people who knocked these buildings down will hear all of us soon."

It was a stirring moment that was pregnant with political consequences. Two Republicans rose to the forefront, as the preeminent "crisis managers". George W. Bush lifted his image in the public mind and Rudolph Giuliani became the hero of the moment, as he trudged through the still dusty and hot remnants of what was once New York's most prominent skyscrapers. Both Bush and Giuliani made the most of the moment by demonstrating an intrepidness and sense of purpose in the midst of a once-in-a-lifetime catastrophe. Giuliani hoisted himself to become the most popular mayor in the country, enough so that he was touted as a serious presidential candidate.

It was also a time of national recognition for New York's suffering. The federal government appropriated an estimated $20 billion towards recovery, 9/11 became a day of commemoration and memorials were planted everywhere. At the same time, 9/11 precipitated a sharp economic recession that lasted several years. In its immediate response, New York City's government shed 5 per cent of its labour force and the stock market closed; within three years overall employment declined by more than 117,000 jobs and the regional gross product fell by over 4 per cent (Chernick 2005: 19; Hill & Lindell 2005: 33).

Among the most devastating effects of this politico/violent crisis was the loss of buildings and office space. The city's estimated property and attendant losses reached as high as $83 billion. The figure includes the loss of six buildings of the World Trade Center and the complete destruction of 13.4 million square feet of office space. Putting this in perspective, the destroyed space equalled the entire office stock in the City of Detroit (Fuerst 2005).

New Yorkers' overriding fear was that those firms and their workers that found temporary space would never come back. Indeed, for a while the office market continued to soften, even in the wake of space shortages created by 9/11. In the two years after 9/11, office vacancies rose in Manhattan and elsewhere around the nation. By 2005, however, office markets had turned around. Mid-Manhattan vacancies shrunk to below 8 per cent, while Lower Manhattan fell below 11 per cent. Manhattan's office markets were not back to the halcyon days of the late 1990s, but they had considerably improved from the devastation of 9/11 and after 2010 they were the envy of much of the world.

The year 2005 also saw other sectors returning, but that was soon set back by the economic recession of 2008. New York's economy had returned by 2010 and went on a surge lasting for a decade. Then 2010 was a pivotal economic year for the region, which could be seen in two critical indicators – gross product and total employment. Figures 2.2 and 2.3 display these trends. Notice the stagnation in the recession period of 2008–09 and the pickup after 2010.

Tourism is also a key indicator because it is a luxurious activity and a willingness to travel demonstrates confidence in the place to be visited. That being the case, a year after the attack tourism dropped by 25 per cent and by the second year it had fallen by more than 29 per cent (Savitch 2008). For a while it appeared the tourist industry would fade, but by 2004 it was back up and by 2005 the industry had fully recovered to its pre-disaster level of 6.8 million foreign visitors annually. By 2018 that number had climbed to more than 13 million foreign visitors, more than twice the number of the pre 9/11 period (NYC Data 2021).[3]

As for the site itself, it has taken more than 18 years to rebuild. Consisting of a 14.6-acre expanse of land, the rebuilding was immensely important, because of its symbolic value and as it sits on one of the most sought-after spaces in the world. Daniel Libeskind, the principal architect laid out a plan to suit that significance. Its centrepiece is a new tower at One World Trade Center that reaches a staggering – and emblematic – height of 1,776 feet, including its spire at the top. Number One, or as it was named, Freedom Tower, is the tallest of four new skyscrapers that have arisen. Also included at what was once "ground zero" is a park, a performing arts centre, a memorial and other facilities.

Enduring effects of 9/11

Even today one can spot the scars of 9/11. The effects can be summed up as a lasting shrinkage of urban space, entailing the blocking off of places that were once freely used. Blocking off can either be obtrusive through the use of physical barriers or inobtrusive, through the application of extensive mechanical or human surveillance (eyes on the street). Public spaces, schools, museums

---

3. Total visits had come close to doubling from the pre-9/11 period of 35 million to 65 million (NYC Data 2021).

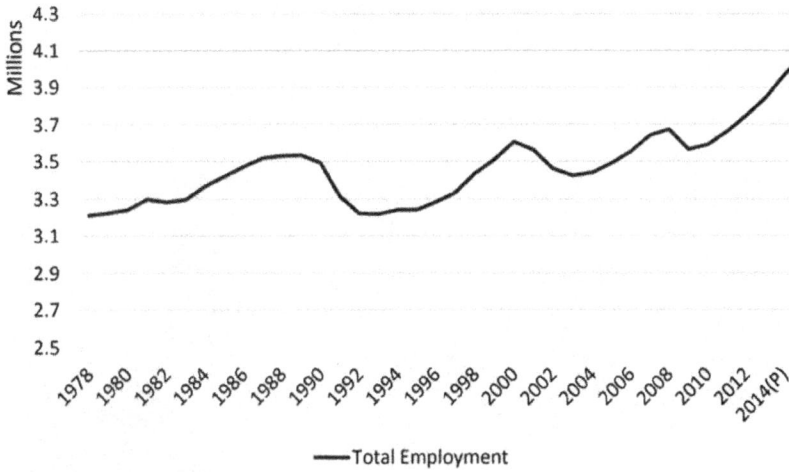

Figure 2.2 Employment rebound in the decades after 9/11.
Source: New York City Planning Department 2015.

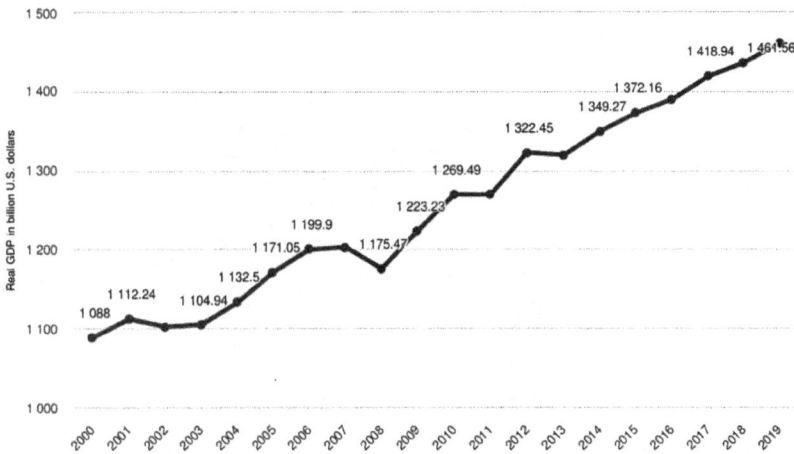

Figure 2.3 Gross domestic product rebound in the decades after 9/11.
Source: Statista 2020.

and other buildings have been "hardened" with gates, bollards, barriers, metal detectors and security guards. Elsewhere, cameras and closed-circuit television cover streets, subway corridors and many corners of the city. Today, an estimated 25,000 cameras of one kind or another can be found in three of the most trafficked boroughs of the city (Manhattan, Brooklyn and the Bronx).

Figure 2.4 Blocking off space at the New York Stock Exchange. Blocking off space has the effect of effectively "shrinking space". Limited space make surveillance against terror attacks easier. It also makes non-terror, social surveillance easier.
Source: Photo by H. V. Savitch.

Figure 2.5 Street barriers in Lower Manhattan. Bollards are employed here mainly to prevent a terror attack via an explosive-laden vehicle. They make it impossible or difficult to penetrate a building.
Source: Photo by H. V. Savitch.

Many of the scrutinized neighbourhoods are African-American or Hispanic, but surveillance can be found everywhere (MIT Technology Review 2022). The average pedestrian in high surveillance areas can expect to be visually recorded scores of times per day.

Of course, the cameras are used for purposes other than terror. Among those reasons are crime-spotting, riot suppression, traffic infractions and "suspicious" social or political activity. New York streets continue to be vibrant but, whatever might be said, public space has not been the same since 9/11. Private surveillance is no better and may be a lot worse. The enclosure of private space is a rising occurrence, with 9/11 often used to justify restrictions. Private surveillance shuts out common use and leaves weary pedestrians without a place to sit or take a brief pause. The most offensive blocking off pertains to the conversion of once usable benches and ledges into uncomfortable, "prickly space" (Flusty 1997). Prickly spaces are found in backless benches, seats that are too high, too hard, steeply sloped or laden with small spikes. The purpose is to keep people away, without individuals having to notice that the spaces are unusually uncomfortable.

In this context we should understand that space is the oxygen of the city and surveillance reduces the room in which it can circulate. Even the most innocuous surveillance dampens that vibrancy. Further to the point, surveillance is surveillance and one cannot always distinguish between whether it is used for "good" or "bad" purposes. Ultimately, the consequences are a net negative for the vitality of the megacity.

Superstorm Sandy

Landfall and its aftermath

What turned out to be the megacity's worst weather crisis began thousands of miles away as a tropical depression in the Caribbean. Within a few days a typical storm was upgraded to a low-grade hurricane, working its way northward towards the Jersey Shore. On the evening of 29 October 2012, superstorm Sandy made landfall near Atlantic City. Just before its arrival a weather official warned a local mayor, "Nobody in the state of New Jersey has ever seen anything like this" (personal interview, 26 July 2017). With winds extending 580 miles from the eye, Sandy was the second-largest Atlantic storm on record. It affected a huge swath of territory along the eastern seaboard in 24 states. Sandy reached as far north as Canada and as far south as Florida. More than anywhere else, Sandy lashed the New York/New Jersey coasts with huge tidal waves.

Dubbed by the popular media as "Frankenstorm", Sandy simultaneously acquired the characteristics of hot and cold temperatures. The hot/cold bipolarities developed as tropical moisture combined with subfreezing air in the core of the upper-level trough. Sandy was at once an extratropical cyclone and a northern blizzard. Temperature extremes varied between 32 and 72 degrees Fahrenheit (Halverson & Rabenhorst 2013). The highest wind gusts swept across the Shore and New York City at 90 to 100 miles per hour. More than a foot of rain drenched the Atlantic shoreline, while 57 inches of snow accumulated in western mountain regions. The flooding was nothing short of immense. New Jersey beaches were overtaken by waves of water as buildings floated like toothpicks on a sidewalk puddle. Gauges at Sandy Hook, New Jersey stopped working after the flooding exceeded 8.1 feet (2.4 metres). It was as if all the cities, towns and villages along the Atlantic seaboard had been dipped into a well.

Seen from above, Sandy came down upon the New York region with unprecedented ferocity. At landfall it ripped up trees, overturned cars, shut down power stations and swept away beaches along the Jersey Shore and Long Island. Major tunnels leading into and out of Manhattan were inundated, as was the city's subway system. Houses and sometimes whole towns were washed away by the severest flooding in centuries. As the rains came down, transformers popped and waters gushed everywhere, spilling raw sewage, gasoline and household chemicals onto the streets. Hardest hit were portions of Lower Manhattan, Staten Island, Queens, Long Island and most of all the New Jersey Shore.

The figures below give us some idea of the geography upon which Superstorm Sandy descended. Figure 2.6 portrays the might of Sandy seen from the upper atmosphere. Figure 2.7 displays the New York-New Jersey metropolitan area stretched along its coastline and its vulnerability to weather disasters. Note a series of anti-flood barriers located on Long Island's South Shore (East Rockaway, Jones Inlet) and at critical points between Long Island's North Shore and the mainland (East River Barrier). These areas had been severely hit by Sandy, especially Rockaway and land adjacent to Lower New York Bay.

As we know, New York was able to grow because of its access to the sea, its rivers and its bevy of inlets and harbours.[4] Its bays, riverbanks and Long Island

---

4. The elongations along south side of the coast are collectively called the New York Bight. The Bight stems from the fact that the Atlantic coast of New Jersey, running approximately north–south, and the southern coast of Long Island, running approximately east–west, form roughly a right angle with the point at the mouth of the Hudson. The Bight Apex is the area including and between the Hudson River estuary and the Raritan River estuary, extending 3.7–4.3 miles (6–7 km) of the coast and includes Raritan Bay and Lower New York Bay.

Figure 2.6 Aerial view of superstorm Sandy.
Source: FEMA After Action Report 2013.

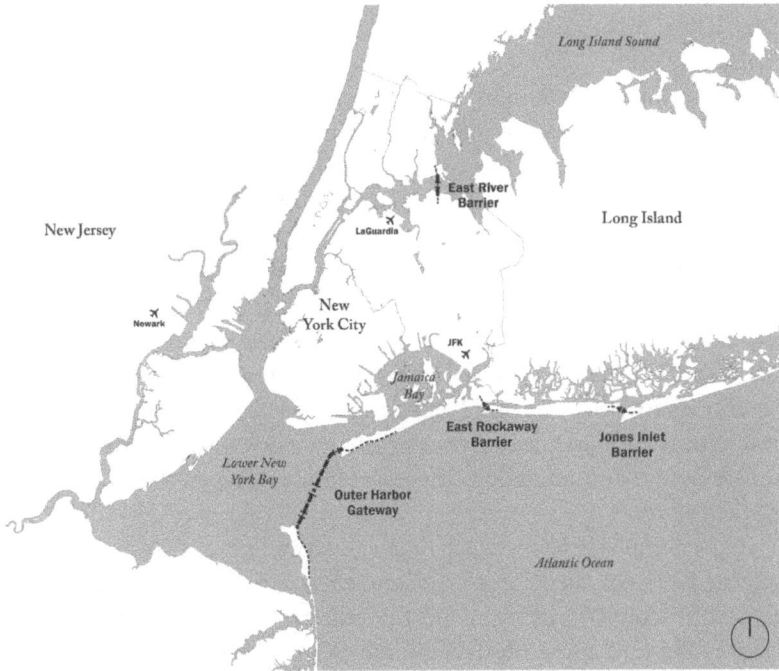

Figure 2.7 Map of megacity barriers.
Source: Wikipedia Creative Commons, at https://creativecommons.org/licenses/by-sa/4.0/deed.en.

Sound express the ubiquity of water. Small peninsulas and tiny islands almost touch one another and, in strategic places, modern engineering has completed the job with bridges and causeways. Along with so many advantages, the surrounding waters can also become a great disadvantage when nature becomes unruly. The most vulnerable sites are also some of its most prosperous commercial and residential areas – the southern tip of Manhattan, the waterfront neighbourhoods of Brooklyn, the southern routes of Long Island heading eastward to Queens and Nassau and Suffolk counties and, not least, the very elongated New Jersey coastline (known as the "Shore").

The rush of the seas did the most damage. Storm surges of 14 feet above the mean lower water mark caused the greatest wreckage (NOAA 2020). At its height superstorm Sandy released 30–32-foot surges (9.1–9.7 metres) in select areas (Savitch & Brown 2017). Sandy took the lives of over 100 people with hundreds more injured. Breaking the numbers down into the megacity's localities, New York City incurred 43 deaths; New Jersey 37, and the Northern/ Long Island suburbs lost 21 people (*New York Times* 2012).[5] Most of the deaths were attributed to drowning, fallen trees and poorly maintained ventilators. The damages in New York City were estimated at $19 billion and another $32 billion in its Long Island and Northern suburbs (*New York Times* 2012). New Jersey incurred similar damages, estimated at $30 billion (Beeson & De Poto 2012).

Within the five boroughs of New York City, one in ten residents lived in a building that incurred flood damage and one in 20 lived in an area where the flooding exceeded 6 feet (Savitch & Brown 2017). In Manhattan, Sandy destroyed Chelsea piers and closed the downtown business district. The storm surge swamped Consolidated Edison's power plant at 14th Street along its way to filling multiple neighbourhoods with waist-deep brine. In Brooklyn the storm wreaked havoc in the waterfront neighbourhood of Red Hook. In Queens the modest beach neighbourhoods of Breezy Point and the Rockaways lost half their houses. Staten Island's heavily blue-collar waterfront neighbourhoods lost 23 residents (Savitch & Brown 2017). All along New York's beach communities, tidal surges shattered windows, split drywalls and swept houses from their foundation. The rush of water clogged streets with sand and blocked sewers.

In northern New Jersey much of Hoboken and Jersey City were under water and the National Guard was called out to help evacuate residents. Some the hardest-hit counties were the most populous. Out of the state's 22 counties, three of the four most affected counties were within the megacity (Hudson,

---

5. Across the largest geographical sweep of the storm 162 people were left dead (FEMA 2013).

Bergen and Essex). Sixty per cent or more of the residents in these counties had no homeowner's insurance and most were high hardship households (low income, high dependency, low educational achievement) (Rutgers University 2013).

The Jersey Shore has always been central to the state's economy. Tourism alone generates more than a half million jobs. Its towns and boroughs serve as large entertainment machines and house thousands of summer tourists and vacation homeowners. During the summer months, the Shore nearly doubles its population, holding more than 700,000 residents, many of whom are New Yorkers. Sandy put that in abeyance. Waterfronts were literally washed away. Bulkheads, jetties and dunes were breached all along the Shore and were of little help in holding back ocean surges. Sandy breached Barnegat Bay and rushed past its connecting bridge. Once the waters receded, most beaches were eroded, many boardwalks were crushed and bridges were shut down.

New Jersey's critical infrastructure was among the first to shut down. The storm quickly put out electrical and utility lines. The lack of power slowed recovery efforts and added significant expense to municipal and household budgets. Estimates show that 2.6 million New Jersey customers were left without power. Some towns were out for as long as 22 days and a large number of other towns were out of power for more than ten days (Rutgers University 2013: 8). Fuel shortages were also rampant, and the governor's office was obliged to adopt a rationing programme. To make matters worse, a good deal of public transit was halted. Some rail lines were knocked out of order for more than a month, affecting millions of passengers. More localized Path Lines to Lower Manhattan were suspended for several weeks (Rutgers University 2013: 35).

Response and recovery

Meanwhile, support for Sandy's victims grew throughout the nation and the region. Celebrities from the world of entertainment held fundraising events. One major telethon dubbed "Hurricane Sandy: Coming Together" featured Jimmy Fallon, Danny DeVito and Christina Aguilera. On another occasion, internationally renowned Mick Jagger and New Jersey's own hero, Bruce Springsteen, gave their talents and time with live benefit performances. The entire chapter of the storm took on a festive air, boosted by placards, T-shirts, and leaflets underscored with the caption, "Stronger than the Storm". The slogan came to define New Jersey and was inscribed into mounds of sand that Sandy had heaped upon boardwalks and nearby streets. Small shops featured the slogan on pins and custom jewellery, and it became the stuff of television commercials and short films.

All this was ideal for politicians, who stood to gain from the publicity. Crises call for the intercession of higher-level authorities. Superstorm Sandy brought to the fore the governors of New York, Andrew Cuomo, and New Jersey, Chris Christie – both becoming the leading crisis managers. They in turn enlisted the support of the President of the United States, Barak Obama. On the New York side, Mayor Michael Bloomberg joined as another lead politician. In a much-publicized event Obama toured the wreckage in each state, with local state politicians at his side. Newspapers and newscasts bannered pictures of Obama-Cuomo, Obama-Christie and Obama-Bloomberg – all of them wearing wind-breakers marked with the logos of their respective offices at the breast pocket. News videos and photos featured each leader gazing upon the debris, as if they were about to clear away the wreckage themselves.

The political payoffs were substantial. For Obama, the post-Sandy tour made him look "presidential" and presented him with an "October surprise" in an election year. Polls registered a "Sandy bump" for Obama; even his rival, Mitt Romney, acknowledged the shift (Koning & Redlawsk 2016: 87). The polls also treated Governor Christie quite well and he enjoyed an 80 per cent Sandy-specific approval rating that helped his re-election (Koning & Redlawsk 2016: 87–8). Sandy also burnished the already high standings of Governor Cuomo and Mayor Bloomberg; both of whom managed to pry loose a generous amount of federal aid.

By the time the crisis had matured, Congress was ready to go along and it passed a $51 billion disaster relief programme covering 12 states. Washington DC and New York City captured the lion's share of the award with $13 billion. New Jersey received considerably less at just $4.5 billion. Not until years later did New Jersey residents discover Christie's ineptitude at securing funds nor did the residents of both states realize that it would be as long as five years before recovery set in. The reasons for the delays and the disparity between the states are multi-fold, having to do with matching funds, the numerous federal departments involved and the higher density of assets in New York City.

If nothing else, politically Sandy was a "wake-up call" about global warming. Polls taken before and after Sandy revealed an 82 per cent rise in the proportion of respondents concerned about global warming. Sandy brought the megacity to a new sense of reality. Three-quarters of those same respondents said it was "somewhat likely" that global warming would cause another natural disaster (Koning & Redlawsk 2016: 83). Since then, New Jersey has strengthened its support for disaster prevention and mitigation with programmes to buy out flood-prone properties, elevate buildings and reduce development in vulnerable areas (Savitch & Brown 2017).

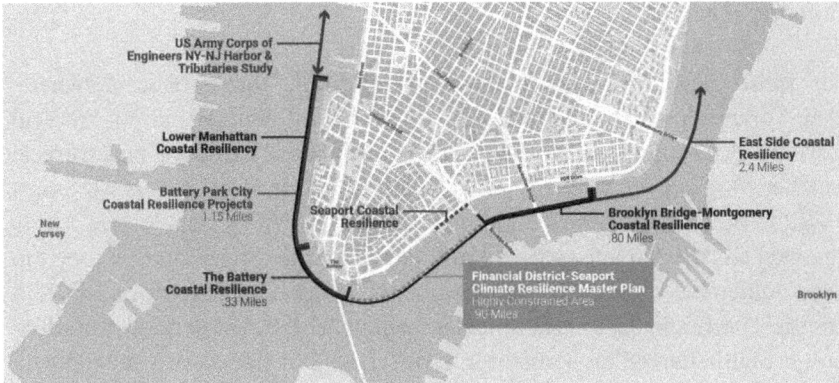

Figure 2.8 Map of Lower Manhattan's U Type Resiliency Projects.
Source: New York City, Mayors Office of Climate Resiliency 2020.

The city came to support a massive re-visioning of its waterfront, initially kicked off by HUD-sponsored projects but eventually gaining a momentum of its own.[6] Emerging from this is an emphasis on recasting Lower Manhattan as a model of urban resilience with both "hard" infrastructure (sea walls, elevated platforms) and "soft" facilities (non-corroding park furniture, plants and shrubs that can live in salt water). Emphasized areas include the Battery, Brooklyn Bridge and neighbourhoods along the Lower East Side. All this is meant to protect New York's financial district and seaport, as well as the commercial heart around the World Trade Center. Figure 2.8 captures that area, along with planned resilience projects.

Estimated to cost a billion dollars in capital expenditure alone, the resilience core takes the form of an asymmetrical U around the tip of Manhattan. Hard infrastructure consists of advanced drainage systems and a raised esplanade at the Battery. Around the Brooklyn Bridge reversable flood walls will be built that normally recede into the floor and flip up to create an enclosed shield. More passive or "soft" resilience allow for the creation of parks and green space over which sea water can glide during a coastal storm (NYC Mayor's Office of Climate Resiliency 2020). Finally, the Metropolitan Transportation Authority (MTA) has invested over $7 billion in submarine doors, Kevlar curtains and mechanical gates. Con Edison has made a similar commitment, constructed Kevlar flood walls and is redoing its control systems so that circuit breaks now stand 35 feet above ground level.

---

6. The project has its roots in a HUD-announced a National Disaster Resilience Competition (NDRC) in 2016. The NDRC programme awarded $1 billion to states and localities in order to encourage resilience programmes begun earlier. New Jersey Shore communities received $15 million to bolster local resilience projects while New York City received $176 million (Savitch & Perez 2016).

Enduring effects of Sandy

For most New Yorkers hurricanes were events that struck elsewhere. New Yorkers have always been ready to write off concerns about tropical storms by claiming that Florida was the designated locale for bad tropical weather. Ten-foot snowstorms could be tolerated, but New Yorkers were supposed to be spared massive flooding and 100mph winds. Superstorm Sandy changed all that and left megacity residents with the realization that they too were vulnerable to hurricanes and massive inundation. The efforts to avoid another Sandy and the broad enthusiasm about "U-type" projects surrounding Lower Manhattan tell us something about the public impact of a superstorm.

Much of this is fed by an emotional component. Just two years after Sandy a study of 600 volunteers in Nassau, Suffolk, Queens and Staten Island showed measurable increases in stress levels. Participants had a mean stress level higher than the general population and 30 per cent of the sample were categorized as "high stress" (Schwartz *et al.* 2016a). Another study demonstrated the long-term effects of post-traumatic stress disorder due to the storm, especially among women and poorer segments of the population (Schwartz *et al.* 2016b). Has this moved the needle to a commitment of total protection? Probably not, but New Yorkers have moved further towards doing something about climate change than Miamians or New Orleanians. As a whole the megacity continues to invest more money in storm protection and mitigation than any of its counterparts (Savitch, Sawislak & Renne 2020).

The Covid-19 pandemic

The contagion strikes

Pandemics spread disease over a wide geography, usually involving multiple countries or continents. By comparison epidemics are geographically limited, although no less different in content and just as deadly.[7] Natural crises brought about by diseases are like no other because they are invisible and their striking or ending time is hard to pinpoint. Contagious disease has an unlimited opportunity to expand and swallow whole segments of a population with debilitating effect on an entire nation. Plague killed nearly a quarter of the Athenian population in 431 BCE, leading to its defeat in the Peloponnesian War and its eclipse

---

7. In introducing the subject, we use both terms interchangeably, but in discussing Covid-19 the term pandemic is more appropriate.

as a great power (Glaeser 2022: 18). A millennium later (541–88) an even deadlier pandemic struck at the heart of the Byzantine Empire. *Yersina Pestis* killed thousands each day in Constantinople and scourged the Mediterranean Basin. Disease travelled even faster in the Roman Empire, with devastating mortality to its principal city. The Black Death was an unalloyed horror for fourteenth-century Florence and nearly destroyed the city. The list goes on: the Bubonic Plague in seventeenth-century Vienna and Prague; smallpox in eighteenth-century Boston and Charleston; and cholera in nineteenth-century London and Paris (Glaeser 2022: 18). By the twentieth century the Spanish flu (1918–19) wreaked havoc in San Francisco, and polio (1908–60) spread rapidly in New York and Philadelphia.

What best characterizes the spread of disease? First, density is necessary for a contagion to expand. The higher the density, the more widespread the infection. The Athenian plague is thought to have spread after Pericles brought the population behind city walls to protect them against sea-borne invaders. It was not war but an invisible pathogen that defeated Athens. Second, travel and internationalization are agents of contagion. Three-quarters of the deaths in Napoleon's invading armies were caused by typhus. It was no coincidence that some of the worst epidemics in history occurred among mobile colonizers and soldiers in the nineteenth century empires of the United Kingdom and France. The Spanish flu was transmitted at the end of the First World War, after European and American troops served abroad and returned home. Third, untreated waste and open sewage are the great incubators of disease. Among the contributions of cities to civilization was their capacity to sanitize living quarters, clean up factory spaces, build sewer lines and furnish clean water to residents.

All this required research, construction and enormous investments of capital. In New York civil engineering worked with epidemiology to build the Croton reservoir and educate the citizenry in public hygiene. The names of New Yorkers Stephen Smith and Peter Cooper achieved heroic recognition because these men were respectively the founders of proper sanitation systems and a free architectural/engineering academy that helped modernize New York. Finally, much as it is difficult to pinpoint the beginning or end of a pandemic, it is also difficult to develop the means for eradicating it. New York and other cities knew how to defeat terror or at least contain it.[8] We know when a hurricane is approaching and have a grip on how to mitigate its effects.

---

8. Terror has largely been defeated as a contagion in major metropolises such as London, Paris, Jerusalem, Moscow and others, although it still can raise its head from time to time as it did in Paris during 2019 (Savitch 2008).

But disease is very different and can take us by surprise. Thankfully, scientists developed a vaccine for Covid-19, but the disease has evolved resistant mutations. While vaccines have helped enormously, they have not been able to stop it.[9]

The current Covid-19 pandemic began with just a handful of cases. Initially it was thought to be a variety of SARS-CoV-2 virus, which led epidemiologists such as Dr Anthony Fauci, and politicians such as Governor Cuomo and Mayor de Blasio to assure the public that the disease posed no real threat to society. Fauci initially played down the disease. Responding to a question on 21 January 2020, Fauci described Covid-19 as "very low risk" and added, "Obviously, you need to take it seriously and do the kind of thing the Centers for Disease Control (CDC) and the Department of Homeland Security is doing. But this is not a major threat to the people of the United States and this is not something that the citizens of the United States right now should be worried about" (Austin American Statesman 2020).

Fauci did caution that this was an "evolving situation" that should be "looked at very carefully" and the government should be prepared to manage it (Catsmaditis 2020). While not putting his finger on the alarm button, Fauci did intend to convey that the dangers of a future epidemic were very real, but he did not believe Covid-19 would be the culprit. The politicians soon followed suit, although not with Fauci's scepticism. More than a month later, Cuomo repeated the "low risk" theory and as late as 8 March stated, "We have a lot of information on this." He added, "There is more fear, more anxiety, than the facts would justify" (Barkan 2021). De Blasio also voiced doubt about the contagion, advising on 26 February that the disease was only transmitted through the closest contact, and he let it be known that "we can really keep this thing contained" (Blake & Rieger 2020).

The policymakers turned out to be wrong, at least through the critical months of February and March. On the last day of February, Fauci repeated the caution that New York was facing an "evolving situation" (Greenberg 2020). All along, Cuomo took his cues from the scientists and once they shifted so too did he. In a 2 March press conference, the governor confessed, "We underestimated this virus. It's more powerful. It's more dangerous than we expected" (Torres 2020). De Blasio also began to recognize the danger posed by the disease but was not prepared for the rapidity of change. On one day he rejected the idea of closing the schools and only six days later he announced

---

9. We do have the know-how and technology for dealing with weather events. Whether we have the political will to fully deal with them is another matter. In the case of epidemics, a cure has never been found for HIV/Aids or Ebola. These diseases have been managed rather than terminated.

their shutdown. New York City has the largest school district in the country and suddenly closing their doors is not an easy matter for teachers, pupils or their families.

The lockdown also aggravated an already bad relationship between the mayor and the governor. Both men were long-time political rivals and had previously argued over the adoption of minimum wages, support for charter schools and the treatment of Uber drivers. Covid-19 raised the issue of who was the better crisis manager. Tempers flared over school closures and reopening and the availability of playgrounds. Cuomo chastised de Blasio over mismanaging the police, as the protests spilled into violence and intersected with Covid-19. The governor and the mayor also clashed over what neighbourhoods to open up or keep under lockdown. De Blasio sought to reclose some highly afflicted neighbourhoods, only to be vetoed by Cuomo, who contended the boundaries for designating a stricken community were insufficient (CNBC News 2021).

Each of the leaders encountered continuing troubles, including personal ones.[10] Cuomo was charged with moving coronavirus patients into nursing homes and worsening the contagion and causing needless deaths. De Blasio was called out for using double standards, when he clumsily threatened Ultra-Orthodox Jews with fines and possible arrest for attending a funeral, yet praised Black Lives Matter and encouraged thousands to march arm in arm on the streets. Both men found themselves tussling with Ultra-Orthodox Jewish communities in Brooklyn over the enforcement of Covid-19 restrictions. De Blasio was especially unpopular. As he was leaving office, the percentage of citizens who disapproved of his mayoralty exceeded the proportion who approved. De Blasio fared better with black and Hispanic voters, but he was deeply disliked by white voters with nearly 60 per cent of outer borough residents holding him in disfavour (Stewart 2019)

Pandemics care little for politics and New York was about to be accorded the unsavoury designation of being the hardest hit city in the country. During the pandemic's infancy New York confirmed more coronavirus cases than China

---

10. Adding to doubts about Cuomo's crisis management were a series of incidents regarding his sexual misconduct. A half-dozen women, including staffers, charged the governor with inappropriate touching. Much to the consternation of the press and fellow Democrats the governor held on, until threats of impeachment brought on his resignation in August 2021. The governor's brother, Chris Cuomo, also became involved in the scandal by trying to use his position as a newscaster to intimidate witnesses. De Blasio's personal indiscretions also took a political toll. The mayor was extensively criticized for using a city-supplied, chauffeur-driven limousine, along with police escort to drive him to a gym for morning workouts. Some politicians might have survived the negative publicity, but de Blasio always seemed aloof from and distrusted by the public. He never recovered his popularity and may never again.

or Iran. Covid-19 was growing exponentially: by 25 March, over 17,800 cases had been confirmed, with 199 deaths. Within just a few days the number of cases jumped to 23,000 and 365 deaths. Within a month that number leapt to more than 72,000 cases and almost 2,500 deaths. At the time, the city's infection rate was five times higher than the rest of the country and accounted for about a quarter of the country's deaths. The megacity region accounted for about a third of the country's deaths (*Economist* 2020a: 19). The most worrying aspects of the pandemic were found in the positivity rates for preliminary antibody testing. Those rates reached more than 21 per cent in the early months of 2020 (NYC Board of Health 2020).

Within the city, the geographic concentration of cases skewed towards lower-middle-class or poor neighbourhoods. Most of affluent Manhattan was spared and the hardest-hit neighbourhoods were found in the Bronx (Mott Haven, East Tremont, Coop City), in densely packed areas of north-central Queens (Corona, East Elmhurst, Rockaway) and sections of central and east Brooklyn (Borough Park and East New York). Some of these neighbourhoods were subject to high crime rates and they housed a disproportionate number of distressed households, whose health needs were underserved. Others contained very large households with adults and children sharing the same living space. In some Jewish neighbourhoods Ultra-Orthodox congregations often crammed into older synagogues and prayed without masks. The infection in these neighbourhoods was six times higher than the rest of the city. Taking Brooklyn as an example, white, affluent Brooklyn Heights and gentrified Red Hook incurred approximately one infection for every 80 residents, while the infection rates for impoverished East New York and Ultra-Orthodox Borough Park were about one in 25 residents (NYC Health Department 2020).

Response and recovery

Thereafter followed a period of massive lockdowns ordered by the governor and mayor. The orders were done by executive fiat throughout the state; they were implemented by city, county and local officials. Only the most essential businesses (pharmacies, grocery markets) could remain open and they were limited to strict crowd controls. Most other businesses were ordered closed. Retail businesses stopped serving customers; restaurants, diners and catering services ceased operations; parks, gyms and theatres were shut; haircutters, beauty salons and personal services went dark. Most government offices were closed, as were universities, schools and public activities. Subways, buses, airports and public transit either serviced a fraction of their ridership or came to a standstill.

Covid-19 was by far the worst and the most unusual crisis of its time. In breadth, duration and relentlessness this pandemic beat everything else. Most of all was its ability to instil mass fear. Eco-fiscal crises could be explained by the familiar turns of the business cycle, hurricanes by the natural course of weather disasters, and terror attacks by the vicissitudes of world politics. But what accounts for the uncontrolled spread of a massive disease in this day and age? For the first time in New York's modern history its streets were emptied for a prolonged and indefinite period. It was as if the entire region were under siege. Governor Cuomo took to the airways with daily reports. His easy style and candid descriptions were viewed quite positively. As a rule, New Yorkers very much accepted the restrictions. Most stayed willingly at home, appearing at open windows, balconies and porches to cheer first responders and health personnel as they returned from work. A 7pm ritual brought Manhattanites to their windows as one musical celebrity stepped onto his balcony and sang inspiriting lyrics from the hit Broadway play *Man of La Mancha*.

In addition to massive shutdowns, New York's lockdowns also included mandatory wearing of masks, social distancing where unrelated individuals must stay at least six feet apart, prohibitions against crowds, stay-at-home orders for school children and other restrictions. From its beginnings in March 2020 to the easing of indoor dining restrictions in February 2021, the lock-down could be said to have lasted for about a year.[11] The arrival of a vaccine and the establishment of huge centres for their administration in early 2021 did ease public tensions.

Looking at the general pattern of the Covid-19 pandemic, the indicators at one time were severe but had eased off, although in a ratchet-like, erratic motion. Thus, at the outbreak of the pandemic in early 2020 the running case average was 62.5 per 100,000 residents; months later, in 2021, that number shrank to a tiny 4.4 cases per 100,000; for a brief period in January of 2022 the proportion shot up again to 486 per 100,000, only to go down again in May 2022 to 45.8 per 100,000. The death toll did drop more steadily, going from 750 per 100,000 in 2020 down to 75 per 100,000 in 2021 and diminishing to 9.1 per 100,000 in 2022. Not shown are positivity rates. These rates at which people tested "positive" for the infection sunk to 6.9 per cent by spring 2022.

All told, the crisis has exacted a steep toll. By spring 2022 New York had suffered 2.4 million Covid-19 cases and over 40,000 dead. The line graphs

---

11. It is difficult to ascertain exactly when the lockdown ended because of its very gradual termination in stages. Thus, public elementary schools reopened in December 2020, but movie theatres did not reopen until three months later in March 2021 (Kerr 2021).

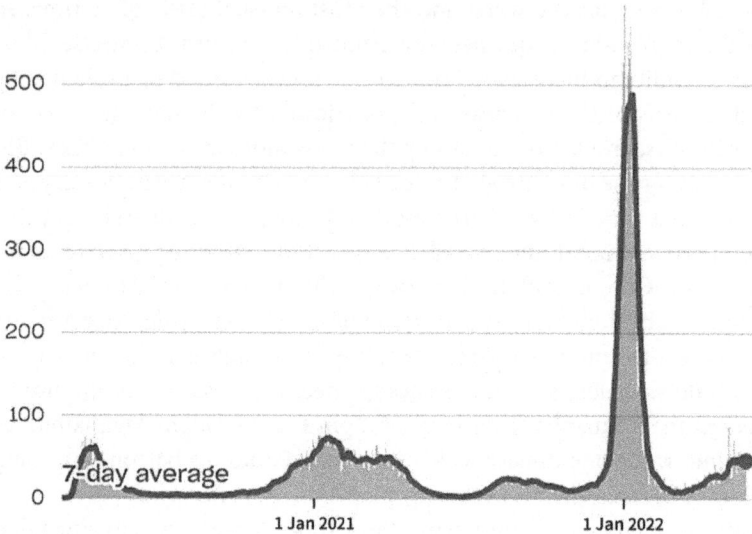

Figure 2.9 Daily Covid-19 cases per 100,000 in NYC, March 2020–May 2022. *Source:* The City 2022.

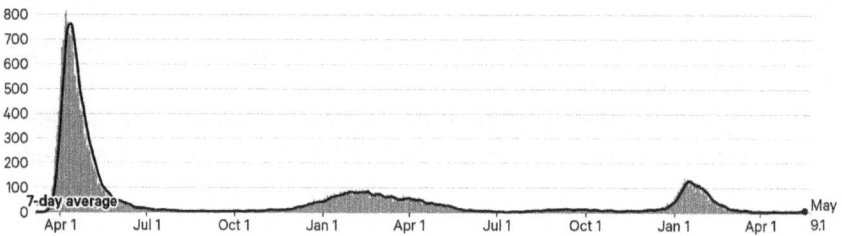

Figure 2.10 Deaths due to Covid-19 in NYC per 100,000, April 2020–May 2022. *Source:* The City 2022.

below show the progression of those cases from March 2020 through the first half of 2022.

Within the 13-county megacity, the human cost has been enormous. More than three million people have been afflicted by Covid-19 and more than 50,000 have died from it (Statista 2022). Most surprising, despite the scientific advance from a century ago, the death rates for Covid-19 are not far from that of the Spanish flu as of 1919. The fatality rate for the 1919 flu was 287.17 per 100,000 of the population, while the Covid-19 pandemic stands at 202.08 per 100,000 persons (Faust, Zengqiu & Del Rio 2020).

Enduring effects of Covid-19

The stereotype of New Yorkers suggests they are an unruly lot, highly individualistic and largely disobedient. A classic book on the city titled *The Ungovernable City* sees its politics as chaotic and its governance as an endless barrage of unresolvable issues piling atop one another (Yates 1977). It may be that crisis brings out the best in us. New York's bout with the pandemic may have debunked at least part of that image.

Confronted with a life-and-death choice New Yorkers showed a remarkable likeness of mind. New York's support for restrictive regulation has been surprisingly high, compared to the rest of the nation and Los Angeles. Particularly interesting are a series of questions, asked at the height of the pandemic in 2020, about the willingness of respondents to sacrifice their freedom for a greater good. This includes a willingness to self-isolate, supported by 85 per cent of New Yorkers compared to 77 per cent for the rest of the country and 83 per cent for Angelenos. Another restriction, the prohibition of indoor dining was supported by 81 per cent of New Yorkers, just 66 per cent of the rest of the nation and 72 per cent of Angelenos. Likewise, mandatory wearing of face masks was supported by 80 per cent of New Yorkers, just 60 per cent in the rest of the nation and 78 per cent of Angelenos. Compliance with mandatory stay-at-home orders, something accepted in Shanghai, was accepted by 86.7 per cent of New Yorkers (Centers for Disease Control 2020). New York had been struck especially hard by Covid-19 and its residents would naturally tend to be more supportive of restrictive measures, but the attitudes do reveal a new willingness to bend its streak of rampant individualism into singular governmentally imposed purpose.

Like so many other megacities New York is still undergoing the pandemic. By now it is less of a shock and less of a headline grabber. It may be a bit of a stretch to say that with far fewer deaths and hospitalizations Covid-19 is now "normalized", but the disease has become part of daily life. In the meantime, Covid-19 has affected every segment of the population. Local government, industry, hospitals, health professionals and first responders have all been cast as players on the public stage. This has been both "good" and "bad". "Good" because it produced a common cause within a population that now realizes the value of collective action. "Bad" because Covid-19 had brought misery to millions of people.

Covid-19's most profound effect comes from its threat to densification. At bottom a megacity is a multi-nodal model of density, proximity and closeness. The evacuation of businesses, schools and public space has been devastating for urban life. Before Covid-19 only 5 per cent of the workforce worked from home. Since Covid-19 that proportion soared to nearly 70 per cent (Apollo Technical 2022). The question is whether New Yorkers will return to their workplaces, their schools, their theatres and the like. At present nearly a third of the megacity's workforce still operates from a distance (Varadarajan 2022). We cannot say for sure whether this "enduring effect" will continue or not. History and experience suggest a return to traditional places and spaces. Schools, theatres, gyms, etc., seem already to have reattracted their clientele. The question is whether business will follow that pattern?

The answer is more complicated than one would expect, mostly because a new generation of workers has grown accustomed to remote work at home. Data continue to point up the advantages to learning and innovation that stem from on-site, in-the-flesh work. Indeed, recent studies show that on-site workers are more likely to earn more money and be promoted than remote workers (De La Roca & Puga 2017). But empirics and human behaviour do not always point in the same direction. Attitudes towards work, life and values also count, especially among "Generation Z". Should remote workers continue to resist on-site work, the consequences for office markets, business and the city would be devastating. A return to on site-work might still leave a residue of depression, which like other crises would fade and leave the megacity restored.

Conclusion: crises and megacity resilience

Crises play a major role in the evolution of cities. Crises stand out because they shape the course of megacity events and influence both the making and unmaking of political leaders. All three crises, 9/11, Sandy and Covid-19, seriously affected the regional economy and its psycho/social complexion. We have noted how both Mayor Rudolph Giuliani and Governor Andrew Cuomo rode the waves, respectively of 9/11 and the Covid-19 pandemic. At one time each of these individuals were among the most popular politicians in America. The Cuomo case is especially revealing because it precipitated the collapse of a family political dynasty and shows that power can be astonishingly ephemeral – compelling at one moment only to vanish the next. We add to this twosome New Jersey Governor Christopher Christie, who also was hailed as a hero, as he toured the state's beaches in the wake of Sandy and hugged then President Barak Obama as a show of gratitude. Just as quickly all three men fell from public favour. Giuliani's fame plummeted because of an ungraceful association with the Trump presidency. Cuomo fell prey to charges of sexual abuse, forcing him to resign from the governorship in utter disgrace. Governor Christie never recovered from the embarrassment of being photographed in an officially closed state park, sunning his ample midriff and enjoying a vacant beachfront with his family while other Jerseyites endured the heat.

Crises also tell us something about the resilience of cities. The onset of a crisis often evokes exaggerated predictions of gloom and doom. Writing at the time that New York City was in the throes of fiscal disintegration, Jason Epstein titled his article "The Last Days of New York". In recalling the city's lost glory, Epstein could only see a future of ruin and abandonment. "The city's problems are by now so complex," he wrote, "that there may be no solution to them at all" (Epstein 1977: 72). At about the same time, noted urbanists George Sternlieb and James Hughes described the region's future as a "bleak one" and concluded it was incapable of stemming the outflow of jobs and wealth (Sternlieb & Hughes 1977: 164). It took a decade to prove the experts wrong, but by the 1990s New York's economy had restructured and sparkled with post-industrial development.

After the attack on the World Trade Center, two eminent urbanists, James Kunstler and Nikos Saligeros, titled their essay "The End of Tall Buildings" and argued that America's infatuation with skyscrapers was over. "We are convinced," they wrote "that the age of skyscrapers is at an end … We predict that no new megatowers will be built, and existing ones are destined to be dismantled" (Kunstler & Saligeros 2001: 1). Since then, New York has gone through an unprecedented boom in skyscraper construction, many of them taller than ever before. Looming at more than 1,700 feet, One World Trade Center defies those who claimed that those tall buildings were obsolete. Elsewhere in the city the number of office towers above 1,300 feet had risen to include nine in 2013, ten in 2014 and 15 in 2015. From a historical perspective, eight of the city's ten tallest buildings were built since 9/11 (Routley 2020). The region has also experienced a surge of tall buildings. Long Island City boasts a 67-storey tower, Brooklyn a 93-story tower and Jersey City now has its own skyline that can be seen from Lower Manhattan.

The predictions after superstorm Sandy were no less catastrophic. Reports by the Union of Concerned Scientists (2018) and Climate Central (2014) described parts of Manhattan and Long Island as facing significant exposure to flooding within the next 20 years. Both organizations predicted that Manhattan's entire Battery and half of the city's subway system would be inundated within the next 25 years. Also included as a "serious risk" were parts of Long Island and large sections of the Jersey Shore, both of which have been subject to recurring flooding.

One might surmise that investors would run from highly vulnerable properties. Precisely the opposite has occurred. At least through to the beginning of 2020, the region had enjoyed a property boom. Office space in Lower Manhattan had been soaked up just as fast as it was ready. Housing prices in Nassau and Suffolk counties rose right up through the onset of Covid-19. Along the Jersey Shore, superstorm Sandy wiped away whole towns and large parts of others. Within a year the same towns were being rebuilt with luxurious single-family houses, constructed to withstand high tides and storms. The newly adapted houses also sold at premium prices. One town saw its destroyed housing replaced with units at triple the former values.

The lesson is that crises are serious matters, but opinion leaders' reactions to them are short-sighted, overstated and most often incorrect. 9/11 and Sandy show the amplitude of false claims and the ease with which they are made. Whether or not Covid-19 fits a historic pattern is still an open question, but our own optimism about the megacity's resilience is firmly rooted in experience.

3

Building a global megacity: corporate-centred urban development and leadership

In this chapter we explore the ways in which leaders have endeavoured to use policy, planning, incentives and regulation to capitalize on these territorial features and manage the resultant tensions that growth brings to people and place (Kantor, Savitch & Haddock 2002). While there is no question that capital, or more specifically corporate interests, have long been viewed as fundamental to the fiscal health of the region, recent history reveals a more complex set of relationships underlying development decisions. Indeed, today it would appear that labour and civil society groups, undergirded by powerful left-wing political actors, have become a force to be reckoned with. Only time will tell if we are seeing a new phase of development in the megacity, a decentring of the growth machine, or perhaps a counterweight is pushing back in the form of an anti-growth collation advocating for people-centred development (Vogel & Swanstrom 1989).

The New York megacity represents a vast "strategic place in contemporary globalization" processes (Taylor *et al.* 2014: 3), where local leaders have endeavoured to manage growth and the inevitable pressures it brings to bear on people and place through bargaining and negotiation. Indeed, one of the unique traits of this powerful city has been its capacity to adapt and change through leadership, policy and planning without compromising its iconic economic and political position domestically or internationally. New York is nothing if not resilient.

New York is first and foremost an economic agglomeration, drawing a diverse range of businesses, a vast pool of labour and extensive flows of capital. As a megacity, it offers the prospect of economies of scale for business. Firms can benefit from proximity to supportive services, competitors and access to supply chains. The global city, as we have seen, is also one that has a wide range of quality-of-life features – ample housing, cultural facilities, public space, transportation and access to educational institutions. Thus it is also presumed to be a place that attracts talent, and by extension serves as a locus for innovation. Finally, it is also the "positionality" of the territory itself, within global economic and political systems, that heightens the desirability of locating in the megacity. In combination, these features serve to frame growth and development of the city over time.

Today, New York has a strong knowledge-based economy that brings together finance, insurance, real estate, communication, information and supportive services, health, education, proximity to competitors, collaborators, international airports, labour, regional transportation systems, news agencies, capital markets and corporate headquarters, which all factor into the calculus of locating in this type of agglomeration (Sassen 2007; Taylor *et al.* 2014).

New York did not simply emerge as an outcome of larger structural forces, but rather through the actions of political, social and economic actors. Not surprisingly, this leads at times to contestation. Although growth offers benefits to some, it also has negative externalities such as increased land rents due to competition for limited space and environmental problems derived from added congestion and use of urban spaces (McCann & Oort 2019: 11–12). As Sassen (2007: 170) highlights: "Global cities are the sites for the over-valorization of corporate capital and the devalorization of disadvantaged workers; but they are also the sites for new types of politics that allow the latter to emerge as political subjects." The story of this region, therefore, is one in which different groups have sought influence, both within the region and in the larger global system. Not surprisingly, local leaders have found themselves in the challenging position of managing the inherent tensions indicative of a locality that is intimately tied to what is at times a turbulent and competitive global economic system.

In what follows we explore economic growth in the megacity through consideration of the development decisions made by local leaders at key points in its history. In each case we consider the tension underlying those decisions and the ways in which adaptation was ultimately achieved. While we could occupy an entire volume on this topic, here we highlight two key moments of crisis/change and the policy interventions taken by local leaders. We then use these cases to consider what lessons they offer us today in 2022, as the region faces what some pundits see as an almost "existential challenge" to the future of a global megacity (Gelinas 2020), as the logic of growth and density are confronted with issues of health and safety, and globalization is being chipped away by national isolationist policies.

Two short case studies are used to reveal the dynamics of leadership in response to the pressures of growth and to highlight the ways in which adaptation to those pressures has been achieved in this megacity. Each highlights the delicate dance that leaders have had to perform in balancing what are at times the competing demands of business, labour and civil society. Endeavouring to anchor and lure a private sector whose interests do not always fit comfortably with others in the polis. Indeed, competing visions have led to distinctly different approaches at different moments in time.

Our first case study explores the megacity from a macro perspective, considering initiatives taken to help the megacity rebound in the aftermath of the fiscal crisis of 1975. The focus in the first case is largely on the local political responses that were promoted in the 1980s and which in many ways set the stage for the emergence of New York as a global megacity. The second case study explores the contemporary politics of development in the megacity through consideration of the failed Amazon HQ2 deal 2017–19. These vignettes represent important moments in the political and economic evolution of the megacity and reveal the nuanced ways in which the megacity's political leaders, private sector actors and civil society have responded to systemic shocks, addressed growth imperatives and, more broadly, the ways in which the megacity city has adapted over time.

Although New York has long held a core position in the global economy, this has not occurred by chance, but rather through active political engagement with the physical, social and economic contours of the region, by the actions of savvy leaders "seizing natural advantages to create regional wealth and power" (Kantor *et al.* 2012: 99). To understand where we are today, we need to begin with a look back at the early history of this megacity's development.

Global megacity long-term economic trends

Early regional development: manufacturing and industry

New York began to set the seeds for its eventual emergence as a global city almost two centuries ago. Even before the consolidation of its five boroughs (core and inner urban) into a single political jurisdiction in 1898, Manhattan had already established itself as global hub of economic activity and a magnet for new populations. Consider, for example, that, during the 1800s, 70 per cent of all immigrants arriving in the United States landed first in the port of Manhattan (Gross 2018). By the early 1840s there were some 40 passenger ships arriving on a daily basis, carrying as many as 1,000 people (Burrows & Wallace 1998). It "became the gatekeeper for new entry to the United States via the Atlantic" (Gross 2018: 233). Not surprisingly, according to the 1860 census, in New York City alone (then not counting Brooklyn), 47 per cent of the population were foreign born. The combined population of the megacity's already urbanized territory (Manhattan, Brooklyn, Newark, Jersey City and Elizabeth) was already 1,193,064 by 1860 (US Census Bureau 1864). By 1890 the megacity had a population of 2.5 million (US Census Bureau 1895).

New York was not simply an immigrant hub, it was also emerging as a central node in global trade. Thus the region was, even at its nascent stages, already a global magnet for population and commerce.

> In 1849 over three thousand ships sailed or steamed into the harbour from more than 150 foreign ports ... and they carried with them half the nation's imports and departed with nearly one-third its exports. In the Gold Rush decade ... tonnage through the port jumped another 60%.   (Burrows & Wallace 1998: 653)

There are a variety of reasons for its early economic dominance, some natural geographic advantages and others by design. The area's proximity to the Atlantic Ocean and the Hudson River meant the ease of access for European traders. Its deep ports created a natural advantage for shipping. Decisions by public and private sector actors to invest in transportation and communication infrastructure were also crucial. Linking the burgeoning metropolis to a regional telegraph system in 1844 meant that information flowed from New York through Philadelphia, to Washington and beyond. By 1858 the United States and British governments, in concert with private sector partnerships, had built the first transatlantic cable system, which connected New York and London (Burrows & Wallace 1998: 676). In 1878 the Metropolitan Telephone and Telegraph Company wired a 33 square mile area surrounding Lower Manhattan for telephone. Alongside of the communication networks were ongoing investments in transit infrastructure (i.e. the Erie Canal, railroads, subways, ferries, tunnels and bridges), which together solidified New York's economic dominance by the turn of the century. The formation of the New York Stock Exchange, alongside the cotton, butter and cheese commodities exchanges in the late 1800s, the passage of legislation supporting the consolidation of small businesses into corporations by the state of New York in 1846 and in 1888 in New Jersey (Freeland 1955), all undergirded the region's emergence as a hub of industry and international finance.

Interestingly, there has also been a long tradition of incentivizing the location decisions of economic actors in the region. As early as 1693, New York State was offering financial incentives to select industries to locate in the urban core. William Bradford, who was responsible for the publication of the first local newspaper, the *Weekly Gazette*, was offered an annual financial incentive to leave Philadelphia and set up shop in New York (US Census Bureau 1902: 586). The pattern of strategic incentive-driven economic growth continues to this day. Not surprisingly, by 1919 Manhattan was home to some 8,000 clothing factories and countless pieceworkers in the tenements. It was the centre for periodical and book publishing, and home to an array of corporate entities supported by vast networks of financial, real estate and legal professionals. Along the waterfronts of Brooklyn and Queens one could find metalworks, ship building and breweries. Moving north towards Westchester one could find carpet manufacturers. By 1900 there were 46,333 manufacturing establishments across the region, employing 557,367 labourers (US Census Bureau 1902).

Across the Hudson in New Jersey there were seven trunk railroad systems with terminals in close proximity to New York harbour, with ferry services tying the surrounding areas to the urban core in Manhattan, later replaced by bridges and tunnels (Gross & Nelles 2018). The region's growth was driven by politics, economics and geography. As Pratt (1911) highlights, already by the turn of the century the urban core was becoming so heavily congested that strategies were required to begin decentralizing outwards to the surrounding areas. Competition to attract industry also became a factor shaping the economic expansion across the region, with cities on the Jersey side of the Hudson attempting to lure business to their areas. By 1900 we begin to see firms moving to the nearby southern side of the region in New Jersey, where land was cheap and rail service plentiful (US Census Bureau 1902: 543). Thus, the geography of what we now refer to as the megacity was already taking shape at the turn of the century.

Economic density was driving up the cost of land on the island of Manhattan, where alongside the dense industrial and trading core in Lower Manhattan, concentrations of workers in overcrowded tenements were generating public health issues, and lack of affordable transportation meant that the core of the region was struggling under the weight of economic growth. Improved transportation, communication, greater regulation of industry and land use, affordable and accessible housing and planning were required to help facilitate the movement of people outwards – to the outer suburban areas of the megacity south of Manhattan to the Gateway region on the Jersey side of the Hudson, north to Westchester and East to Long Island. While, at the same time, it was essential that these new communities remained connected with the urban core, in order to anchor and shore up the economic agglomeration.

Transitioning from manufacturing to advanced producer services

New York has also maintained its economic position, by virtue of its ability and capacity to diversify and adapt to larger structural shocks (i.e. economic

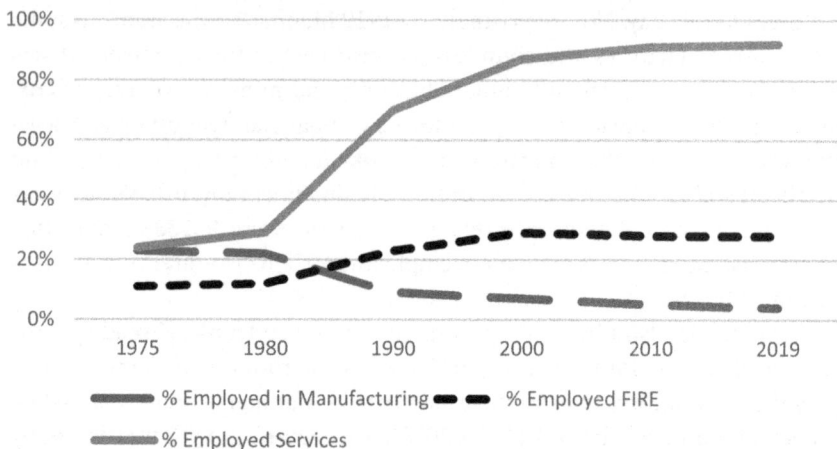

Figure 3.1 New York megacity employment by sector, 1975–2019.
Source: US Bureau of Labor Statistics (n.d.), Quarterly Census of Employment and Wages, county high-level.

restructuring, recession and depression) to the global economic system. Technology, land, labour, housing and transportation policies all influenced the megacity's response to the massive redistribution of manufacturing, both within the megacity and subsequently out of the region to the southwest of the United States and to other parts of the world. "By 1966, fewer than half the manufacturing jobs in the New York metropolitan region were in the city itself" (Phillips-Fein 2017: 21). At the same time, as Figure 3.1 illustrates, although manufacturing leaves, other sectors fill the economic void.

Although the economic losses in the 1970s were significant for the region, the seeds of revival and transition to a megacity were sown early on in its history. Through the cultivation of these resources, the region was able to successfully navigate economic shifts and survive the recession and economic crisis of 1975 that was to follow.

As Mollenkopf (1994: 50) highlights, when industrial firms began to relocate, "they left behind an unparalleled array of advanced corporate services firms that serve clients on a regional, national and global scale … The rapid growth of employment and earnings in investment banking had a strong multiplier effect on other sectors". Accounting, information, real estate and back-office support services. All flourished across the region. As Berg (2007: 22) comments:

> First, the decentralization of economic activity, especially manufacturing, on a global scale created a need for greater centralized

management, planning, and control. Although the location of manufacturing and economic activity became decentralized throughout the prior decades, ownership was not decentralized. In addition, centralized control became necessary to deal with the increasing involvement of governments in the regulation of economic activity on a multinational scale. Second, as global economic activity became more decentralized, support services developed and were produced to assist the corporations in controlling their decentralized enterprises. These support services included telecommunications, computers, advertising, and legal and financial services. These new producer services needed to locate near clients.

What this brief foray into the long-term history of the regional economy reveals is the rather diverse economic base on which the megacity rested, and its resilience in the face of change. As Figure 3.2 shows, with some small exceptions, such as the drop between 2007–10 during the "great recession", private sector employment has continued to grow over time – until the pandemic in 2020 (to be discussed in the concluding section of this chapter).

Thus, while a substantial portion of manufacturing may have decamped from the region by the mid-1970s, private sector employment continued to grow. FIRE (finance, insurance and real estate), transportation, information, education and health services and low-skilled support service sectors continued to fuel economic growth, and became critical strategic resources for leaders of the megacity to bargain with during periods of economic tumult, like the fiscal crisis, and most recently in relationship to the Amazon HQ2 negotiations.

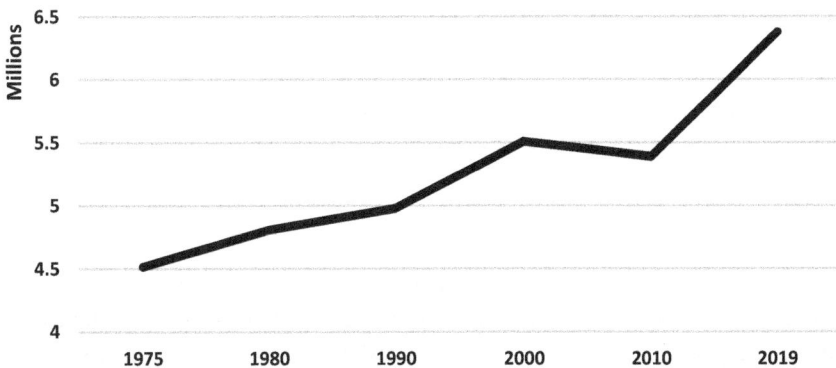

Figure 3.2 Annual average private sector employment, 1975–2019.
Source: US Bureau of Labor Statistics (n.d.), Quarterly Census of Employment and Wages, county high-level.

The corporate economy and public policy

Economic growth does not occur in a vacuum. Rather, it is shaped by policy, planning and leadership. Cities use incentives to attract, infrastructure to support, land use laws and regulations to help manage development. It is supported by an executive and legislative system that endeavours to balance and give voice to competing interest in civil society. It requires programmes to generate and regulate the production of housing to accommodate its workforce, education systems to build its base of talent and an environment that encourages innovation. Finally, it demands a legal system to ensure fairness, policing to support the creation of secure environment, and investments to support the creation of a vibrant quality of life.

The first case explores the megacity response to fiscal crisis, focusing specifically on the Koch administration and the efforts of political leaders to directly engage the private sector actors in the management of growth and development (1978–89). The second case explores the more recent failed effort by Amazon to build its new HQ2 headquarters in the region, and the civil and political response to this privately led development effort. In both cases, while our focus is largely on leadership at the centre, we also consider the role played by actors on the geographic periphery, and vertical power dynamics initiated by state partners of the megacity

Each case reveals distinctly different sets of leaders with unique policy and planning agendas. All were clearly seeking to manage the inevitable tensions inherent in a megacity region of "gargantuan" proportions. The cases expose the diverse and at times conflicting set of interests, needs and demands indicative of a megacity. While social dynamics and housing are clearly a central feature of growth, that topic will be taken up more directly in Chapter 5 on neighbourhood diversification and gentrification.

Case 1: Adaptation in the aftermath of the fiscal crisis: macro-level growth and development in the global megacity

Growing pains

Our first case focuses specifically on the ways the megacity has managed economic decline (aka the shrinking region). This period is an important one in the lifecycle of the region. It was a period of adaptation to significant economic restructuring, characterized by a redistribution of jobs and industry across the megacity territory. As Figure 3.3 illustrates, only two counties experienced population growth, while most experienced shrinkage. White wealthy

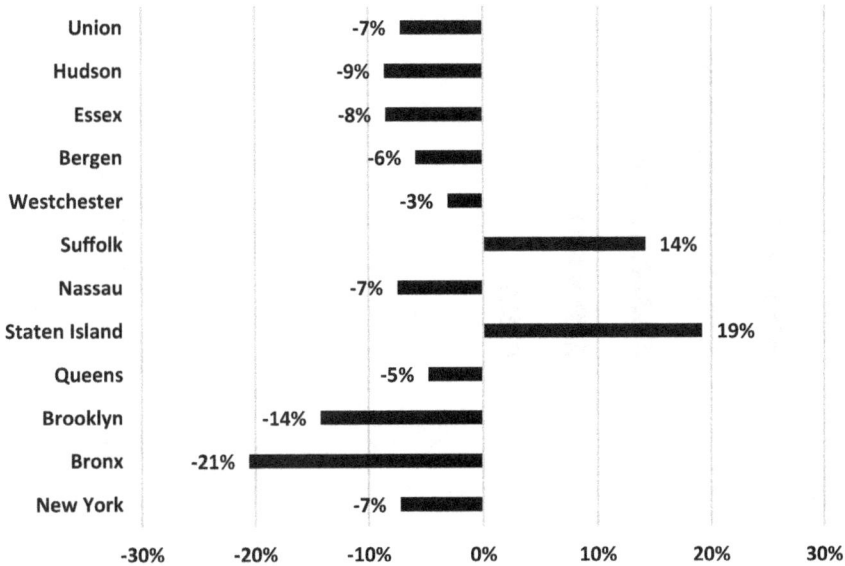

Figure 3.3 Population growth rates within New York megacity, 1970–80.
Source: US Census Bureau 1970; 1980.

residents moved out to the suburbs, leaving a poorer minority population in the core. It was, as Drennan (1991) highlighted, a period of "churning".

Alongside the population declines, the area also experienced rising poverty rates. As Figure 3.4 shows, the highest poverty rates were experienced in the more urbanized portions of the megacity. Note that both Essex and Hudson counties, located in the outer ring of the megacity, have large urban areas, including Newark and Jersey City.

Between 1970 and 1980 Manhattan alone had lost some 110,950 residents and saw its poverty rate increase by 4.5 per cent, and in the surrounding inner-city areas the increase was greater. By 1980, 28 per cent of the Bronx population were living in poverty, 24 per cent in Brooklyn, 22 per cent in Manhattan and 11 per cent in Queens. Across the Hudson on the Jersey side of the megacity, poverty rates had reached almost 18 per cent in Essex County and 17 per cent in Hudson. Deindustrialization had taken its toll. The outer-ring suburban counties of Long Island and Staten Island in New York fared better, with poverty rates remaining below 9 per cent, a reflection of the previous decade of suburban flight, and Bergen County saw no change in its poverty rate of 4.1 (US Census Bureau 1970, 1980). The megacity economy, not surprisingly, suffered. Between 1969 and 1979, for example, the New York megacity region lost some 55 corporate headquarters (Ward 1994: 476) and, across the region, economic decline ensued.

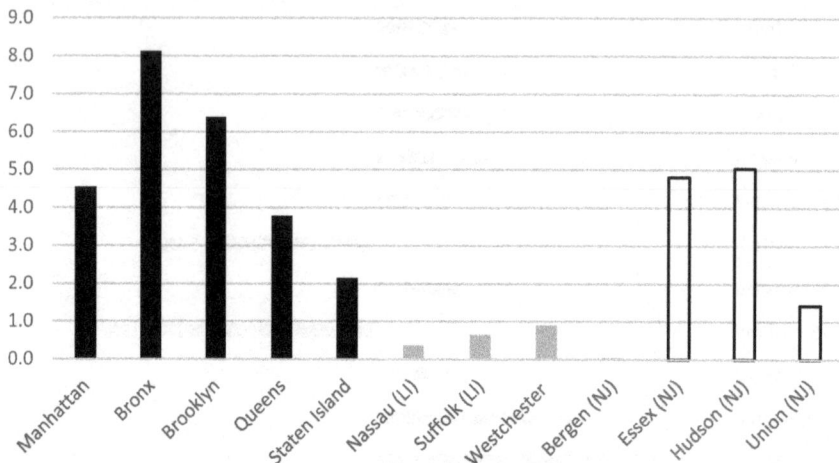

Figure 3.4 Change in poverty rate by county, 1970–80.
Source: US Census Bureau 1970; 1980.
Note: Black bars = 5 New York City counties (urban core and inner urban); grey bars = New York suburbs; white bars = New Jersey gateway counties (suburban and urban).

When Ed Koch became the 105th mayor of the City of New York, this was his backdrop. In the nearby counties of Essex and Hudson, similar pressures were being felt, with abandonment following race riots in Newark (Essex County) and Jersey City (Hudson County) in the late 1960s. New York City teetered on the edge of bankruptcy (Nussbaum 2015). Although ultimately the federal government did provide assistance, the period was one of austerity. It also exposed the tenuous relationship between the megacity and the federal government (a theme we will return to in Chapter 4), and stirred up bi-state competition within the megacity region between municipalities in New Jersey and New York. More broadly, it opened the way for the growing influence of the private sector and the importance of the entrepreneurial mayor. Koch (1984a) described himself as "a fiscal conservative who kept New York from squandering its income and thereby restoring its credit". In his 1984 State of the City speech, he comments:

> We cannot afford to be complacent. Neighboring states are moving actively to lure our financial-service industries and capture our back-office jobs. Too many of our jobs are going to non-residents. And we must also find suitable space for the manufacturing firms which can no longer afford Manhattan's high rents. (Koch 1984a)

Indeed Koch himself referred to this being a "complex [time] … because it reflect[ed] a city in transition" (Koch 1984b). His city was shrinking, thus his task would be to balance the tensions of a fiscally strapped city and population, against the needs for investment and growth. In addition, there was the added tension of needing to convince higher levels of government that the city could balance its budget and increase its credit rating.

Tensions

The tensions at the time were significant as the region faced a period of economic decline and shrinkage. Austerity further fuelled the flames. In the core, subway fares were increased to cover cost, there were pressures to abolish rent control, and demands to eliminate free tuition at the City University of New York. There were closures made to several public hospitals, and public wage freezes. According to Ron Nessen, Ford's press secretary, the federal mindset was that it "was not a natural disaster or an act of God. It is a self-inflicted act by the people who have been running New York City" (Nussbaum 2015). The importance of this statement revolved around the fact, that it essentially meant that the region was being left to its own devices to remedy and stabilize the economic situation. And, while regional collaboration might have been beneficial, competition ruled the day.

Tensions in large part related to a need for economic growth and a desire to maintain services. Obviously the two go hand in hand. In the aftermath of the fiscal crisis, the city faced an increasing demand from higher levels of government and the private sector to reduce costs and balance the public budget. At the same time the region was experiencing greater need for social services and affordable housing. Tensions mounted and pitted communities against one another. Parts of the region, such as the Bronx, had been devastated by deindustrialization, population decline, arson, decay and lack of investment.

The private sector interests in finance, real estate and producer services all sought a reduction in costs of doing business in the region. Spending on services for the poor and low income sectors were deemed by some to be the cause of the city's fiscal woes. Public sector labour unions were also fighting for survival, in an environment that was increasingly hostile to organized labour. Wealthy New York suburban communities sought better transportation infrastructure, and nearby New Jersey communities saw New York's dilemmas as an opportunity. Meanwhile, the corporate sector sought reductions in the cost of doing business in the region and threatened to move out.

Adaptations

In the aftermath of the fiscal crisis, the megacity underwent a period of major adaptations. This was evidenced in changing priorities vis-à-vis public sector spending and austerity. The period was characterized by the formation of governance regimes of public, private and non-profit actors brought directly into decision-making. In 1975 the Uniform Land Use Review Process (ULURP) was approved and became a part of the New York City Charter. ULURP was introduced in part as a response to the backroom approach that Robert Moses had taken in the past to land use decisions. ULURP provided communities greater voice in resource allocation and land use decisions. With that, a more democratized process for land use decisions was created, with local populations being given the right to express advisory opinions about changes to their neighbourhoods. Thus, it was also a period in which the city began to rely more heavily on publicly informed, privately led economic growth and housing development.

When Koch became mayor of New York in 1979 there was already a series of public and private partners actively engaged in policy and planning around the fiscal crisis in the region. Thus, the crisis was not wholly managed from the offices of the New York mayor, but rather involved a cast of players from higher levels of government (the state government of New York), as well as key private sector partners from the financial, real estate and insurance sectors, and of course local communities. And, although centred in the core of the region (New York and the inner-ring boroughs), partners from the larger megacity in the suburbs of New York and New Jersey were also active partners in the political and economic response to the crisis.

In regard to governance regimes, a core group of private sector actors in finance and real estate became advisors to political leaders across the region. Here, in keeping with the works of Logan and Molotch (2007), actors came together (public and private) in a form of growth coalition with the intention of increasing land value. Many were themselves commuting from the nearby suburban counties of the region. David Rockefeller (who lived in Westchester), and leading figures from Chase Manhattan Bank, Morgan Guaranty Trust, the First National City Bank (who were given the moniker "Jersey Mafia" to reflect the fact that they lived in the nearby New Jersey suburbs but worked in Manhattan (Jensen 1975)), were at the centre of the mix. FIRE sector leaders became members of a "financial community liaison group" created to push the municipality towards a balanced budget and adopting austerity measures around public spending. The financial community was actively involved in efforts to raise the municipal credit rating and secure the city's bond ratings. The Municipal Assistance Corporation was created by the state of New York to provide oversight and assistance, and was led by Felix Rohatyn (a partner at the international investment bank Lazard Frères & Co.).

The policies and programmes adopted by local leaders in the aftermath of the fiscal crisis "largely set the script for the way municipalities would respond to crisis for many years to come" (Enright 2014: 4). Thus, it was a period in which policymakers increasingly relied on incentives to spur the physical development of the region, tax abatements to capture private sector industry, managerial changes to provide more efficient and transparent management of the budget, and active engagement with the FIRE sector. At the same time, efforts continued to be made to balance budgets and cut public sector spending. And while civil society groups were also consulted, they remained the weaker partners, able to advise but not to veto land use decision and budget choices.

The megacity witnessed a period that can only be described as one of economic austerity and economic restructuring. In addition to building stability in the economy, this period also revealed the ongoing tensions of governance across a region that, although economically tied, was internally competitive with each community seeking to hold on to its own piece of the pie (this theme will be discussed in detail in Chapter 4, which explores governance).

Mayor Koch's approach was to rely heavily on the private sector. But to do so he needed to create an environment supportive of business. To this end he put forward a set of policies designed to create a favourable tax base for business, to reduce energy costs and to promote investments in the creation of office space in "downtowns" across the five boroughs (core and inner-ring boroughs). These strategies were also designed to prevent business from moving across the Hudson River to New Jersey, or out of the region altogether.

Koch's focus was largely on the urban core and the surrounding boroughs. Because of this, he has been described by some as "parochial" (Soffer 2010: 310). He used commercial and industrial tax incentive policies to support development across the five boroughs, specifically in the downtown commercial corridors. As Fainstein (2001: 38) highlights, between 1981 and 1990, 243 million square feet of office space was added to the urban core, representing a 20 per cent increase. Major development projects to create back-office space were initiated in the Brooklyn Downtown: MetroTech and Atlantic Terminals. Here a private developer (Forest City Ratner) was the builder, and tenants were offered in some cases more than 20 years of tax rebates to locate there.

He viewed the nearby northern New Jersey areas as competitors, who were also actively engaged in their own efforts to promote growth through redevelopment. Thus, rather than seeing them as being a component of the megacity, they were seen as a potential threat to the global city's nodal positioning. So, while he endeavoured to create a more geographically diversified economy, including efforts to hold on to industry and commerce, he did so firmly within the confines of the urban core and the inner-ring boroughs. And he did this through investments in the development of office space and alongside the now familiar line of many a politician – "no new taxes". By the mid-1980s, when he felt that the city was safely beyond the fiscal crisis, he then promoted investments in education, policing, sanitation and the like.

Meanwhile, across the Hudson, the New Jersey side of the megacity was actively engaged in major waterfront redevelopment of its own. In 1980, for example, Jersey City in Union County re-zoned its waterfront from manufacturing to allow mixed uses (commercial and residential). As the decade unfolded, a series of projects were built. Two 60-storey towers, and a new commercial district and residential complex was planned. As Lueck (1989) reports, "dozens of projects" were being planned "for the back office operations of banks and securities concerns" in locations with direct access to Wall Street in Lower Manhattan. Similarly, over in Essex County, Newark was also engaging in a redevelopment of its waterfront, which had over the prior decade been slowly replacing its industrial sector with business in the FIRE and service sectors (City of Newark 1983).

Although Koch began the first of his three terms as mayor of New York with efforts to cut spending, he "became a pro-growth mayor" who spent significantly on the promotion of property-led development, re-zoning, services and housing, viewing areas such as education and public safety as important for investment to support the local economy, and to attract tourists. But, more than anything else, one must remember his leadership as one that increasingly relied on private sector partners to restructure the urban economy. Not surprisingly, he increased annual spending "in economic development by 207.9%" (Weikart 2009: 57).

Mayor Koch endeavoured to manage the tensions in the five boroughs by stabilizing the economy through cutting public costs, re-zoning some areas from manufacturing to commercial uses, using the powers of eminent domain in areas deemed to be "blighted", and through significant economic support of private sector-led redevelopment. In the process business districts emerged across the megacity: Metrotech in downtown Brooklyn, Long Island City in Queens, the South Street Sea Port in Lower Manhattan, the Javitz Convention Center on the west side of Manhattan, etc. It was a process of "property-led urban economic development ... defined as a public sector strategy to encourage economic growth ... by creating conditions under which real estate investors are drawn to and can extract value from a place" (Wolf-Powers 2005: 380). Thus, Koch followed the adage that "if you build it they will come", expecting a trickling down of benefits to the locality from property-led development. By the end of his three terms in office, "the city granted tax abatements worth $650 million" (Weikart 2009: 61). In the process some credit this approach with important outcomes such as enticing Chase Manhattan Bank to move its 6,000 person headquarters to Brooklyn's Metrotech and, similarly, using abatements to generate the construction of new office space and luxury housing across the megacity.

Case 2: The Amazon HQ2 deal: drilling down to the micro-level

The Amazon case reveals a different side to the competitive nature of economic development in the twenty-first century and the new challenges that leaders face in this post-industrial global megacity. Whereas the previous case explored the challenges of economic development in the context of a shrinking region, this case reflects the challenges of managing development in the face of rapid growth. Not only does the case reveal the ongoing tensions between municipalities within the megacity, but the case also points to the possibility that the global megacity may well be "on the verge of a sea change in [the use of] corporate tax incentives" as tools of economic growth (Charleston & Randall 2019).

The Amazon case can be looked at in three phases, all of which reveal a great deal about growth patterns, the shifting nature of power and influence over economic development policy, land use planning and the economy of the global megacity. The first phase concerns a series of land use changes that reshaped Long Island City (the site selected for the Amazon HQ2 headquarters) into a mixed-use development site, and opened the door for massive population increases. This early history also helps one to understand some of the reasons behind selection of this area as a potential site for HQ2, as against hundreds of others.

The second phase came after the Amazon deal was announced in 2017, and concerns the ways in which different municipalities within the region competed with one another to win the bid. A unified proposal offering multiple New York location options, both in the core, inner ring and suburban parts of the megacity was put forward by the state of New York. Multiple independent proposals came from other parts of the megacity in the surrounding counties in New Jersey, with one garnering state support from the New Jersey governor. The disparate and competitive proposal process, as will be seen, was reflective of the geopolitical tensions endemic to this megacity.

The third phase will take us into an analysis of the local backlash, the political battles and the decision that Amazon made to withdraw. This phase highlights an emerging tension wrought by rapid population growth within the region, and the emergence of conflicting visions about how economic development should be pursued and in whose interests.

Growth: be careful what you wish for

In some regards, we can begin the discussion of the HQ2 deal and Long Island City, where the previous case ended. Long Island City was a neighbourhood that had been zoned almost exclusively for manufacturing in 1961 and then became the poster child of deindustrialization by the late 1970s. Rather than attempt to lure manufacturing back to the area, a strategy of restructuring for back-office services ensued. Long Island City was among the communities that then was viewed as ripe for new development. A surplus of vacant space in 1982 opened up an opportunity for land speculation. The match that lit the flame was a large investment banking firm that got permission from the city to convert two industrial buildings into one million square feet of office space (Henry 1982). Ultimately, this development proved problematic as it was unable to lure the expected private sector back-office businesses to the area and was subsequently tenanted by public agencies. However, one could see the start of a transition towards high density and mixed use.

When manufacturing left the megacity, neighbourhoods such as Long Island City, which had been zoned for manufacturing, experienced significant growing pains. Spaces like these were targeted for urban development. With massive amounts of empty industrial space, the area began to attract artists interested in large and affordable studio spaces. Then, in 1986, in keeping with the citywide efforts to use zoning as a tool to attract and anchor service-based industry, a small three-block area was identified for high-density commercial and residential development (Kober 2019).

In 2000, with Mayor Bloomberg at the helm, the strategy of business-led development and re-zoning continued. In keeping with past practices, a broad-based governance coalition of public and private sector actors came together to strategize about how to shore up the megacity as a node in the global economy. To this end, the "Group of 35" was formed with support from federal, state and locally elected officials, economic development agencies and core members of the FIRE sector (Group of 35 Task Force 2001). The group identified Long Island City as one of three areas ripe for commercial development. But, for this to happen, more significant re-zoning was required to allow for mixed uses.

In 2002, of the 21,059 acres of land zoned exclusively for manufacturing across the megacity's core and inner-ring boroughs, Queens had the largest number 9,418 acres (NYC Planning n.d.). Just four years into the Bloomberg administration, "the city ha[d] lost roughly 20% of its manufacturing land" (Davis & Renski 2020: 4). Whereas some formerly industrial parts of the megacity in both the core Manhattan and nearby inner ring in Brooklyn underwent surges in property-led redevelopment, Long Island City, despite its prime location on the waterfront and close proximity to the urban core, took almost a decade longer to transition.

Even when the city implemented an industrial business zone (IBZ) policy in 2006, which incentivized industry to move to designated industrial zones such as Long Island City, there was little change. Indeed, researchers found that the business that moved to Long Island City through this programme, "largely catered to residential and commercial support needs … supermarkets; specialty food stores; dry-cleaning and laundry services; and gift, novelty, and souvenir stores were among some of the non-industrial businesses that received incentives within IBZs" (Davis 2018). After a series of fits and starts, however, the area did grow, but only after developers began opting to convert buildings into largely residential towers and some back-office space, resulting today in one of the fastest growing areas in the larger megacity (Kober 2019). This growth also brought more affluent residents into the area.

According to the American Community Survey, there were 2,784 residents in the area in 2000; by 2010 that number was 4,949. In 2019 there were 170,000 residents living in the area (Long Island City Partnership 2019). Long Island City saw a 155 per cent growth in its populations between 2006 and 2018. Today it is also home to 6,600 businesses, employing over 115,000 people, in 8.5 million square feet of commercial and industrial space (Long Island City Partnership n.d.).

The decision to re-zone the area for higher density mixed use in 2004, the support for residential conversions, the inclusionary housing programmes of 2005 and even the 2006 (elaborated upon in Chapter 5 on neighbourhood development), and the IBZ programme may well have sown the seeds for the tensions that emerged among residents and businesses, and shaped the subsequent Amazon HQ2 battle that was to come. Since that time the area has had additional re-zonings, most recently Mayor de Blasio's administration identifying this as one of seven neighbourhoods that the city would allow additional up-zoning in support of affordable housing.

As will be illustrated, it was ultimately this new residential population, alongside long-standing labour interests, that may have scuttled the Amazon deal, and may be redirecting policy in the megacity towards development that supports "equity and economic justice" (Fitzsimmons 2020).

Tensions

The Amazon HQ2 case was played out on a terrain characterized by a wide range of tensions – economic, social and political. The pressures of growth discussed above left the area with a variety of economically and politically induced tensions between sectors, between communities and between populations. Structural shifts in the economy, and policy and planning choices made in response, set the stage for this contentious battle over the siting of Amazon's headquarters within the global megacity.

Long Island City, where the fight ultimately played out, was a community that had a long history of "tug of war" between those seeking to sustain a small last bastion of manufacturing in the megacity and those seeking to transition to a post-industrial service-based economy. The FIRE sector ultimately appears to have won this battle, following the development path set by the local growth coalition in the 1980s, and supported by the zoning and land-use policies and economic development programmes of city and state government. In turn, the area became a site in which public policy created the conditions for speculative private sector-led back-office development and deindustrialization (Wolf-Powers 2005).

The case also revealed horizontal tensions within a region beset by competition to lure and attract economic growth. Long Island City and other former industrial locations within the larger megacity were actively engaged in efforts to use the tax incentives available through the IBZ programme of the Economic Development Corporation to lure and anchor what remained of industry and manufacturing. An illustration of the ways in which this programme helped to stoke geopolitical tensions within the megacity can be found in the case "Fresh Direct".

Prior to the Amazon HQ2 competition, in 2012 Fresh Direct had threatened to move out of its home in Long Island City in search of a larger space. The company was initially offered an incentive package to relocate to Jersey City. That offer was then countered with a bigger set of tax incentives from the Bronx. In the end, Long Island City was not able to anchor this company, and Newark failed to lure it across the Hudson. However, Fresh Direct, which employed some 2,000 workers, did opt to move its facilities to the Bronx, after being given a more lucrative counter-offer valued at $130 million in tax benefits (Johnson 2019). The result was a redistribution of business within the urban core. Bronx's benefit was Long Island City's loss. Thus, the IBZ programme generated horizontal tensions between localities across the megacity. When it came to the actual HQ2 competition in 2017, not only was Long Island City among the bidders, but so too were the outerring suburbs of New York and the urban parts of the New Jersey gateway. Parochial competitiveness, therefore, was spurred by past policies and the ongoing pressures of economic growth.

Jumping ahead now to the HQ2 competition itself that was launched in 2017, we find Amazon as the instigator of the development battle (rather than the municipalities). Amazon put out a call for proposals from localities to be the site of its second headquarters in the United States (aka the Amazon HQ2 competition). This request for proposals resulted in an inevitable bidding war, within and between localities across the United States, Canada and Mexico.

More directly it tapped into the ongoing legacy of competitive economic development within the global megacity region.

According to the request for proposals, Amazon sought a metropolitan area with a population of more than one million, within 45 minutes of an international airport, close proximity to major highways, access to mass transit, and space for an initial build of 500,000 square feet, with expansion possibilities to grow to 8 million square feet. Amazon also expressed an interest in being located in a community with a diverse population, a strong educational arena and a skilled local workforce (McDonald 2019).

Seven bids came from New York State, three within the megacity area – New Rochelle, NYC-Long Island-Hudson Valley and Westchester. Because the request for bids came a private entity as opposed to a public request for proposals, only some of these bids were made public. As Jensen (2019) reminds us, "corporate [led] selection processes remain outside the public eye", thus only a handful of the bids were made public due to laws regarding public disclosure of economic development projects. Thus, while 238 bids were made, only 26 were made public.

The New York and New Jersey proposals were among the publicly disclosed group. There were some interesting differences relating to those coming from the New Jersey municipalities as contrasted with the New York ones. In New Jersey there were eight proposals submitted, which included Bayonne and Jersey City in Hudson County, and Newark in Essex County. Only the Jersey City proposal also got the endorsement of the state of New Jersey. As an indication of the internal megacity competition, its proposal promoted the idea of Amazon being able to become a part of the "New York skyline without paying Manhattan prices" (Kofsky 2018). In New York a joint proposal was put forward by the Empire State Development agency, with four potential regions across the state identified. This included one proposal for a site within the borders of the megacity. That proposal included options in the core and inner urban ring (Long Island City, World Trade Center, Brooklyn Navy Yard, DUMBO – Down Under the Manhattan Bridge Overpass – in Brooklyn, and Midtown Manhattan West) and in the nearby New York suburbs on the periphery of the megacity (Long Island and the Hudson Valley).

Geopolitical conflicts between localities to attract the lucrative headquarters ensued. Thus, the second phase of the Amazon case revealed the competitive nature of economic development across the megacity. The subnational state played a central role in the competition, with New York opting for a more collaborative approach in support of regional growth, while on the New Jersey side of the megacity each actor fought for its own interest with little regard for the regional dynamics. As will be discussed in Chapter 4, the global megacity has a long history of internal tension, thus shared governance has always been beset by competition and often requires the intervention of high levels of government to facilitate a regional collaboration (Gross & Nelles 2018).

Following site visits by Amazon to the 20 finalist cities. Long Island City was selected as a location for 50 per cent of the planned HQ2, with the remainder going to Arlington Virginia. At the same time, Amazon generated a memorandum of understanding laying out the terms of its agreement for the City of New York, the NYC Economic Development Corporation and the Empire State Development Corporation, estimating the creation of 107,000 jobs and tax revenues of $14 billion for the state and $13.5 billion for the city over a 25-year period. In return, Amazon would receive some $3 billion in incentives (New York City Council 2019a: 4).

Long Island City's proximity to the region's core, access to the vast global megacity transportation networks (air, sea, road and rail), extensive educational facilities, housing options, cultural offerings and space for additional buildouts over time were but some of the reasons for this decision. But what Amazon failed to factor in was an understanding of the socio-economic tensions present in the community. Nor did they consider the political expectations of elected officials, local communities, businesses and trade unions for voice and transparency in the location process.

This highlights another important aspect of economic development in the megacity, which began in the aftermath of the fiscal crisis. Today, New York residents have expectations that economic growth must directly factor in their needs and interests. This aspect has been given added emphasis by recent political leaders in the urban core. In 2011, for example, a participatory budget pilot project was piloted in four communities, and under de Blasio the number grew to 31 (out of 51 community districts). In 2020 there were 33 council districts participating in this programme, managing some $35 million in capital funding (New York City Council, n.d.). On the New York side of the megacity, then Mayor Bill de Blasio placed even more emphasis on the importance of community voice in decision-making. In 2018, for example, a commission was created, "The New York Civic Engagement Commission", to promote trust in local government and to support the citywide implementation of participatory budgeting. These programmes and policies are an indication of an important change in the way public business is being done in the megacity and the growing expectation of communities in regard to voice in policy and planning decisions.

The New York City Council's Committee on Economic Development held its first hearing about the proposal in December 2018 and the second in January 2019 (New York City Council 2019b). The first hearing focused on demands for transparency, the second explored the costs, benefits and equity of the proposal for the community and the megacity more broadly. The first hearing was held to clarify the proposal itself, which was negotiated largely behind closed doors with the state of New York. As the speaker of the New York City Council commented, "the process circumvented the uniform Land Use Review Process", which would have required a series of public hearings and an environmental impact assessment to inform the proposal and decision (New York City Council 2019b: 5). Thus, no analysis of the impacts on housing, schools and the community overall was conducted. As the hearing progressed, additional concerns were raised by the Long Island City Councilman (Jimmy Van Brammer) regarding Amazon's anti-union stance, and concerns about providing Amazon with massive incentives at a time of "growing income inequality" (New York City Council 2019b: 14).

The Amazon HQ2 competition that played out between 2017 and 2019 did so on a terrain of internal and external tensions, and within a competitive and divided political arena. Thus, when Amazon came to the megacity to close the deal in 2019, it encountered heated pressure from communities and local politicians. The decisions made and the demands placed upon Amazon reveal "competing visions for the city" and a situation in which "business [was] on the defensive" (Fitzsimmons 2020). The mayor and governor supported the deal, the council member and speaker of the city council opposed it, and the Long Island City population and business communities were divided. Some saw the behemoth as a threat to small business, others saw it as a generator of business. Some viewed the move as likely to enhance land values, while others feared its presence would displace them. Some felt it would place undue burden on local services, transportation and local school systems, others saw it generating ample local revenues to enhance local services. Some community groups even proposed that Amazon should pay a gentrification tax to offset the impact of its vast workforce on local infrastructure (Goodman & Fitzsimmons 2018).

As the battle lines were drawn, it was evident that the social and economic tensions induced by rapid population growth, gentrification and structural change in the local economy all served as context for local opposition. And it was here that things began to fall apart, which ultimately led to Amazon's decision in February 2019 to abandon its deal with New York to locate its headquarters in Long Island City. The private corporate entity was unwilling to make the concessions being demanded by local interests and unwilling to "run the gauntlet of community engagement and public process ... part of the cost of doing business" in the global megacity (Municipal Arts Society 2019).

Adaptation: policies, planning and governance

Adaptations to the pressures of growth were revealed across the three phases of development in the Long Island City case. The first phase of this case took us back to 2001, when the tools that had been developed in the aftermath of the fiscal crisis to encourage growth – zoning for land-use planning, deregulation and tax-based incentives for private sector-led economic development – were used to promote growth in the area. We also saw how some programmes, such as the IBZ programme created in 2006, to support efforts to anchor existing business, facilitated the redistribution of industry within the megacity and highlighted the fragmented and competitive nature of economic growth in the global megacity. Programmes, policies and plans tended to favour the demands of developers and FIRE sector business over local community demands for equity.

Tools such as these continued to be used to prompt private sector developers to invest in localities within the megacity and, in many ways, became the basis on which the Amazon deal was played out. Thus, when developers opted to build high-density luxury housing, that brought with it a more affluent residential population to the community. The zoning changes in 2001 started the transition, leading to a building boom that began in 2010 and generated 41 residential apartment buildings by 2017, before the Amazon deal was struck.

New populations to the area helped fuel pressures emanating from the bottom – civil society and local labour – who subsequently organized opposition through grassroots activism, lobbying of local elected officials and then the public hearing process to push back against the Amazon deal. Thus, these popular pressures were in many ways the result of the adaptations that the city made to zoning and programmes to support development and restructuring of the area to a mixed-use district. The unanticipated outcome was a more affluent millennial population, who appear to be generating pressures for a much broader change in the economic development approach that had long characterized the region.

Some believed that the opposition to the deal was coming from outside the neighbourhood itself: "elected officials and young progressive activists with an anti-corporate agenda" (Kilgannon & Piccoli 2019). But others highlighted the growing tensions within the area between affluent newcomers and long-standing working-class and low-income residents of the area. The area was not only home to a new millennial community but also to Queensbridge houses, the largest public housing complex in the nation. So concerns about gentrification were brewing.

For some there were questions about the degree to which Amazon would hire locally, having initially suggested that it would take on 30 residents of public housing in its call centre. Given that New York has more than 400,000 such residents, this offer seemed meagre (Goodman 2019). However, for others the prospect of 25,000 new jobs for the community was more important, even if those jobs were taken by others in megacity. Thus, the deal pitted those who feared displacement as land rents grew against those who feared that they would not be able to afford to more expensive luxury shops that would arrive to service the newer communities. And for some elected officials, the idea of providing Amazon with $3 billion in incentives (state and city) seemed unacceptable.

There was a wide cast of characters engaged in these negotiations – mayor, governor, city council members, union leaders, residents and local business. Pundits argue that Amazon failed to understand the complex politics of the megacity and the "growing influence of the progressive left" (Goodman & Weise 2019).

The core story here – massive growth of housing and development – made the area desirable according to the core themes of the HQ2 competition. But that growth in many ways generated a new set of tensions, which manifested in pushback from some in the community and highlighted a fundamental challenge to corporate-led economic development in a city with a strong history of labour organizing and an emerging base of community activism.

Conclusions

In this chapter we explored the ways in which economic growth and development have occurred in the global megacity over time. It is a topic that could occupy an entire volume on its own, so we inevitably had to find ways to abbreviate and cut corners in the telling of this portion of the story. A rapid overview of the economic trends experienced by this megacity over time and two short cases studies were used to highlight the ways in which policy, planning and leadership came together to shape and manage growth.

What becomes clear is that New York is a megacity that has evolved, adapted and diversified over time. It has successfully transitioned from commercial trading corridor to manufacturing centre, to a largely service-based economy. The most recent endeavours have revolved around efforts by both the Bloomberg and the de Blasio administrations to encourage growth in sectors outside the mainstays of FIRE. In addition, the theme of equitable growth is also becoming a priority of many of the region's civic leaders today (as evidenced in current housing programmes and zoning for equity and affordability – two themes that will be discussed in Chapter 5 on neighbourhoods and housing). The most recent economic growth endeavours have been centred around effort to lure business to the city in the information and high technology sectors. Programmes are being implemented to create innovation spaces and to support start-ups in digital technology and cyber security (De Blasio 2020).

In January 2022, Eric Adams took office as the second African-American mayor of New York City. Thus far he has sought to position himself as a supporter of both the corporate sector as well as civil society, campaigning on a platform of being a "friend of both business and working class New Yorkers" (Geringer-Sameth 2022). De Blasio, a more left-wing leader with a pragmatic focus on building equity, had begun to steer the megacity towards a more progressive focus on policies supporting use value for the people of the city. By contrast, Adams appears to be more of a centrist, with a corporate-centred development lens. Early indicators suggest that Adams will be more heavily focused on promoting policies in support of enhancing exchange value in the city. One sign of this came during his campaign, when he received more contributions from the real estate sector than any other candidate (Murphy 2021). He has subsequently created a "corporate council", which brings together some 60 corporate and political leaders to serve as an advisory council. Interestingly, Adams had endorsed the Amazon deal, as well as another controversial plan around the re-zoning of the Brooklyn waterfront in Industry City when he served as Brooklyn borough president. Entering office at a very challenging time for the megacity, in the aftermath of the pandemic, this new mayor is clearly working to shore up the region's economic core while also supporting the users of the city spaces, with efforts to invest in the workforce and job creation. Thus, while more centrist, the current mayor continues to focus on issues of equity, but he does so through targeted investments in workforce development.

The global megacity has clearly been moulded though a complex mix of policy choices designed to promote economic growth, encourage targeted private sector-led development and incorporate community voices. The tools that have been used include land-use decisions around zoning, environmental regulations, economic investments, participatory budgeting, community planning and targeted tax-based incentives. Leaders from the public and private sectors have taken the reins as partners in some instances and competitors in others.

New York is nothing if not resilient, having successfully weathered many crises. Indeed, one of the unique traits of this powerful city region has been its capacity to adapt and change, through policy and planning, while maintaining its iconic economic position as a node in the global economy. Today the region is facing unique challenges in the face of increasing nationalism, global isolationism, social unrest and a health pandemic. Although this future is still unfolding, we conclude this chapter by consideration of what lessons its past choices can offer for our understanding of the economic future of this megacity in light of the pandemic impacts on the megacity economy.

Just before the pandemic, the region had witnessed a ten-year period of economic expansion. However, since the pandemic hit, New York State has reported that the core and inner rings have experienced a loss of 758,400 jobs in services, hospitality, education and health, FIRE, professional services, information, transportation and manufacturing. Unemployment was 20.4 per cent in June 2020 (New York State 2020). In April, the Federal Reserve reported that business activity declined for 85 per cent of the firms doing business in the megacity region, half of all firms cut payroll though staffing, and 60 per cent of service sector workers were working from home (Abel, Bram & Deitz 2020). At the same time, the NYC Comptroller reported that Wall Street had its "most profitable quarter in over a decade" during the first quarter of 2020, benefiting from market vulnerabilities (Stringer 2020). The real estate industry reports are more sombre. In 2020, New York had the highest vacancy rate on record (-3.67 per cent), leading to reduction in rent and incentives for commercial leasing (Falcon 2020). Public agencies were also asked to make massive cuts themselves, with impacts on planning, transportation and all other public services.

Although the economic future of the megacity is clearly uncertain, what is clear is that there is a strong base upon which to build. A global pandemic, rapid economic shrinkage, alongside a national geopolitical arena that was hostile to globalization and diversity (we will address this later theme directly in Chapter 4 on governance), does appear to be turning around. And what is clear is that the tools of economic growth – zoning, regulation, incentives and participatory planning – remain. Business is once again being courted by current political leadership, but this appears to be through a reframing that also acknowledges the critical importance of equitable development in support of working-class and black residents (who were most severely impacted by these trends). How these tools are adapted to these new conditions remains unclear. As long as the virus continues to be a threat, it remains impossible to fully assess the needs of the region.

Early signs seem to suggest that the megacity is bouncing back. By 2021 the partnership for the city of New York reported almost a 6 per cent growth in employment as compared with 2020, with the largest gains to be found in hospitality, information, services, retail and healthcare. Unemployment rates by the end of 2021 had dropped to 9 per cent (Hughes 2022). And land rents are once again on the rise. Residential real estate prices have experienced roughly a 17 per cent growth rate across the region (Hughes 2022). Commercial real estate remains more of a question, as businesses readjust and more employees are working from home.

The megacity is no stranger to the political and economic pressures of growth and shrinkage. New York stands as a territory whose wealth, power and people have allowed it to make its mark globally and, more importantly, have enabled it to overcome even the most daunting of economic challenges. Its resilience is derived from its adept leaders, powerful communities and innovative approaches to land use, policy and planning. Thus, while things will certainly change, New York has long demonstrated that it has the capacity to meet most challenges.

4

Expanded governance in the megacity

Governance across New York is perhaps one of the most counterintuitive features of the region. Given the size of its economy, the vast range of services that must be performed on a daily basis, the scope of its transportation networks and the sheer numbers of people and goods that circulate through the megacity (not only locally but nationally and globally), one would expect that, beneath this living breathing behemoth, there would be a unified, well-organized and coherent governmental system. One would imagine a clear set of institutions in place that would oversee, manage, plan and coordinate these activities. One would anticipate a political system characterized by collaborative leaders, working collectively to adapt to the tensions inherent in growth, and a political system that would serve to keep things moving. One would expect an institutional ensemble that was poised to face the challenges wrought by climate change, terrorism, global economic shocks and health crises. But, in fact, when we turn our gaze to the administrative and political scaffolding that supports the megacity, what we find is something quite unexpected.

This highly productive region appears to operate in the absence of a unified or coordinated structure of governance. Regional institutions operating both across the entire region and within each state coexist alongside a plethora of more localized county and municipal governments, special districts and neighbourhood-level institutions. Governance in the region is so very complex that it does at times seem almost miraculous that the megacity is able to cohere around critical needs, and yet it does.

The megacity contains, literally, thousands of entities, some formally defined in law (*de jure*) and others informally emerging (*de facto*). The historic evolution of governance in this dynamic region mirrors the patterns discussed in Chapter 3. Governance has been shaped by ongoing competition between localities to capture a larger share of economic growth, popular pressures over equitable representation and administrative pressures to cut costs and increase efficiency in the delivery of services. It is not simply economic competition that has driven processes of expanded governance, but, as discussed in Chapter 2, necessity has also served as a driver during moments of crisis (environmental, economic, health). The New York megacity is a complex cacophony of formal and informal institutions, public and private actors, often competing, occasionally collaborating but, in the grand scheme of things, largely able to find ways to keep the ship afloat. It is to this, the "expanded governance of the megacity" that we now turn our attention.

As the megacity has grown and changed, and needs extended beyond the formal political boundaries of its constituent parts, there have been efforts to reconfigure power within and across the megacity. Indeed, the complex, competitive and dynamic institutional architecture that underpins processes of expanded governance in the megacity can be seen most clearly during moments of collaboration and conflict over institutional adaptation. By focusing on governance, we draw attention to the ways in which "multiple actors and agencies [endeavour to] come together to achieve public purposes" (Gross 2017: 560). What is evident is that this megacity is a "highly differentiated polity" with multiple stakeholders each vying for control or influence (Gross 2017: 563).

In what follows, we will first endeavour to provide an overview of the formal structures of government underpinning processes of governance in the megacity. We will then explore the battles over institutional adaptation, highlighting the relationship of said changes to cycle of growth. Expanded governance of the region is meant to highlight the challenges of institutional adaptation within the urban core (considered to be the driver of economic growth in the region) and across the surrounding older urban and suburban communities on the periphery in New York and the Gateway region of New Jersey. This chapter also explores more explicit efforts to build regional governance, touching both upon the roles of regional economic development entities such as the Empire and New Jersey State Development Corporations, the metropolitan planning organizations, the Regional Plan Association (a non-profit civic organization) and, of course, the Port Authority of New York and New Jersey (PANYNJ). We use these regional entities to illustrate the unique ways in which this often balkanized and bifurcated region has come together to manage and build critical regional infrastructure, respond to shared crises and to shore up the megacity's dominant role in the global economy. In combination, this will paint a picture of what expanded governance of the New York megacity looks like. We use the case of congestion pricing to illustrate these dynamics. Finally, we end with a consideration of the implications of expanded governance for grappling with problems that do not conform to the megacity's institutional architecture.

Structures of government and processes of governance within the megacity

The federal system of government in the United States poses unique challenges when it comes to megacity governance. In a system of fragmented and differentiated political power, the megacity must chart a path that allows it to navigate through this complexity. In New York, struggles for political control and the capacity to govern have not only pitted the constituent parts of the megacity against each other but also with higher levels of government at the state and national level.

One of the important nuances of local government in the United States is that it is absent from the formal documents that define government nationally. There is no mention of it anywhere in the federal constitution. The structure, powers, functions, taxing and borrowing powers of local governments in the United States are, by default, in the hands of the state governments. These arrangements were initially spelled out in an 1868 court decision by Judge John F. Dillon in Iowa, who ruled that all local governments be treated as "creatures of the state", and thus subordinate to the state and federal governments. Several years later, in 1871, Judge Cooley of Michigan, put forward a different interpretation, suggesting "a fundamental principle of local self-government", based on the fact that many local governments pre-existed the formation of states. Thus, Cooley argued that they should be protected from state control (Reock 1985: 6). Since that time there has been an ongoing tension between state and local government, played out in battles over balance of power, distribution of functions, design and legislative influence. There have been periods of centralization and periods of decentralization, often correlated with periods of growth and decline.

The basic frameworks of local government in this megacity are laid out in the state constitutions of New York and New Jersey. This is central to understanding the first hurdle that one faces when it comes to governance of the expanded region. Local stakeholders must navigate two different state government systems. They must work with two different governors and two different state legislatures, and operate within the confines of two different state constitutions. Local governments are nested within these systems. States set the broad parameters, counties provide services that cross local jurisdictional boundaries within states, while cities, towns, villages and hamlets take on more localized responsibilities. Interstate compacts are required in order for any formal policy, planning or programme coordination to occur between localities situated in different states.

County governments in the suburban areas on the New York side of the region (Nassau, Suffolk and Westchester) are considered municipal governments in their own right, with elected county executives and legislatures. In fact, each of these counties has its own charter, authorized by the state, which allows it a limited degree of autonomy. Here, county governments have been empowered by the state to adopt local laws, acquire property, collect rent and fees, and to perform comprehensive planning (New York State Association of Counties 2015). Similarly, on the New Jersey side of the region, counties are also considered municipal governments. They administer the state's social service programmes, prisons and courts, colleges and vocational education, parks and bridges. Counties across the megacity also participate in the governance of economic development, workforce development, consumer affairs, waste collection and recycling. In both New York and New Jersey, counties have seen their responsibilities grow over time in areas such as cooperative purchasing, emergency management and policing (New Jersey Association of Counties 2020). This devolution of responsibilities is part of a larger trend indicative of the neoliberalism in the United States.

Currently, the three New York suburban counties each have governmental systems that divide powers between an elected county executive and a legislature (17–19 elected members). These systems were designed both to promote fair representation as well as to check and balance the power of the county executive. But they did not start out this way. Originally, all three systems fused executive and legislative functions into a single body (i.e. a board of legislators or county supervisors), allowing for power to remain highly centralized. In some cases one representative was chosen per municipality, regardless of changes to the population size, leading in some cases to inequities in representation. As these counties grew, they endeavoured to use their regulatory powers to shape settlement patterns. Tools such as zoning were used to keep property values high, and control where poor and minority populations could settle. Over time some parts of the counties grew rapidly, while others restricted new growth. Some areas became spaces of concentrated poverty, while other areas became enclaves of affluence and exclusivity. Although population growth was occurring, county government systems were slower to adapt (and some were resistant). In turn the more densely populated lower-income areas found themselves marginalized in the county decision-making bodies.

Because few sitting power holders were willing to cede their authority, changes did not come easily. Indeed, most of the changes to county government came as a result of lawsuits brought by communities that were either excluded or marginalized (contravening the principle of "one person one vote"). Most of the county-level institutional changes required the involvement of the federal courts.[1] Changes were legally mandated for Nassau County in 1963, Westchester in 1965 and Suffolk in 1991. Executive and legislative powers and functions were subsequently divided (i.e. executive council forms), and legislative seats were apportioned more fairly.

The courts found in all three cases that the voting district boundaries and system of representation failed to meet the needs of the changing population and, thus, broke the equal protection clause of the US Constitution by denying the principle of "one person one vote". In the case of Suffolk, for example, the town of Hempstead had 56 per cent of the population of Nassau, but controlled 70 per cent of the voting power (McQuiston 1993: B5). A similar decision was made in the urban core in 1989, when the courts ruled that the "board of estimates", which served as a shared county-level governing body in the urban core, violated that same law. In the core, the board of estimates was abolished and its responsibilities were shifted to an enlarged legislative body, the New York City Council.

The counties at the core of the region (Manhattan, Bronx, Brooklyn, Queens, Staten Island[2]) are unique. Each have an elected borough president and a borough board (peopled by the borough president, city council members from the borough and the chairs of each of the borough's community boards). These entities lack real power, serving more in the form of advisory groups to inform and shape city policy, planning and budgeting. Thus, they do not each have their own general purpose governments, as is the case in the rest of the region, rather they are governed by a unified city government that extends across all five boroughs and takes the form of a strong mayor-council, with representation for each of the boroughs.

On the New Jersey side, the counties of Hudson, Essex, Bergen and Union were created before the American Revolution. Passaic county was created out of parts of Essex and Bergen in 1837. They are today among the most populous counties in New Jersey. Counties on both sides of the region have historically been seen "as an arm of state government, serving state purposes" (New York State 2018: 210). The New Jersey gateway count governments were also

---

1. See, for example, *Reynolds* v. *Sims* (1964), *Baker* v. *Carr* (1962) and *Wesberry* v. *Sanders* (1964).
2. Note, we have used the vernacular names of each of the urban counties in the core of the megacity. Thus, New York County is referred to as Manhattan, Kings County as Brooklyn, Richmond County as Staten Island. The remaining counties, Bronx and Queens, have no vernacular alternative.

reformed in the aftermath of the supreme court decision mentioned above. While on the New York side each county negotiated its own reform process, in New Jersey the state government passed enabling legislation in 1972, giving counties the power to modify governmental structures from systems that fused executive and legislative power to those that divided these powers. County reforms were instituted in Essex and Hudson in the mid-1970s and in 1986 in Bergen. The division in powers was seen as an important fix to overcome problems of efficiency and fragmentation (Hanley 1986).

Changes in the structure of county governments on the New York side of the megacity were resisted by county and local political elites. By contrast, in the case of New Jersey they have most often been pushed by state legislators and local political parties. Union County's freeholders selected a county manager form of government in 1976, based on the assertion that this form of government would overcome patronage by hiring a professional manager to oversee county operations. This change was pushed by the county's Democratic Party organization (*New York Times* 1975). At the time they argued that such a system would be more "responsive to the people". Passaic has maintained its colonial form, with a body of freeholders (akin to a commission form) and no separation of executive and legislature.

Across the megacity region, both states have moved from requiring special acts to create municipal governments, to the creation of general laws laying out a series of choices among government types for local populations to choose from. Mirroring county structures, at the municipal scale there is yet another layer of more localized governments. At this scale we find three general institutional forms: mayor-council (strong or weak), council-manager and commission forms of government. These systems also vary in terms of electoral arrangements – partisan and non-partisan, district and at-large elections. Generally one finds that, in the regions cities, the mayor-council form is most common, with partisan elections. Whereas smaller village jurisdictions are more likely to adopt council-manager forms of government, which fuse executive and legislative functions, and tend to opt for at-large or non-partisan election.

All told, the New York megacity extends across two states and encompasses some 297 general local-purpose governments (12 counties, 23 cities, 69 boroughs, 38 towns, 34 townships and 121 villages), alongside a plethora of public-benefit corporations that manage specific services. There is one bi-state regional entity (the PANYNJ) charged with overseeing commerce, trade and security of the seaport and airports. There are two federally authorized, and state led, metropolitan transportation planning organizations as well, the New York Metropolitan Transportation Council (NYMTC), and North Jersey Transportation Planning Authority (NJTPA). These organizations are peopled by agency leaders and elected county representatives. As Kantor *et al.* (2012: 100) comment, "most local governments [in the region are] … used to create a favourable climate for investment and economic growth". Land use and zoning have largely been understood to be local functions, whereas taxation and finance, although locally collected, tend to require state approval. Municipalities are generally tasked with local service provision and powers to regulate land and public order. These groups also come together at times of crisis around environmental and public health concerns.

To summarize, below state-level are county governments, which have adapted and changed over time. Adaptations have been made in institutional structure as well as functional responsibilities. They have roots in the colonial period of the United States when they were charged with overseeing defence, law and order within their boundaries. Over time the responsibilities of counties have expanded to include the management and oversight of services such as transportation, social welfare, parks and recreation. They serve as arms of enforcement for the state governments and manage the conduct of elections. In general, counties manage those policy areas that extend beyond municipal boundaries or that are beyond the capacity of more localized levels of government to manage or finance.

Today, in the megacity, local governments provide a wide array of services in the locality, funded through taxation (property and income), state and federal direct aid, fees for services and own source revenue. There are significant differences in local government revenue sources for localities in New York as compared with New Jersey. As Figure 4.1 illustrates, New Jersey relies far more heavily on property taxes. Tax rates are set by the county, collected by municipalities and approved by the state. Due to the heavy reliance on property taxes, one should not be at all surprised to find that the system promotes greater competition between the parts as each seeks to carve out its own piece of the economic pie, attract maximum growth and anchor its more affluent tax-paying residents and businesses.

Municipal charters detail the structures, powers and functions of government at the local scale, and these are designed in accordance with the frameworks set at the state and county levels. The result of these arrangements is "that the balance between state and local powers is not a static phenomenon. It changes constantly as conditions change and as new constitutional and statutory provisions are enacted … powers have been granted to local government units and they have been withdrawn" (Reock 1985: 6).

While municipalities have the capacity to draft and modify their charter, this must be done within the limitation set by their respective state governments. Any change in the division of powers within and between local governments has in general come with some local opposition. Those

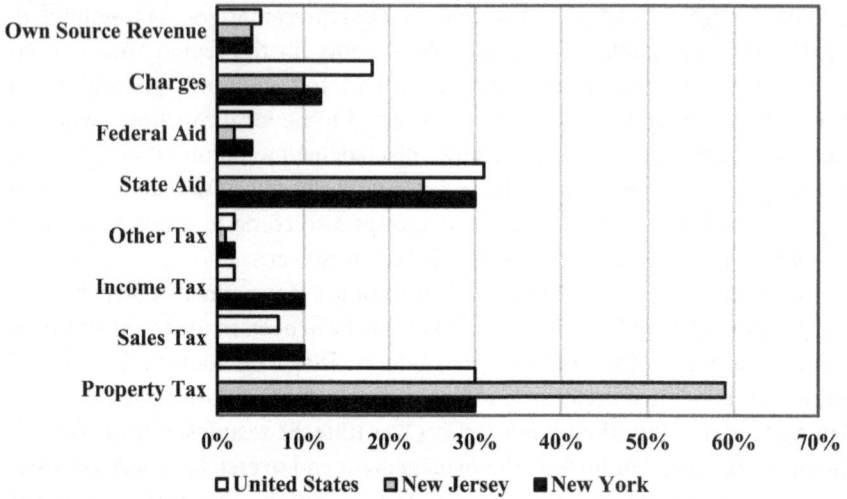

Figure 4.1 Sources of local general revenue for New York, New Jersey and the United States, 2017.
Source: Lincoln Institute of Land Policy 2022a; 2022b.

in power are less than happy about the prospect of losing it or sharing it with new stakeholders. Local efforts to garner greater control over local affairs are known as "home rule initiatives" and, as will be illustrated below, "the courts, more often than not, sided with the state legislature" when it comes to the interpretation of these laws (Viteritti 1995). These tendencies, we would suggest, have emboldened the state governments and governors within the region to take a heavier hand in the control of localities, particularly during moments of social and economic crisis, or when wicked environmental and health problems generate negative externalities that cross municipal or state boundaries.

The shifting balance of power: institution adaptations and charter reform in municipalities

The urban core (New York City five boroughs): charter reform in the early years

The urban core of the megacity as we know it today took form between 1821 and 1898, through a series of charter reforms, although formal amalgamation of the territory did not begin until 1857. Devolution from states to localities and then centralization of power at the city scale began in 1821, when New York State authorized Manhattan's legislature, the city council, to select its own mayor from among its members. In 1834 the city was given the power for its people to elect the mayor, creating the system that continues to exist today, a mayor-council form of government. In 1849 executive and legislative functions were separated, and in 1853 the mayor was given the power to appoint department heads, with city council approval. Ongoing corruption by political machines at the time resulted in this power being taken over by the state in 1857, thereby solidifying state domination of local affairs (Viteritti 1989).

The state set the ball rolling for expanded governance at the core of the megacity region in 1857, when it "combined the police, fire and health departments of the cities of New York (what we now refer to as Manhattan) and Brooklyn" (Burrows & Wallace 1998). Then, in 1874, portions of Westchester County to the north of Manhattan were annexed to New York, making up what is today the western portion of the Bronx. At the time, the area was physically a somewhat pastoral bedroom suburb, linked to Manhattan by the railroads, which had attracted people in search of single-family homes. Due to the strength of the regional economy, the continuing influx of new immigrants from Germany and Ireland, and migrations north in the aftermath of the civil war, these areas were experiencing rapid population growth. Consider that this portion of the Bronx had grown from a population of 441 in 1849 to almost 23,641 by 1875 (Gonzales 2007: 29). The "region's most populated sections suffered from inadequate police, fire protection, poor sanitation, and a scarcity of water" (Gonzales 2007: 17). The eastern portion of the Bronx, along with Brooklyn, Queens and Staten Island, were annexed in 1898. Together this created what we today refer to as the City of New York (the core of the megacity).

The consolidation of the urban core of the megacity was a move designed to support and sustain the area's economic supremacy over cities like Chicago, Cleveland and Pittsburgh. At the time, local elites in Manhattan argued that the only way for the region to be able to maintain its position as a centre of commerce and manufacturing, and to have the space needed to accommodate its ever-growing immigrant population, was through consolidation of its powers and lands. The reforms received overwhelming support from the voters. Municipal power was subsequently consolidated into a centralized system, with a mayor at the helm. A five-member body called the "board of estimates" was created to oversee the budget, and an assembly to serve as the legislative body. The board of estimates was to be controlled by the mayor, comptroller, corporation council, president of the city council and the president of the department of tax and assessment.[3] Up to this point, all changes to the city charter required state legislative approval and, more often than not, the legislature also demanded popular approval as well. "Between 1900 and 1921, more than 1,600 such special laws were passed regarding New York City. Of these, thirty-six were passed over the mayor's veto" (Viteritti 1989: 25).

The first locally formulated charter for the five counties making up the urban core was passed in 1936. Prior to this time, municipal government in New York was largely a top-down affair, codified in the state constitution but requiring popular approval. In 1963 mayoral powers were increased, leading to what we currently refer to as a "strong mayor-council system".

In 1975, at the height of the fiscal crisis, the state's charter review commission promoted a series of changes that would weaken the power of the mayor, while enhancing the power of neighbourhoods. It was a period of tumult in the urban core. Population loss to the surrounding suburbs, increasing debt and a great deal of unrest led to a new push for adaptation. As Stetson (1975: 35) pointed out, during the 1960s the city's budget had "quintupled ... welfare roles ... tripled, [and] city cost soared". The charter revision commission argued that "the alienation of citizens in the communities from a distant city bureaucracy, ha[d] created deep citizen dissatisfaction." Subsequently, 59 community boards were created and a public review process was created to oversee land-use change (also known as ULURP). Institutional changes were induced by declining population and suburban flight, which together resulted in a shrinking tax base alongside rising costs for services to those who remained in the core. Thus, we begin to see a period of increasing decentralization and efforts to encourage greater popular participation in urban governance processes.

Urban core: contemporary charter reform – growth and adaptation

Contemporary charter reform can be viewed as a highly political and strategic process. In New York, charter reforms can be initiated by the executive (i.e. mayor) or the municipal legislature (i.e. city council). Each has the power to create a commission to review the existing charter and make proposals for its revision. Reform, however, requires that any proposed change is ultimately referred to the voters in the form of a referendum. The mayor's ballot measures take precedence, so if there are competing commissions, only the mayor's ballot proposals will be moved forwards. Not surprisingly, charter reform is a highly political process. Because of this, it offers an interesting lens through which to view the ways in which public and private stakeholders have endeavoured to

---

3. The Greater New York Charter, 1897, Title 5, Section 226.

reshape the formal institutions of governance, in the context of uneven growth in the megacity.

Between 1980 and 1990, as the megacity began to recover from the fiscal crisis, population in the core slowly began to grow. By 1990, the trends of the previous decade were reversing and the urban core added some 250,000 new residents, representing a 4 per cent increase. Brooklyn and Queens accounted for 58 per cent of the growth, and Manhattan 20 per cent. Foreign population in the core grew from 1.7 million in 1980 to almost 2.1 million by 1990 (a 24 per cent increase) (NYC Department of City Planning 2020). Thus, the city was continuing to grow and diversify. Not surprisingly, this led to demands from the inner-ring boroughs for greater representation and responsiveness to community needs.

In 1988 Ed Koch was serving as mayor of the city of New York. The charter revisions introduced during this period were designed to bring greater voice in policy and land use to local residents, through an enlargement of the city's legislative body. The legislative body operating in the urban core, the city council, increased its size from 35 to 51 members. Reforms were also introduced to strengthen the powers of the mayor in land-use decisions by expanding the size of the City Planning commission (the majority of whose members were to be selected by the mayor). This, therefore, could be viewed as a period in which institutional change was tied to pressures for representation of community interests, alongside the mayor's efforts to maintain control over core policy areas. The system adaptation therefore created a more representative and, by extension it was hoped, a more responsive local government system. Changes in campaign finance were proposed as a way to open the door to future generations of elected officials.

The first set of reforms were tied to an effort to grapple with corruption in local political processes. In 1986 a scandal involving New York city officials, government employees, party leaders and economic elites occurred. All had been involved in payoff schemes relating to parking violations. The mayor in turn appointed a commission that recommended charter revisions to New York's campaign finance reform system. The reform was designed to level the playing field and to prevent candidates for office from being overly reliant on private money and open to the possibility of corruption. The popular referendum passed easily and a system was created in which candidates could opt into a matching system where the city would match contributions ($1,000 or less), and in exchange the candidate would limit spending and large contributions. Today, almost 80 per cent of candidates for office have opted into the system (Eide 2015). The reform was also designed to create an avenue to enhance representation of the growing minority population across the urban core, by providing funding opportunities for younger and less politically connected candidates, who until that point had a difficult time unseating long-serving incumbents. Thus, it could be viewed as a reform that was designed to ensure fair representation in the face of population change.

The most significant charter reform in modern times, however, came in 1989, in response to a court decision, discussed above in relationship to county reform. In 1986 the US Supreme Court ruled that the board of estimates (a body that played a central role in budgets and land-use decisions in the city) was unconstitutional. Because each borough had equal representation on the board of estimates, regardless of population size, "Staten Island voters had 78 per cent more power on the board than voters from Manhattan" (Soffer 2014: 372). Residents of the more populous parts of the urban core were not being fairly represented in the system. Here, the mayor again created a commission to study the situation, this time with extensive outreach to the community. Over a two-year period, some 140 public hearings were held and, with that, a referendum was held, which eliminated the board of estimates, expanded the legislative body for the city to 51, removed powers from borough presidents and created the position of public advocate (Rivlin-Nadler 2018). These changes had far-reaching impacts in terms of representation, transparency, participation in budgets and land-use control at the core of region.

In 1993 a very well-funded private civic group brought forward a proposal to create a two-term limit for the mayor, city council members, the public advocate and the comptroller. This was the first ballot reform initiative to have come through a public petition process. Opponents included most elected officials and the trade unions, who argued that change would weaken the power of government at the core (Myers 1993: A41). Supporters argued, however, that the system was becoming stagnant and, even with campaign finance reform, it was still in need of fresh blood. The majority of council members at the time had already served for eight years, and the advantages of incumbency increased the likelihood that they would remain. The ballot passed despite efforts by the city clerk (whose main function is to ensure that laws enacted by the city council are in keeping with its charter) to prevent it from moving forwards. And, when in 1996 the city council subsequently proposed to extend this to three terms, the voters this time rejected the change, keeping the two-term limit in place.

The Giuliani years (1994–2001) brought a very different approach to the use of the charter reform. One of the interesting nuances of charter reform in New York relates to the fact that the initiatives can come from the city council, the mayor or via public petition. If there are duelling proposals, the mayor's charter reform proposals take precedence and will knock out any competing proposals, preventing them from being brought before the public for a vote. Giuliani used this power strategically throughout his time in office to prevent the city council from being able to put forward its own proposals. He did this in 1998, 1999 and 2001. These power plays offer a clear illustration of how the core's strong mayor system operated.

In 1998 the city council announced plans for its own ballot proposal to modify the charter in relationship to public funding for the development of a new stadium for the New York Yankees in Manhattan. "The proposal would [have] prohibited the City from using public funds to obtain property or make contracts for building a new stadium for the New York Yankees in Manhattan. The proposal would not [have] prohibited the City from using public funds to repair Yankee Stadium or build a new Yankee Stadium in the Bronx or in any borough other than Manhattan" (New York City Campaign Finance Board, n.d.). The mayor, a long time Yankees fan, argued that moving the stadium to Manhattan would spark redevelopment along the Manhattan Waterfront and bring increased revenue from tourism and the like. The city council felt that these new developments should be more equitably spread across the greater megacity area. The mayor opposed the council's efforts to protect borough interests. To prevent this, Giuliani put in his own ballot proposals, targeted at the campaign finance reforms that had been implemented during the Koch years, which the mayor had already tried to veto but had been overridden by the city council. The mayor's new proposal included efforts to modify the campaign finance law and ban corporate money in local elections. "But his ban applie[d] only to candidates who agree[d] to accept public matching funds" (New York Times 1998). This referendum was opposed by the city council as well as a wide range of civic groups, who viewed this as a "stealth proposal" designed to weaken access for minority candidates. By pushing for this ballot reform, the city councils' ballot proposal was blocked. The referendum failed but it also stopped the city council's reform ideas as well.

In 1999 Giuliani used this approach again to ensure that if a mayor left office before their term was up (to, for example, take a seat at a high level of government), a special election would be required within two months. At the time the Republican mayor was considering a run for Senate and he feared that then Public Advocate Mark Green, a Democrat, would automatically assume control of the executive office (in keeping with the existing charter at the time). In fact, alongside this, the mayor peppered the ballot proposal with a variety of other changes, likely to garner popular support. For example, the ballot also promised to create a permanent agency for immigrant rights and for children's services, and create gun-free zones near schools, and require safety locks on all guns. There were additional components concerning crime control, gambling and licensing. However, by tying all of these things together into a single vote up or down for the entire proposal, the complexity actually resulted in the entire proposal being defeated by the electorate.

In 2001 Mayor Giuliani made two significant strategic changes in his approach to charter reform. First, he tied his proposals more directly to the 911 crisis; and second, he chose to separate out each of his charter revision proposals for a case-by-case vote. Not only did this allow him to prevent the council from putting forward its own reforms yet again, but it allowed him to pass many of the revisions that had failed earlier. Thus, this time, he succeeded in centralizing some of his powers by merging several executive agencies and created new executive agencies with permanence: the Mayor's Office of Emergency Management, the Mayor's Office of Immigrant Affairs, the Department of Children's Services. He was also able to institute gun-free zones and other gun laws to protect children; a core component of his mayoralty had been crime control.

When Bloomberg became mayor there were a series of what some refer to as good government proposals. These were initiatives in which the underlying goals concerned efficiency and transparency in the system of governance at the core. They also included initiatives that strengthened the power of the mayor significantly by shifting control of the public school system from the city's community districts, created during the Lindsay years, to the mayor. This change came through negotiations at the state level. The mayor's office shifted its focus to the state senate in this case and was able to persuade the body that centralized control would enhance the efficiency and improve the school system across the core. The mayor was given the power to appoint the new Schools Chancellor and with that generate significant centralization over one of the largest school systems in the United States.

In 2003 Bloomberg (who himself had been politically fluid throughout his career, being a Democrat prior to 2001, Republican during his period as mayor and then Independent in 2007) endeavoured to introduce non-partisan elections, streamline the purchasing processes for the city and create ethics reviews for administrative judges. These proposals were defeated in the elections. In 2004 he put forward ethics reforms again and sought to mandate financial audits of the city; this time both passed.

In 2008, when the financial crisis was at its peak, there was a popular petition put forward to extend the mayor's time in office from two to three terms. The argument at the time concerned the need for a leader with strong financial acumen. However, this time, the community felt that it had already made its feelings heard in the prior referendum and, not surprisingly, the reform failed. But the city council decided to override the popular vote and then opted to do this on its own through legislative processes. It tied these changes to the confluence of Bloomberg's term with the financial crises. Thus, in October 2008:

Mayor Bloomberg, seizing on the notion that the financial crisis was an emergency requiring him to remain in office, crafted a onetime-only deal with the City Council, which narrowly passed a local law permitting those holding city offices at the time to run for a third term, including Mayor Bloomberg and the very City Council Members who had approved the law. As part of the deal, the two-term limit was placed back on the ballot for a referendum in 2010. The voters would restore the two-term limit with a third decisive vote.

(Mastro 2013: 140–1)

Now, moving forwards to the de Blasio administration. This time, the mayor has used charter reform as a means of "strengthening democracy to make city government more accessible to New Yorkers" (Billy & Gewolb 2019). The focus specifically for this charter revision commission was on making government accessible to underrepresented populations (immigrants, homeless, disabled and the incarcerated). De Blasio in many ways was promoting greater decentralization following a long period of centralization. Thus, in 2018, three proposals were put forward, all of which passed: greater limits on campaign finance for those opting into the matching system, the creation of a "civic engagement commission" to support participatory budgeting and boost civic engagement citywide, and term limits for community board members.

In 2019 ranked choice voting was approved to ensure a winner and save the city money in run-off elections. The Civilian Complaint Review board's power was expanded and the number of members increased in an effort to confront claims of police misconduct. Limitations were placed on the ability of former elected officials to take jobs as lobbyists. The city was also given the power to create a "rainy day" fund, to guarantee budgets for borough presidents and the public advocate, and to impose budget deadlines on the mayor. And finally, the time allocated for public review of land-use decisions was expanded.

De Blasio's final charter reform legacy, approved by voters after his term had ended in November 2022, focused on racial, social and economic equity in New York. Three ballot proposals were put to voters in New York City. All sought to enshrine a progressive commitment to address structural racism and inequality. Some aspects of the proposals were aspirational, as in the first ballot proposal, which enshrines a commitment to address historic legacies of racism and promote a more equitable future for all New Yorkers. Two ballot items were structural, one creates a permanent office to oversee issues of racial equity and support the creation of biennial race-equity plans for city agencies. These reforms were made in an effort to overcome the legacy of segregation that continues to shape the neighbourhoods of New York (as discussed in

Chapter 5). The other focuses on economic equity through the addition of a requirement that the city develop a more accurate cost of living measure to inform budgeting, policy and planning in the New York metropolitan core (NYC Votes, n.d.).

The new mayor, Eric Adams, will likely have his own set of charter reforms, but it is still very early in his administration. Currently, mayoral control of the New York City schools is once again on the agenda as this reform is set to sunset. But the early signs are that mayoral control will be extended by the current New York State Governor Kathy Hochul. Other areas we are likely to see in this arena concern criminal justice, a central pillar of Adams' political agenda for the core.

What we see, from this brief overview of charter reform, are the ways in which leaders have used this arena as a mechanism through which to respond to challenges that emerge in response to growth, crisis and change. In each case, we can see efforts to streamline and build efficiency during moments of fiscal stress on the city, while in other instances we have seen mayors endeavour to centralize power at moments of crisis such as 9/11. Most recently, amid waves of popular protest and demands for more responsive and democratic local government, we see efforts to devolve power downwards to local communities. These same processes can also be seen in relationship to governance in the greater megacity region.

New Jersey's local government system

The full complexity of expanded governance across the region cannot be appreciated without some attention to the evolving structures of government on the New Jersey side of the megacity. These localities are intimately tied with the regional economy, yet are also competitively engaged in efforts to capture economic benefits flowing through the region.

In New Jersey, charter reform can be achieved in one of two manners. Voters can approve a charter study commission, which then puts forward its recommendations for change in a ballot ordinance. Reform is also possible through direct voter petition. So, the process in New Jersey is more closely linked with local electoral processes, without empowering either mayors or councils to self-initiate (as is true on the New York side). This difference is a reflection of New Jersey's strong home rule based in the Cooley interpretation of home rule discussed above.

In the 1800s, as New York was beginning the process of consolidation, northern New Jersey townships were already emerging as "satellites of New York

City", first connected by ferry and later via rail, road and tunnel. "By 1860, a million rail passengers travelled annually between Newark, Jersey City and then across the Hudson to New York" (Salmore & Salmore 2008: 234). Thus, populations of the megacity were already becoming increasingly tied together in the growing regional economy.

In New Jersey, municipalities emerged in a more ad hoc manner than was the case on the New York side. Prior to the passage of the Faulkner Act in 1948, each local government required separate legislative approval from the state. However, while in the case of New York, in general, the municipal form was tied to population size, service demands and levels of development, in New Jersey things are not quite as straightforward. "Though New Jersey has towns, boroughs, townships and villages. New Jersey is unique in that these types do not differ in their rights, power or duties" (Salmore & Salmore 2008: 237). Towns in some cases date back to the colonial period, whereas boroughs have roots in the late 1800s when parts of towns split off over conflicting local views around prohibition ordinances and taxation demands. The result is that today there are five types of municipality and 12 forms of government on the Jersey side of the megacity region.

In order to bring greater cohesion to the system, the state passed legislation in 1948 to streamline things a bit and to create more professional capacity at the local level to manage local services and be more responsive to local needs. The Faulkner Act promoted the separation of legislative and executive functions, alongside increased power for local executives. Localities were offered two basic designs: mayor-council and council-manager. They could opt for a council with five, seven or nine members, partisan or non-partisan elections, concurrent or staggered terms and wards or at-large elections (Salmore & Salmore 2008: 238). Interestingly, as Reock points out, "The approach reportedly was followed because ... of concern[s] that the state courts might regard the grant of full choice to the local level as an unconstitutional delegation of legislative authority" (Reock 2015: 3).

In 1950 most local governments operated under laws set in place before 1900. With the passage of the Faulkner Act, most opted to create weak mayor-councils in cities, towns and boroughs, and committee forms in smaller townships. In 1981 the Optional Municipal Charter Law was passed. This law gave localities additional options concerning the timing of elections, districts structures, council size and partisanship in elections.

The cities on this side of the megacity have, like New York, seen small efforts at centralization, but not on the scale seen in the urban core. And change has tended to shift control up to the state, rather than shifting control between legislative and executive officers at the local level.

In 1989 the state assumed control of the school system in Jersey City and then did the same in 1995 in the case of Newark. Supporters of the move at the time argued that schools were failing, so state control was put forward as a more efficient way of effecting change and bringing the resources required into the municipality. These reforms also opened up the system to private charter schools. Researchers suggest that the initiatives may also have had a more subtle underlying reason. The reforms not only centralized functional and financial control over education in these districts, but also closed down an avenue through which minorities had begun to gain access to local political systems through their local school boards (Morel 2018). They also opened the way for a greater private sector role in education. These changes remained in place for a decade. Operational power was returned to localities in 2007, and fiscal control in 2014. By this time a large proportion of children had moved into private charter schools and, at the same time with a smaller number of students in the public system, improvements in outcomes could be seen.

The use of charter reform is less pronounced in this part of the megacity, but here we see the state as being the critical vehicle for such change, rather than changes being initiated at the municipal level. The school reforms were opposed by elected officials in 1989, and yet supported in 2007 and 2014. Private sector actors were also important in putting their support behind these changes in governing systems.

Pulling the threads of government together: governmental forms

Today we find that the older, more urbanized areas on the New Jersey and the New York side of the region have for the most part opted for a mayor-council form of government. Members of the council tend to be elected with staggered terms to ensure continuity over time. The exception to this is Jersey City, which elects its officers concurrently. Smaller municipalities in the more rural suburban areas tend to opt for council-manager forms of local government. In this type of government, the council appoints a manager to oversee operations but decision-making is controlled by the elected legislative council.

Across the megacity, in mayor-council systems, the executive is tasked with responsibility for the preparation of budgets, the appointment of department heads and the like. Mayors have veto powers, but councils can override these vetoes if two-thirds of its members vote to overturn the mayor's veto. Council's tend to serve as the locality's legislative body. Together then, local governments are tasked with regulating land use through zoning laws and special purpose authorities.

What we can see from all this is how incredibly complicated governance is across the megacity. There are variations that are derived from state differences, historic differences, from county variations and, most importantly, from the choices made in response to the pressures of growth and development. One important difference to be found in relationship to the municipalities of New Jersey is that, with the exception of education in select parts of the region, the state seems to take a weaker role in terms of oversight than is true of municipalities in New York.

Here we simply suggest that in New Jersey there is greater connection to the Cooley interpretation of local government in support of strong home rule provisions, while on the New York side of the region Dillon's rule tends to prevail, putting the state in a much more influential position than is true of the New Jersey municipalities. Although the governors of New Jersey are reported to hold "the most executive power in the nation" (Sutton 2020), they have tended only to intervene directly in localities during periods of crisis – fiscal, environmental, security and health. We will return to this theme in our discussion of governance in the greater region in response to Covid-19.

Finally, before turning our attention to regional governance, we would be remiss not to mention that, alongside these formal institutions, one can find an even wider array of public, private, non-profit and non-governmental organizations that are also actively involved in megacity governance. These include quasi-governmental agencies such as the Economic Development Corporations of New York, Jersey City and Hoboken. Beyond this, one can also find an extensive network of more localized partnerships that bring the private sector more directly into governance processes in the megacity. For example, there are 130 Business Improvement Districts serving as more hyper-local, placed-based governance partnerships managing space and development in small commercial, retail and industrial areas of the region. And finally, there are countless community-based organizations, all involved in the governance of development and growth across the territory. These arrangements remind us of the highly decentralized nature of local governance in the United States and remind us of the challenges that one encounters with efforts to work across these entities. We will revisit this aspect of governance in the megacity in Chapter 5 when we drill down to explore the neighbourhoods of the megacity.

Regional governance in the megacity

Regional governance in the megacity is concentrated around issues of transportation, economic development and environment needs. And while there are a variety of bi-state agreements and institutions in place, one tends to find that the competitiveness and complexity within the region also shapes the nature of regional collaboration in the expanded area. Actors tend to adopt parochial attitudes and are more likely to be engaged in defending their locality's interests in policy, as opposed to searching for shared collective outcomes. This is even true within regional institutions. What we find at the regional scale are public benefits corporations, which are often charged with the task of wrangling the parts together behind the shared needs of the greater megacity.

The PANYNJ, for example, was created in 1921 through an interstate compact to coordinate the ports, commerce and trade in the megacity. As Gale points out, the PANYNJ "became a forum for discourse, permitted both states to air political and economic issues of mutual concern … [and] the primary engine for economic development in Greater New York" (Gale 2006: 21). When created in 1921, it was given responsibility for the oversight and development of the most critical transportation arteries in the region.

The problem with this entity as a mechanism of expanded governance relates to its political structure. The governors of each state each appoint six members from their own states to the governing board, and the governors themselves each have veto powers. And, while the PANYNJ has remained the singular entity within the region with the power to plan, manage and finance infrastructure across the larger megacity territory, its political design in many regards has hampered its effectiveness as a unifying body in a politically divided and diverse metropole. As Gross and Nelles (2018: 124) point out:

> Though in principle, its oversight of core regional infrastructure projects offered the PANYNJ economic power, it lacked capacity to overcome the political fragmentation endemic to the region … While a formal regional institution of governance [was] created, the informal political divisions … left it as a weaker than hoped for tool of regional cooperation and planning for all but the lowest risk projects.

As a bi-state entity, its members have for most of its history leaned towards parochial competitiveness rather than regional collaboration and have more commonly exposed the contentiousness of a deeply entrenched and diverse set of stakeholders. This has also meant that even its most successful initiatives have often ended up taking far more time and have been far more costly to achieve. This is not to say that the PANYNJ has not achieved some impressive outcomes: the Holland and Lincoln Tunnels, the PATH commuter rail system, the development of the World Trade Center, the development and management of Newark, JFK and LaGuardia Airports are all success stories tied to the PANYNJ. Indeed, these projects lie at the heart of the region's success, as they enable the flow of people, goods and services to move within, through and beyond the region. Without it, the region is unlikely to have achieved the massive economic growth and vitality that we have depicted here. But analysis of this institution reveals that it has often required the intervention (fiscal and political) of the federal government to overcome deadlock and push initiatives forward (Gross & Nelles 2018).

The parochialism indicative of the region has also impacted other efforts at regional planning. The Metropolitan Regional Council, created by Mayor Lindsay in 1956, for example, fell apart after two decades, when suburban partners believed that the urban core was exerting excess control (Miller 2016). Other entities engaged in governance at a regional scale are the two federally mandated metropolitan planning organizations, the NYMTC and the NJTPA. The NYMTC is made up of county representatives from all the megacity counties and includes representatives for the New York City departments of planning and transportation. All decisions are based on consensus. It also includes non-voting members from the federal transportation and environmental protection authorities, the PANYNJ and NJPTA. The NJPTA oversees federal transportation projects in northern New Jersey. As with the NYMTC, its membership comes from the counties of northern New Jersey, and it has non-voting members from the PANYNJ and from the governor's office. These bodies really serve as conduits for the allocation of federal resources within their respective territories and, as they are "splintered" by state, they lack a broader vision of the region.

The same challenges beset efforts to consider economic development regionally. Here we find two state-level development entities: the Empire State Development Corporation and the New Jersey Economic Development Authority. Both entities are public benefits corporations whose job is to support economic development, workforce development, marketing and tourism across their respective states. They are competitors rather than tools of collaboration in the governance of the greater megacity.

Finally, we need to mention the Regional Plan Association, an independent civic organization that has been advocating for regional planning around economic, environmental, housing and quality of life concerns across the region for almost a century. Although this organization may lack the formal power found in the public benefits entities mentioned above, it has been at the root of regional thinking for the megacity for a very long time. Although covering a much larger terrain, with the inclusion of Connecticut, it has been advocating for long-range regional planning since 1929. Its membership is diverse, including corporate, academic and community leaders. They not only conduct research, but they also partner with these same groups to implement and advance their projects. This body has played an important role in governance through its ongoing advocacy around regional needs.

What should now be evident is that expanded governance in the New York megacity is incredibly complex. There are many actors engaged in these processes and there are few incentives for these actors to come together to collaborate. Thus, the governance of the region is best viewed as competitive. Collaboration is driven by self-interest and most likely to occur at moments of crisis, as seen in Chapter 2. We end with one short case study of the regional efforts to grapple with traffic through the lens of congestion pricing.

Congestion pricing and commuter taxes: expanded governance

The case of congestion pricing offers us an interesting window into the politics of expanded governance in the region and the role played by state and regional actors in achieving programmatic and policy outcomes in arenas that cross jurisdictional boundaries. The transportation system (i.e. rail, roads, tunnels and bridges) has long been seen as a core component of development and growth in the megacity. It is considered to be a critical piece of national and regional systems of commerce, trade and defence. The system is the backbone to the regional economy, providing what might in essence be considered the arteries through which people, goods and services flow. It also connects and binds the disparate geographical parts together. The simple recognition that the heart of the megacity, Manhattan, is an island, connected to the inner core and suburban ring by a series of bridges, tunnels, roads and rails, puts this in perspective. Given transportation's critical role in growth, one should not be at all surprised to discover that it represents a highly political and contested terrain of governance in the greater megacity.

In 1966 the city's corporate economy was robust but, at the same time, suburbanization meant that the fiscal landscape for the core was problematic. A growing proportion of the labour force was working in the city but paying property taxes in their residential suburban locales. Republican Mayor Lindsay projected a $500 million deficit for the city, which would significantly impact transportation systems and service provision. Mayor He sought a solution that revolved around a series of tax code changes, in order to capture revenues from suburbanites who were working in the core (Viteritti 2014).

Due to the governing system in the region, such a change not only required support from the Democratically controlled city council, but also that of the Democratically controlled state assembly and Republican Governor Rockefeller. As one might expect, the policy was controversial. Opposition could be heard not only from the suburban legislators – but from the corporate and real estate interests based in the urban core, who threatened to move their

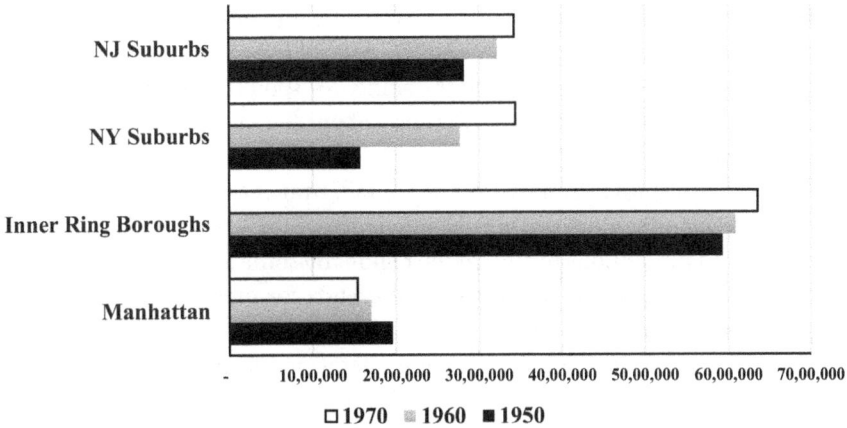

Figure 4.2 New York megacity: population change, 1950–70.
Source: US Census Bureau, 1950; 1960; 1970.

headquarters elsewhere. At the time, the governor intervened and enabled this controversial bill to pass. With its introduction, New York City levied a 0.024 per cent payroll tax on suburban residents who worked in the urban core. Although the percentage was relatively small, it yielded an important revenue stream that was used to maintain the region's transportation infrastructure. The tax, as one might expect, was highly controversial.

It was done at a time when the region had experienced significant losses as manufacturing left the city and when an equally large number of residents decamped for the suburbs. The result was a declining tax base to support and maintain the vast infrastructures that kept the city moving. As Figure 4.2 illustrates, between 1950 and 1970, while the urban core lost population, all the surrounding areas, both the inner ring and the nearby suburban communities, saw population growth. And, while residential population was shifting, employment remained concentrated in the core.

This tax remained in place for the next three decades, with little outcry until it became caught up in a state legislative race in 1999, when both Republican and Democrat candidates endeavoured to outdo the other with promises of tax breaks. It did not matter who won, because all candidates had promised to eliminate the tax if elected. In the end, the issue was taken up by the state legislature, which chose to abolish it shortly after.

Since then the only form of commuter tax on suburban residents of the megacity has been levied by the PANYNJ through tolls, as opposed to levying a more general tax, which would likely incur the ire of voters during election cycles. In this way the cost of commuter use is distributive rather than redistributive – a policy that tends to be less politically controversial than other approaches. Moreover, as the PANYNJ has control over tolls at the crossings, there are in reality fewer cooks with the ability to "spoil the broth". Governors are supportive, as it helps to defray the costs of upkeep of essential transportation systems.

Attempts to capture revenue from road, rail, tunnel and bridge use and to apply it to the costs of upkeep and maintenance of this critical infrastructure has a long and tumultuous history in the region. By some accounts, congestion pricing has been on the megacity political agenda for more than "half a century" (Schwarz *et al.* 2008: 594).

Congestion pricing reflects the next iteration of the commuter tax. Initially proposed in the spring of 2007, it was a policy that was folded into then Mayor Michael Bloomberg's sustainability plan. While the policy was promoted as a component of sustainable development, as well as an effort to bring more revenue into the urban core during the financial crisis of 2007–08, it could in reality be traced to the post-war development of an extensive network of roads, bridges and tunnels. Between 1920 and 1950, this resulted in a 105 per cent increase in the number of river crossings to and from Manhattan. The core continues to be a magnet for economic activities, thus even when it experienced a decline in population between 1960 and 1980, the region saw a "94% growth in vehicular river crossings" (NYC Department of Transportation 2016: 10),

Although the commuter tax was in essence a flat tax, congestion pricing was a tax tied to geography. The goal was to levy fees to those entering heavily congested commercial areas of the city during a high traffic period. The proposals also included the idea of adding tolls to the East River crossings. It was this element that caused the greatest backlash within the urban core. The boroughs of Brooklyn and Queens would have been most heavily impacted, not only by the fees that their residents would now be charged but also by the traffic that would likely ensue when new tolls were put in place. And, although in 2007 there was a large coalition of supporters – public, private and civic: "Mayor Bloomberg, former Governor David Paterson, a coalition of 135 civic, business, labour, environmental and advocacy groups and the editorial boards of all four major newspapers" (Schaller 2010: 6), there was an equally large backlash from stakeholders in the expanded megacity region.

We would argue that its failure to be implemented at that time fell squarely on the shoulders of the complicated and competitive governance systems. It is here that one can best understand the rocky road that this policy initiative has faced. Dillon's Rule in New York meant that the passage of a commuter tax would today require the support of the New York State legislature, the governors of New York and New Jersey, the New York City Council, the mayor and all the municipalities that would be impacted in the larger megacity region.

In fact, congestion pricing was once again proposed in 2015 and in 2017. This time, Mayor de Blasio and Governor Cuomo engaged in more extensive discussions. Buoyed by the success of similar initiatives in other global cities, such as London, and with the advocacy of former Mayor Bloomberg, a new plan emerged. The project got the support it needed from the state and in 2019 an agreement was reached. The money generated would be spent on the upkeep of the New York City subway, regional buses and the Long Island and Metro-North Commuter rails. And, with no direct ties to New Jersey, there was no need to bring them into the decision-making process.

Although the policy was passed and the project was added to the state budget, it still sits in limbo. Because the project involves the highway system, it also requires federal government approval, which had been blocked due to the tensions between the megacity and President Trump.

Thus, what we see in this case is that congestion pricing, like many issues that the megacity faces, can only be understood through the lens of regional complexity. Expanded governance in the region tends to be caught within an ongoing fiscal and political battle that was directly tied to the pressures of megacity growth outwards, coupled with the concomitant impacts of depopulation in the urban core. Although the need for congestion pricing was evident, the process continues to be stymied by a region clogged with a plethora of institutions, each of which are fighting for their own survival.

Conclusions

It would appear then, when we consider expanded governance in the megacity, that the system itself becomes very problematic. Vertically, the region is caught within a matrix of competing and conflicting institutions. The fact that the region crosses two states is perhaps the central challenge. This alone means that any shared fiscal collaborations will be met by very parochial demands. Where success has been more evident is around more tangible infrastructure projects and more recently in regard to environmental and health crises, as revealed in Chapter 2.

As mentioned earlier, the bridges, tunnels, rails, roads and airports might perhaps be seen as the arteries through which people, goods and services flow. But, in addition, we might also see these as serving as the glue that binds the disparate parts together. The shared reality of these necessary building blocks for a regional economy has revealed the region's capacity to reach agreements and to build new projects. But this does not occur easily and often demands some twisting of arms by state and federal officials.

At moments of crisis, a more positive side of the megacity is revealed. Collaborations in the aftermath of 9/11, hurricane Sandy and now the pandemic reveal a region that can do great things together, when it can find an elevating goal that moves these stakeholders beyond their parochialism.

The scaffolding that underlies governance of this megacity is rarely stable or solid. The spaces for breakdown are extensive. But even so, the region continues to function, more by necessity perhaps than by design. But in the end it is perhaps the shared recognition that all can benefit from the competitive advantages that the region has long held in the global economic system. Thus, as a region, much has been achieved, although always through complex, difficult compromises and challenging collaborations among stakeholders in the public, private and non-profit sectors.

5

Neighbourhoods, diversification and gentrification in the megacity

New York has always been a magnet, not only for economic development, commerce and trade, but most importantly for people. Immigration and migration have fuelled growth and also helped to stabilize this diverse region during moments of instability, crisis and decline. In 2020 there were an estimated 4.95 million foreign-born residents in the region (58 per cent naturalized), 21 per cent entered the United States after 2010, and 67 per cent entered the United States after 1990 (US Census Bureau 2019, 2020a). The Great Migration between 1910 and 1970 from the south of the United States brought a 27 per cent increase in the region's black populations. Puerto Rican migration grew during the post-war period, immigration from South America came in the 1990s (NYC Mayors Office of Immigrant Affairs 2021b), and today the fastest-growing ethnic groups in the megacity are of Asian and Pacific Islander origins (NYC Mayors Office of Immigrant Affairs 2021a).

On the New Jersey side of the region, the cities of Newark, Jersey City and Elizabeth situated in the older urban areas of the gateway region are home to the largest foreign-born populations in the entire state of New Jersey. Despite ebbs and flows over time, the megacity is not only home to the largest immigrant population in the United States, but also the largest black population (Mollenkopf 2017). According to the 2020 census, the megacity was home to almost three million African-American residents (US Census Bureau 2020b). Not surprisingly, the megacity has prided itself on being a locus of diversity. While the forces of migration and immigration have been central aspects of megacity growth and diversification, public policy and private markets have been used to influence how these forces overlay onto the region's neighbourhoods (Leibbrand *et al.* 2020).

Neighbourhoods have served as critical points of access for new populations, connecting people to jobs, housing, social networks and education; however, the history of neighbourhoods in the region also reveals tales of exclusion and disinvestment. As sociologists Mary Waters and Phil Kasinitz argue, "this diversity is characterized by paradoxes that emerge due to the 'intersection of race and immigration'. It is at the neighbourhood scale, that these paradoxes are experienced" (2014: 147). Thus, although New York is a diverse megacity, it is also a territory of inequalities, as documented throughout this book. Cycles of growth and decline have been met by both progressive and regressive policy choices. As a result, this megacity is not a monolithic territory, but one composed of diverse neighbourhoods that are being constantly remade.

Neighbourhoods are viewed as the containers within which people, infrastructure and economic activity coalesce. The neighbourhood represents a geographic space, made up of assets (physical, economic, social and political), which are shaped by policies that directly (and indirectly) structure the flow of people and their settlement patterns. In combination, the mix of people, policies and amenities have served to attract, lock in and to exclude or repel populations. Thus, "neighbourhoods are places ... with overlapping systems of oppression and affordances" (Roy 2018: 62). It is at this most local scale that one can begin to understand how New York became a region characterized by both diversity and segregation.

The patterns we see today are the result of policy choices made regarding land-use, zoning and housing. In combination they have influenced how and where people live, what is built and what is not. Tenement laws, public housing, rent regulation, affordable housing (incentivized as well as mandatory), zoning (comprehensive, exclusionary and inclusionary) and immigrant integration policies have all played a role in shaping the neighbourhoods of the megacity. Figures 5.1, 5.2 and 5.3 portray the neighbourhoods of the megacity through the lens of race and ethnicity.

This chapter takes a longitudinal lens, exploring policy impacts over time, capturing the ways in which policies have shaped neighbourhoods as they navigate between cycles of growth and decline. This is followed by two short cases that explore the ways in which neighbourhoods have endeavoured to preserve and promote diversity over segregation. The first explores efforts to institute rent control in one of the New Jersey gateway communities, Montclair. The second highlights recent efforts to create mixed income communities through mandatory affordable housing policies in Brooklyn. Together this data reveals the challenges that policymakers and advocates face in their efforts to reframe neighbourhood settlement patterns in more equitable ways.

Figure 5.1 Total population: Black or African-American alone ACS 2019 (Five-year estimates).
Source: Social Explorer 2019 Black or African-American Alone, based on data from US Census Bureau.

Figure 5.2 Total population: Hispanic or Latino ACS 2019 (Five-year estimates).
Source: Social Explorer 2019 Hispanic or Latino, based on data from US Census Bureau.

Land-use, housing and neighbourhoods

Zoning concerns the public regulation of land-use, whereas covenants are agreements among private sector actors to control access to land, housing

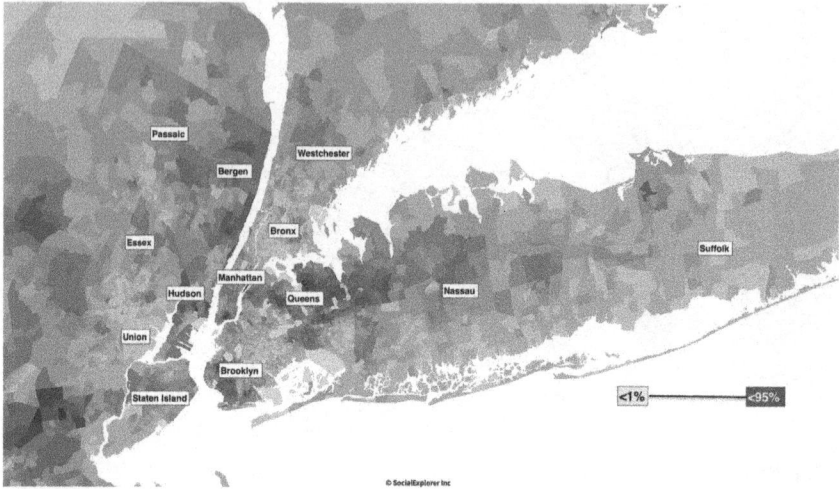

Figure 5.3 Total population: Asian alone ACS 2019 (Five-year estimates).
Source: Social Explorer 2019 Asian Alone, based on data from US Census Bureau.

and even finance within neighbourhoods. Land-use and housing policy in the megacity has taken three broad forms: regulation, incentives and direct provision. Here we explore how these tools have been used to shape the spatially segregated megacity that we have today.

Early history

New York has long a long history of using zoning policy to regulate and control land-use. The "Commissioners' Plan of 1811" (also known as the grid plan), created for the urban core, laid out the streets of Manhattan north from Houston Street to Harlem. At the time, these parts of the city had yet to be fully developed. The plan could be seen as an early effort to control growth through the creation of a more orderly street grid and to provide a framework for the development and sale of real estate. Prior to the plan, Lower Manhattan south of Houston Street (already the economic core of the emerging megacity) had evolved somewhat organically though private sector choices resulting in a haphazard street pattern. This created challenges for the movement of people and goods throughout the city. Dense residential areas grew in close proximity to employment centres. New arrivals tended to settle in neighbourhoods with like populations, through processes known as chain migration. New arrivals were drawn by cultural ties and access to employment, housing and transportation. Neighbourhoods were also structured by private property owners, who steered new arrivals to housing.

The 1811 plan laid out the streets and avenues, and while it proposed lot sizes, it did not mandate use, density or bulk (Baics & Meisterlin 2016: 1155). The suggested "standard lot was 100 feet deep (half the block depth) and 20 or 25 feet wide" (Ballon 2011: 87). Lots could also be combined, with no requirement for setbacks from the streets or space for yards. As a result, densely packed tenement housing was built by the private sector in those parts of the urban core that offered easy access to the nearby industrial jobs, while single-family homes were built on the periphery of the built-up areas. The latter emerged in locations more distant from the grittiness of factories, to accommodate more affluent, primarily white residents. A similar pattern of housing development occurred in and around the economic hubs on the New Jersey side of the megacity. As in the core, tenement housing was built by the private sector to capitalize on the massive waves of immigrants and migrants arriving in search of jobs and opportunity.

These early zoning plans were considered to be utilitarian, created for the purposes of economic growth and development (Rose-Redwood 2011), while also serving to shape the early physical contours of the megacity and its neighbourhoods. Because these grids did not require back yards, natural light, ventilation or even plumbing, what emerged were crowded tenement communities, which "were private, profitable and often unsafe" (Martens 2009: 7).

While local governments created a loose regulatory framework for where housing would go, the actual development and construction of housing was largely left to the private and philanthropic sectors. By 1867 there were some 15,000 tenements in the core (De Forest 1914: 9), which by 1894 would accommodate 143.2 people per square mile (Marcuse 1980: 153). Similar conditions were also found in the older urban parts of New Jersey's gateway neighbourhoods such as Newark, Hoboken and Jersey.

In a study of tenement housing in Jersey City at the turn of the century, neighbourhood "conditions were found of such seriousness ... to warrant and demand interference by the board of health" (Sayles 1902: 32). Tenement housing was built to accommodate three or more families. Often the ground floor would be used for commercial activity. Over time, the poor health conditions at the neighbourhood scale created pressure for a more detailed set of regulations to ensure the health and safety of the megacity's residents and its economy. At the same time, housing policies were created to address issues of access and equity in neighbourhoods.

Tenement housing laws were introduced in New York State in the late 1800s, in response to scathing reports about tenement life (Riis 2011). In 1860, for example, ten people were killed when their tenement in Lower Manhattan caught fire. At the time there were 24 families residing in the building. When its ground floor bakery caught fire, there was no infrastructure to allow the firefighters to scale the building, and their ladders were not tall enough (Apmann 2012). This was not an isolated incident, and in response the first tenement safety laws were initiated, requiring that all new developments would include fire escapes and windows in every room. Across the region, leaders also equated tenements with poor health and crime, leading not only to efforts to regulate, surveille and police their form and populations, but later this would be the basis for the decisions to create the largest public housing system in the United States.

In 1879 housing law was modified to require that windows be placed near sources of fresh air and light. Then in 1901 tenements were required to include exterior spaces for garbage and at least one toilet for every two families (Apmann 2016). These requirements also resulted in the construction of taller residential buildings (often seven storeys in height), adding density to the region's urban neighbourhoods. In 1904 New Jersey's gateway communities followed suit, in response to the same dynamics. In Jersey City, Newark and Hoboken, tenements were deemed to be dangerous and overcrowded places (De Forest 1914).

These earliest efforts to regulate the privately developed built environment could be seen as direct responses to migration and immigration, and the pressures of economic growth. The replication of policies that were initiated in the urban core, in New Jersey's gateway neighbourhoods, were a reflection of the shared experiences and policy synergies that would characterize and influence neighbourhood development in the megacity to this day. Thus, while collaboration was often difficult around economic development and growth, proximity did shape the flow of ideas and even advocacy between neighbourhoods, counties and the municipalities of the megacity, inducing replication.

Between 1913 and 1914 the states of New York and New Jersey created enabling legislation to allow municipalities greater local control over the regulation of land-use, through zoning ordinances. Zoning continued to be seen as an important corrective to the problems indicative of the types of private unplanned housing development that had plagued the region and resulted in overcrowded immigrant and migrant communities. New York continued to use zoning regulation as a means of controlling physical development in the Manhattan core and inner-ring neighbourhoods of Brooklyn, Queens and the Bronx, as did the surrounding urban and suburban municipalities in Staten Island, Long Island, Westchester and in northern New Jersey.

New York's 1916 Zoning Resolution introduced municipal controls on development, and for the first time regulated space by uses – residential, commercial and industrial. This policy was described as a tool of "rationalization" rather than one of exclusion (Fischler 1998: 171). It was meant to create healthy residential communities that did not suffer the negative externalities emerging from proximity to noxious industrial uses or crowded commercial areas.

At the time there was great debate concerning the role of public versus private sector actors when it came to land-use control. The courts tended to support the principle of zoning as being a reasonable exercise of public power over private markets. The use of zoning for public purposes emerged on the New York side of the region first and then in 1927 New Jersey introduced comprehensive zoning to municipalities across the state (Costin 2019). These patterns illustrate the ways in which policy principles flowed across the megacity.

The next significant application of zoning did not come until 1961, with the passage of the New York City Zoning Resolution. This time zoning was used in the urban core to separate residential, commercial and industrial uses by neighbourhood. It also introduced the use of incentives for development. Here a carrot rather than a stick approach was used to encourage the creation of public spaces in new developments. Builders were incentivized to add things such as public plazas, and in exchange they were granted the right to increase the floor space built for housing. The laws also allowed for additional density in the commercial parts of the core, while reducing density in residential areas located on the periphery. The stated goal at the time was to use zoning to stabilize the region's residential and commercial communities and to encourage development in a managed and healthy way. Unstated were the ramifications of these policies for poor and minority populations, who were often locked into specific neighbourhoods and denied access to others on the basis of income.

Regulation was also used by policymakers in the megacity to rein in markets and respond to popular pressures for affordable housing. In the immediate aftermath of the First World War, for example, rents skyrocketed, vacancy fell to almost zero, inflation was rampant and population continued to grow. Popular unrest over rapidly rising costs and fears of displacement led to thousands of rent strikes, not only in the tenement neighbourhoods in the urban core but also in Hoboken, Newark and Jersey City (Fogelson 2013: 60.) Policymakers responded with the passage of a series of emergency regulations to prevent eviction and to pressure landlords to keep rents reasonable.

Rent regulation was used as a tool to stabilize housing costs and prevent displacement, a supply-side approach (Bloom & Lasner 2016: 37). These laws were only in place for a short time. Pressure from the real estate sector emerged, and legal challenges were mounted to push back against public intervention in the housing market. The courts ultimately ruled that by 1926 the post-war emergency situation was over and these emergency laws would be allowed to expire. While the poorest were protected for a few more years, the laws were allowed to sunset in 1929. Although short-lived, these laws are mentioned because they had enduring implications for neighbourhood development. Various forms of rent regulations would return to the megacity, often in response to crises, becoming one mechanism that low income communities across the megacity have continued to fight for, to support access, prevent displacement and in some cases to promote racial and ethnic diversification when markets failed to do so.

As was true in the case of corporate-centred urban development, the carrot has been much more popular than the stick when it comes to governmental efforts to control growth, housing and neighbourhood development in this megacity. For example, New York State passed the Limited Dividend Housing Companies Act (1926), which created a mechanism through which the state would offer 20-year tax abatements for home improvements, in exchange for controlling rent in the urban core.

Public decisions about development, location and access to public housing have also had lasting impacts on neighbourhood development. In the aftermath of the Depression, governments became more active in the provision of housing. With the support of federal government funding, many localities began to respond to housing crises through programmes of direct provision. The New York City Housing Authority, created in 1934, was the first of its kind in the United States. Under the leadership of then Mayor Fiorello LaGuardia, this agency oversaw the development of what would become a vast public housing sector in the urban core. Public housing authorities were subsequently created across the megacity: in Yonkers (on the northern border of the urban core in Westchester County) in 1935, in 1938 housing authorities were formed in the gateway cities (Jersey City and Elizabeth), and Hoboken in 1949. In Long Island, public housing has been more contentious, left to county and more local-level governments, and subject to significant pushback from local residents.

To this point our focus has been on housing and land-use policy and how they impacted the development of neighbourhoods across the megacity. But, as mentioned above, race intersects with income in powerful ways at the neighbourhood scale. The neighbourhood of Harlem, for example, had already become one of the most densely populated African-American and Latino communities in the megacity by the early 1930s. These migrant populations found their way to Harlem through the pull of chain migration, the push of Jim Crow in the south,[1] and exclusion from access to housing in neighbourhoods of the megacity itself. As Biondi (2007: 1) reminds us:

---

1. Jim Crow refers to state and local laws implemented in southern states to segregate African-American populations.

Segregation in New York was not only widespread and lawful, but government and public policy sanctioned it and helped to create it: there were whites-only signs in Manhattan apartment buildings, racially restrictive covenants in property across the region, whites-only classified job advertisements, whites-only hotels and restaurants in the heart of Manhattan, and segregated seat assignments by American Airlines at La Guardia.

Similar patterns were also to be found in New Jersey. Large African-American and Latino communities were concentrated in the older urbanized parts of the New Jersey, in Newark, Jersey City and Paterson.

These patterns of racial and ethnic residential concentration were shaped by private land owners feeding off chain migration and immigration. Unscrupulous landlords packed these populations into smaller and smaller spaces, while realtors steered populations into specific neighbourhoods such as Harlem, while excluding them from accessing housing elsewhere in the region. During the Depression, as conditions deteriorated, popular unrest grew. Riots broke out in Harlem in 1935 due to the poor conditions of these areas, rising unemployment, policing and segregation (Frazier 1935). In response, city leaders in New York announced plans to develop public-provided housing, but it did so in a manner that reinforced racial and ethnic segregation.

The first public housing in the region was built in the core of Manhattan on the Lower East side. "First Houses" was a relatively small unit, with some 125 apartments. It was located in one of the most densely packed immigrant communities in the region (Thompson 1999). Screening processes were used to ensure that only low-income working families would have access (Ferré-Sadurní 2018). Income restrictions were used to ensure that the very poor and the affluent were kept out. Harlem River houses opened in 1937, and the Ten Eyck Houses in Williamsburg in 1938. Importantly, these two development were completely segregated by race, with Harlem River restricted to black families, and Williamsburg to white families.

From the Depression through to the early 1980s, many of the suburban communities in the region instituted policies to promote residential growth, but also to preserve the lower-density suburban lifestyle. Thus, even though public housing was introduced, in most cases it was placed in low-income areas where migrants and immigrants were concentrated, and in neighbourhoods that had the lowest land value, fewest services and fewest amenities.

Interestingly, whereas in the urban parts of the region zoning was used to control building heights and setbacks (i.e. distance to the street and other buildings) to allow for air to flow more easily and to aid the municipalities in the management of their physical infrastructure, in many of the region's suburban communities during the interwar years, public zoning was often used to control growth, increase land values and restrict population movements based on race, ethnicity and class. In combination these produced very different racial and ethnic residential patterns across the megacity.

In the suburban counties of Nassau, Suffolk and Westchester, African-American and Latino populations were only able to purchase land in those areas that were unincorporated (outside county boundaries), or rent substandard tenement housing (Wiese 1995: 63). According to researchers, out of some 300 private housing developments built in and around Long Island and Westchester between 1935 and 1947, "56% had racially restrictive covenants" (Rothstein 2017: 79). Then, in the early 1940s, many of these municipalities used urban renewal funds to clear these populations by designating these low-income communities as blighted. With this designation, communities across Nassau and Suffolk counties rebuilt at lower density (i.e. Glen Cove, Long Beach, Freeport, Hempstead, Manhasset and Port Washington) (Wiese 1995: 63), while concentrating African-American and Latino residents into smaller and smaller spatially segregated spaces.

The private property owners and developers used racially restrictive covenants to shape who had access to land or homes (for purchase or rental). Zoning was used to prevent multi-unit housing from being built and to regulate land development to large single-family homes on large lots. In doing so they increased the cost to rent or purchase housing. Many suburban communities used these regulatory tools to exclude access to communities of colour and to low-income populations. Historian and policy analyst Richard Rothstein found that these tools had a profound impact on the emergence of the segregated spaces of the megacity (Rothstein 2017).

Perhaps one of the more pernicious tactics used by both public and private sector actors was redlining. During the early 1930s, the approach was initially used by the real estate sector, and then subsequently by governments and banks. Between 1935 and 1940, a series of maps was created by the Home Owners' Loan Corporation (a federal entity), which earmarked some neighbourhoods as creditworthy and others as risky. The neighbourhoods identified as risky were largely low-income areas, while the wealthier suburban communities became sites for residential investment. These maps were used by financial institutions to determine where mortgages and home loans would be provided. The result was that little money flowed into the low-income neighbourhoods. Thus, it was minority-dominated urban neighbourhoods that suffered the most under these policies, while largely white suburban neighbourhoods became key places for investment (Ware 2021).

Geographers Mitchell and Franco found that these policies had lasting impacts on the types of segregation we see across the megacity today (2018).

Federal subsidies for the highway systems helped to further these divisions by enabling the development of roads, which municipalities used in some cases to separate black and white neighbourhoods, reinforcing residential segregation. Legal scholar Leland Ware argues that "for most of the 20th century, redlining prevented African Americans from securing mortgage loans". Later, "minorities were targeted by lenders (reverse redlining) … resulting in defaults, massive foreclosure, and the loss of billions in home equity" (2021: 98).

Prior to the Depression, the public approach to housing was largely regulatory, leaving development and provision to the private sector. The Depression served to open the door for a far more activist public sector role in both the provision and regulation of housing. The decisions about where to build, how to build (density, height, etc.), what funds to offer and who had access had an enduring impact on neighbourhoods and segregation.

Tax-based incentives were used to encourage private sector housing development, while urban renewal was used by the public sector to take control of and clear the land of human and physical obstructions (Podair 2002). In the mid-1950s, programmes such as Mitchell-Lama provided developers with abatements, low-interest mortgages and a guaranteed return on investments (Bloom & Lasner 2016). Some 80,000 units of working-class housing were in place by 1960 (Podair 2002: 13). Public housing was increasingly built to accommodate low-income African-American and Latino populations, and subsidized private housing for middle-income, white, working-class populations (Alexander 2011). Quota systems were used to allocate housing in these developments and served to maintain these patterns of neighbourhood segregation. These same tools were used across Long Island to remove or concentrate poor communities of colour. The development of Levittown in Nassau County, Long Island, was an example of this. Here a massive private development was built (17,400 homes), sold almost exclusively to white families only (Institute on Race and Poverty 2002).

Exclusionary zoning policies were ultimately challenged in the now famous New Jersey court case of NAACP (National Association for the Advancement of Colored People) versus Mt Laurel NJ. The courts ruled that zoning was being used by municipalities to make it "physically and economically impossible to provide low and moderate income housing", and that these mechanisms "would reproduce systems of segregation and fortify it with zoning ordinances" (Dantzler 2016: 657–8). The courts ruled that the state had a responsibility to ensure that all municipalities be responsible for providing their fair share (relative to the state) of such housing. Although Mt Laurel Township was not within the New York megacity itself, the decision had significant implications for the neighbourhoods located on the New Jersey side of the region because, as Dantzler (2016: 659) highlights, the ruling exposed the fact that "zoning power ... [should] be used to further the *general* welfare as opposed to the welfare of one particular, local segment of society". Of course, it would take another decade and two additional lawsuits to actualize these policies, but the framework was set.

Contemporary neighbourhood development

This history provides us with a context to understand the racial, economic and ethnic segregation patterns of neighbourhoods in the contemporary megacity. When the fiscal crisis hit the region in the mid-1970s, the urban neighbourhoods on the New York side of the region "lost over 800,000 residents" and city government took "ownership through tax foreclosure of over 100,000 units, 60,000 in vacant buildings and another 40,000 ... in occupied and semi-occupied buildings ... As a result, the Department of Housing Preservation and Development became the second largest landlord in the city", only the New York City Housing Authority surpassed it as the "largest public housing authority in the country" (Furman Center 2006: 2). Suburban white flight contributed to the region's precarious economic position. The declining tax base, economic restructuring (discussed in prior chapters) and public policy would continue to shape neighbourhood demographics and patterns of residential segregation.

Perhaps the most infamous case of this could be seen in Yonkers, a neighbourhood located north of the urban core, in the suburban county of Westchester. Although some 6,000 units of subsidized housing were built there in the post-war period, all were built in one small quadrant of the neighbourhood. The result was a concentration of African-American and Latino residents in an area that was roughly one square mile of the 29 square miles of land that the municipality occupied. Other parts of Yonkers used private covenants and racial steering to prevent access to these populations. The case is infamous because it took another 30-plus years for Yonkers policymakers to respond to this situation. In 1980 the courts ruled that racial discrimination in housing and education had indeed occurred in the areas, and in 1985 it was deemed to be intentional. Despite this the area continues to struggle to overcome this legacy and build more economically and racially integrated neighbourhoods (Gershman & Haub 2017).

In Brooklyn, Queens, the Bronx, Staten Island, Hudson, Essex and Union, pockets of concentrated poverty and minority concentrations grew. At the same time, the suburban neighbourhoods of Westchester, Nassau, Suffolk and Bergan counties became increasingly white, working class and more affluent (Savitch 1985: 164).

As Marcuse astutely observes (1987: 280), this became a period in which neighbourhoods endeavoured to "treat" decline through incentives for commercial investments in central business districts (as discussed in Chapter 3) and investments and bonuses for housing development in upper income areas. The expectation was that the benefits of luring more affluent residents would then "trickle down", buoying the socio-economic foundation of the megacity, while, at the same time, a "triage" approach was taken in low-income areas by cutting expenditure in areas such as housing, education, transportation and health. Not surprisingly, researchers highlight that, while the region's economy would ultimately revive and boom by the1990s, it did so in a highly uneven manner, resulting in the growth of income inequality (Sites 2003). Thus, policy and investment choices reinforced the spatial segregation of the megacity by race, class and ethnicity.

On the New Jersey side of the region, many of the municipalities that were losing population turned to the use of rent regulations as a mechanism to stabilize neighbourhoods, but also to protect property values in the face of decline. The areas that were gaining population turned instead towards the use of exclusionary zoning tools as a means of controlling who would have access to these areas. In turn, the patterns set over the prior half-century would continue to influence patterns of neighbourhood development across the megacity.

Neighbourhoods and the contemporary uses of control, regulation and subsidy

The fiscal crisis in the mid-1970s in many ways represented a turning point for the megacity and the ways in which neighbourhoods, diversity and segregation would be addressed. Economic restructuring had generated changes in the labour market, due to the shift from manufacturing to producer services. These processes were overlaid by public policies that continued to be used to selectively open and close neighbourhoods to populations. In some cases access was restricted based on income, and in other cases based on race and ethnicity. White populations were pulled to suburban areas of the region via incentives, amenities and opportunities. Minority populations were restricted or denied access through private covenants and public decisions regarding land use, housing and access to public financing and mortgages. In the process the minority populations found themselves locked into inner-city neighbourhoods in the inner-ring boroughs, and older urban industrial parts of the region. As Alba, Logan and Crowder (1997: 884) comment, the process could be "linked to invasion and succession in inner city neighborhoods by minorities, chiefly new immigrant groups" and migrants from the south. And while it is true that market forces were important to the way neighbourhoods were shaped, and the locational choices that residents made, public policy played a critical role in shaping these so-called choices.

In the aftermath of the fiscal crisis, efforts were made to move away from direct public sector provision and management of public and affordable housing towards neoliberal approaches that might encourage private and non-profit sector partners to fill the void. Tax abatements, density bonuses and the increased use of incentives became the preferred methods to increase the supply of "affordable" housing.

The fiscal crisis had brought in policies designed for "planned" yet targeted shrinkage vis-à-vis neighbourhoods. Austerity measures were introduced in low-income minority communities, urban renewal in areas deemed to be blighted, and in the more affluent white suburbs a series of policies and programmes to anchor affluent homeowners, while preventing access for lower-income minority populations. As the income bases of neighbourhoods shifted, so too did the tax base, which led to increasing inequities in public education (funded through property taxes). This would have lasting impacts on the ability of minority residents to become upwardly mobile.

Ed Koch was elected mayor in New York City in 1978 on a platform supporting gentrification as a response to the population losses during the fiscal crisis and the growing number of abandoned housing units across the megacity. In his inaugural address, Koch argued for the importance of private sector development and middle-class residential investments as a fix for neighbourhoods deemed to be "blighted" due to high poverty rates, abandonment, poor housing conditions and high service demands. Arson was also common during this period, as property owners began to burn down their buildings to reduce liability and to be able to build market-rate homes. Researchers reported that between 1974 and 1984, across the five boroughs of New York there were 10,000 arsons each year (Gottlieb 2019: 393).

This was also period of public sector austerity, thus efforts were made to minimize public sector expenditure, while endeavouring to tap into private markets as a tool of neighbourhood revitalization. Koch, for example, created a programme for "density bonuses", which were tax incentives given to encourage private sector development of affordable housing. City leaders also began to provide cleared tracts of land to community organizations, which became housing developers during this period. In and around the region's core, specifically in older urbanized areas that had lost population to nearby suburban communities, new housing was being developed. In some cases this was by the private sector directly, and in other cases in partnership with non-profits. Of importance here is that, while these programmes were highly successful in creating housing for working families, they did little for those living below the poverty line. The mid-1980s, not surprisingly, also witnessed the growth of homelessness, in the core on the New York side and in the older urban areas of the New Jersey gateway.

The first years of the Koch administration saw vacancy rates decline, and rental rates increase by 26 per cent in core and surrounding urban areas (Soffer 2010: 257). The development of privatized housing through tax-based incentives and subsidies served to stabilize some neighbourhoods, push up housing costs in other areas outside the core, while also preventing additional population loss. A voluntary inclusionary housing (VIH) programme was instituted in 1987 in an effort to encourage private developers to create more affordable housing. Developers were enticed through the promise of being able to increase the density and height of their developments, if they included 20 per cent affordable housing. The VIH Program, however, did not produce the amount of affordable housing required to meet the needs of lower-income residents in the core of the region, as the luxury markets were too hot. As a result, some of the peripheral areas with easy transportation access to the core began to attract these new high-skill service workers.

By the end of the Koch years (1989) the region had returned to a period of growth. By 1989 Koch's housing programmes had produced 3,000 renovated apartments, another 13,000 apartments in construction and plans for 20,000 more (Soffer 2010: 303). Not surprisingly, the next two mayors in the core (Dinkins and Giuliani) followed a similar policy path, although little of this impacted the ongoing racial, ethnic or economic inequities within the megacity.

The New Jersey side of the region mirrored the New York experience. Many of the older urban areas of the New Jersey gateway communities were labelled blighted and became sites for the development of new housing as well as being the locus for new highway construction. As Newman (2004) points out, in places such as Newark, highway development would cut up 78 neighbourhoods. Urban renewal projects were used to bring investment into the central business districts of the region to increase shares of highly skilled service-based employment. Tax rebates and incentives were used to spur partnerships to oversee development and management of housing, with non-profits tending to take on these roles in the poorer neighbourhoods and private sector partners in the more affluent areas.

Another force shaping neighbourhoods revolved around a set of battles between owners and renters in relationship to rent control. At the time, existing tenement housing on the New Jersey side had largely been rent controlled, an outgrowth of Depression-era responses to rising housing costs. Battles ensued between property owners and developers seeking rental decontrol, and low-income communities seeking to solidify these protections to prevent displacement. Hoboken in New Jersey introduced policies to allow for decontrol when properties were vacated, and rent increases were allowed if hardship could be displayed by the owner. This in turn fuelled a spate of arsons to remove tenements completely and make way for the development of new market-rate housing. In Hoboken there were 500 fires set between 1978 and 1983, displacing 8,000 largely low-income Latino residents (Gottlieb 2019).

Public–private partnerships were used to leverage funding from governments to neighbourhoods for housing development. The targeted application of these resources to specific areas helped to shape development patterns moving forwards. An article in the *New York Times* reported that, by 1988 in Newark, for example, there were 73 private housing projects underway, although only a small portion was reserved for low-income residents. As then Mayor of Newark, Sharpe James commented, "For Newark to progress it cannot remain a city just for the poor" (Garbarine 1988). And, like New York City, in these areas municipalities used their powers of public land taking (i.e. eminent domain) to gain control over properties in foreclosure and to convert these areas into sites for redevelopment. Later tax abatements and low-cost property sales were promoted to entice private sector partners to build.

Growth in the urban core added pressure on neighbourhood housing markets in the periphery. Housing prices for a single family jumped 25 per cent between 1984 and 1985, and 78 per cent between 1981 and 1985 (Kilborn 1985). As the service sector grew, affordable housing stock was not able not meet demand. VIH in the core was not being used, as developers opted to build market-rate housing. The result was that new workers began to look for housing elsewhere, and in the highly accessible yet peripheral parts of the region the pressure was most intense. Hoboken, in New Jersey, for example, was a ten-minute ride from the World Trade Center (the financial heart of the region) via the PATH rail systems. By the late 1990s, "40% of the residential population in Hoboken worked in managerial or executive positions" (Gotttlieb 2019: 415).

When incentives failed to produce affordable housing, regulatory approaches were again turned to. In 1985, Mayor Vazzetti of Hoboken promoted the use of rent control as a tool to anchor low- and moderate-income residents, and instituted a programme of mandatory inclusionary housing (MIH). The programme demanded that 20 per cent of all new and renovated units be held for low-income residents. Vazzetti unfortunately died in office in 1988, and his programme was discontinued. Hoboken would follow the path of many other areas located proximate to the urban core, as developers jumped on the luxury housing bandwagon. Housing became increasingly unaffordable and the lower-income minority communities were once again at risk of displacement. In nearby Jersey City, rents were being deregulated, housing costs were increasing and low-income populations were forced into smaller and smaller parts of the region, concentrating poverty and wealth and perpetuating more segregated neighbourhoods.

New York continued to be a megacity of economic inequality, which increased competition between neighbourhoods across the region for population and development. Tensions at the neighbourhood level grew. Racial conflicts, conflicts with police, inequities in education and health, were all viewed as indicators that "the city's decade long economic recovery … had [also] produced increases in poverty, inequality and racial segregation" (Sites 2003: 50).

While the Koch plan endeavoured to generate housing through partnerships with community-based organizations as well as the private sector, it did little to relieve the neighbourhoods that had experienced the greatest losses. Low-income minority and immigrant neighbourhoods were not buoyed by the successes at the urban core, while the more affluent suburban communities were.

As Mollenkopf and Castells (1991) argue, New York was becoming increasingly polarized, a *dual* city. Economic recovery was uneven, with some areas thriving and others failing.

It was the growing inequality between neighbourhoods that led to the election of David Dinkins, the first African-American mayor in the core, in 1990. Dinkins' electoral campaign focused on the need to bridge the divides between minority neighbourhoods of concentrated poverty and white neighbourhoods of affluence. Although the core had recovered economically, racial and ethnic segregation persisted across the entire megacity region.

Dinkins campaigned on a "promise to end the racial divisiveness of the Koch years" (Sites 1997: 547). The core issues he faced were homelessness, educational inequities, affordable housing, and race relations (Arian *et al.* 1991). Dinkins' ambitions never matched the outcomes. Thus, while he modified the housing plan for the city, by focusing more heavily on affordability and on partnerships with the community-based organizations rather than private partners, he continued many of the Koch tax-incentive programmes and actually cut public spending for housing. Gentrification pressures continued to escalate, while affordable housing stagnated. Incentives and bonuses were not creating a market for affordable housing. As a result researchers report that "between 2000 and 2010, the city's segregation rate grew" (Samaha 2013). But now populations were also being displaced from the inner-ring boroughs as well as older urban parts of the region, as property values increased in areas that were proximate to the urban core.

Property values in East Harlem increased by 222 per cent between 2002 and 2013 (Rodriguez 2013). And, while some affordable housing was being built, other properties were becoming unaffordable and many communities began to allow for decontrol of rent-regulated and rent-controlled apartments, both in

New York and New Jersey. Families were forced to pay an increasing proportion of their income on housing, more than 30 per cent. Policy continued to focus on supply and, when Giuliani was elected mayor of New York in 1994, a policy of removing the homeless population altogether ensued, rather than create temporary housing in shelters or voucher systems.[2]

Although zoning had been used as a tool of neighbourhood development for decades, VIH continued to hold traction. During the Bloomberg mayorality (2005–14), there was also a major effort to re-zone some neighbourhoods for growth, and for preservation of low density in others. Between 2002 and 2013 "more than a third of the city [core and inner ring] was re-zoned in 122 targeted neighbourhood actions" (Stein 2019: 106).

Re-zoning came in three forms: some areas were up-zoned to allow for taller and denser development, some areas were downzoned to restrict densities and height, and in some instances there was a mix, with some areas (such as commercial corridors) up-zoned, and other areas (often residential) downzoned (Walters 2021: 17). There was also a racial dimension to these neighbourhood re-zonings. According to Stein (2019: 103): "White upper-income homeowners tended to see their blocks downzoned or contextually zoned (i.e. historic preservation), while working class tenants of color tended to see their blocks upzoned." Yet again, this reinforces the socio-economic and racial segregation patterns of the megacity.

The 2005 VIH Program allowed developers a 33 per cent density bonus if 20 per cent of the housing produced was made permanently affordable – at or below 80 per cent of the area median income (AMI). This housing could either be located on site or off. This meant that the affordable component could be placed in another area altogether, so long as it was a part of development plan. It was applied to new construction, rehabilitated or preserved housing (Newman 2018: 135). As with previous efforts, zoning for VIH tended to have only modest impacts due to the strength of real estate markets in the region. The tax benefits were not great enough to offset the perceived losses. Moreover, for those that did take advantage of the programme, most often the affordable housing was placed in distant neighbourhoods where lower-income residents could be found, thus reinforcing spatial economic inequality rather than overcoming it.

When affordable housing was included, rental rates were based on the AMI for the entire region, thus suburban and high-income neighbourhoods were

---

2. Voucher systems are programmes that allow the recipient, in principle, to use the voucher for housing in the neighbourhood of their choice. In New York there are a range of conditions of loopholes under which landlords can deny access to voucher holders. Thus, the recipient is publicly enabled but may be privately restricted.

also factored in. Not surprisingly, affordability was relative. Studies found that these programmes were more likely to support middle-class housing needs than poor or working-class residents. "Most of the new apartments were reserved for households making 80 percent of AMI, or $66,000 … [when in reality] 80% of New Yorkers median income would have been just $39,000" (Stein 2019: 112–13). VIH was designed to "achieve socially desirable outcomes" through market-based incentives.

De Blasio was elected mayor in 2014, on a platform similar to Dinkins, highlighting rising inequality among neighbourhoods. He replaced VIH with MIH in areas that had been up-zoned. Affordable housing was made mandatory for new developments located in neighbourhoods that had been up-zoned (to allow for taller and denser development). As of September 2020, six neighbourhoods had been re-zoned, and an additional nine were in the process. The re-zoned areas were largely in low-income minority communities such as East Harlem, East New York in Brooklyn, Far Rockaways in Queens and the like. Bloomberg had already re-zoned almost a third of the entire city. Because much of the low income parts of the core and inner ring had already been up-zoned, they were also then ready for the introduction of MIH. Since implementation in 2016, "the city created 2,247 housing units in total … Manhattan 453 units, for the Bronx 943 units, for Brooklyn 649 units and for Queens 752" (Kully 2020).

In 2016 MIH was touted as a tool to attack issues of affordability. As Newman argues, these programmes "fit well within the shift to market-based programs but it also acknowledges the need for public subsidy to achieve social objectives" (Newman 2018: 131). Of this housing, 19 per cent is considered to be affordable, and of the group considered affordable, 28 per cent is identified as "deeply affordable" (serving populations with income levels at 50 per cent of the AMI and below), while 81 per cent are market rate (Walters 2021: 6). This suggests that even the shift from VIH to MIH has been minimal, albeit better than earlier periods, and its impact on breaking down neighbourhood segregation is questionable (as the case of MIH in East New York reveals below).

In regard to the production of affordable housing, the Association for Neighborhood & Housing Development (Block 2022) found that neighbourhood re-zonings have had very little impact on the creation of affordability, instead site-specific (or spot zoning) tended to generate higher rates of affordable housing (Walters 2021: 6). Neighbourhoods that are majority low-income African-American and Latino did generate the largest number of affordable units in relationship to market-rate housing units, whereas moderate/high-income, majority white neighbourhoods had much lower rates of affordable housing (Walters 2021: 6). Thus, while affordability may be generated in small areas, these programmes do not seem to break down the racial, ethnic and economic barriers between neighbourhoods in any meaningful way. Indeed, in some cases they have spurred new forms of speculation and displacement.

So, the story of land use, zoning, rent regulation and housing policy reveals that the inequalities to be found in the region's neighbourhoods are not easy to overcome. Where one lives can have a profound impact on one's life chances. Although we have had to abbreviate a great deal here, what should be evident is that this is a region that is diverse, but its neighbourhoods tend to be largely homogenous. As containers they hold affluent white populations in some locales, and concentrate the poor in other areas. There are exceptions, of course, but the vast majority of the region's neighbourhoods do fit into these patterns. All of this is overlaid with a history of institutional racism that has allowed patterns set in the early days of development of the megacity to largely persist. At earlier points in history one can certainly point to these processes as being *de jure* (using the policy intentionally to create communities of similarity). Today these patterns are perhaps *de facto*, and more difficult to manage given the deep roots, and complex trajectories.

The New York megacity has been an area with a long history of immigration and migration. While the region has a strong magnetic pull that continues to fuel its diversity, at the neighbourhood scale one continues to find that some populations have access while others do not. These same patterns have been experienced in virtually every part of the region (Stirling 2016). Zoning, land use, rent regulation, incentives and inclusionary housing have all played roles in these processes.

We are today at yet another turning point in the face of the Covid-19 pandemic. The demand for less density, and for suburban lifestyles certainly grew during the early stages of the pandemic, but in 2022 the residential return to urban areas is once again on the rise. The pandemic, however, has also exacerbated and made the region's inequalities highly visible. According to the Association for Neighborhood & Housing Development (Block 2022: 6), "during the pandemic, the rate of eviction filings in majority-people of color zip codes has been over twice as high as majority white zip codes".

The pandemic also led to high unemployment and some abandonment. At the start of 2021, in the core and inner ring, there were 200,000 eviction cases pending, as an estimated one million residents lost employment, and there was some $2 billion in rent arrears (Henning-Santiago 2021). Thus, one can see that the demand for affordable housing is likely to grow.

Meanwhile, the region's suburban communities have seen housing prices soar. For example, Bergen County in New Jersey saw home prices increase by as much as 18 per cent in some neighbourhoods (US Census Bureau 2021), and in Westchester sale prices had increased by 11 per cent during the first quarter of 2021 (Kolomatsky 2021). Some of the increase has been spurred by residents of the core moving outwards in search of single-family homes, and some is due to speculation fuelled by outside investors (domestic and international). Given that a much larger proportion of African-American and Latino residents in the region are renters, they are also "most likely to be displaced when neighborhoods change", a claim that early evidence on eviction filings in the region supports (Mironova, Stein & Baiocchi 2022: 2).

Affordable housing will be on the agenda of many for the foreseeable future. Between January 2021 and 2022, rents in the core rose by 33 per cent (Zaveri 2022). Eric Adams became mayor in January 2022 in the core of the region, as only the second African-American ever elected in New York City and, as a former police officer, there is a great deal of speculation concerning what role he will play in this segregated megacity. In June 2022 he put forward his housing vision, titled "Say Yes to City". He indicates that with this he hopes to tackle some of the housing needs in the region by working with the powerful real estate sector, while targeting communities in greatest need. He has announced plans to increase the amount of money being allocated for the unhoused, voiced a desire to convert underutilized office space to housing, and an intention to continue the use of up-zoning to increase housing supply in neighbourhoods of all incomes, across the core (Honan & David 2022).

Adams has campaigned for the development of affordable housing in New York's wealthiest neighbourhoods, using many of the tools already discussed, but applied to different neighbourhoods than in the past (Adams 2021). However, pressure from the real estate community and pushback from the city council are likely to prevent any radical changes. He also proposed repurposing vacant office buildings for affordable housing, allowed for the creation of smaller housing units, conversions of basement dwellings, and investments in housing specifically for the homeless in the areas that they were displaced from. Investments in voucher programmes are also a part of his plan.[3] Finally, he points to the importance of creating zoning laws that allow for more mixed-use, live-work communities, rather than single-use.

This leads us to the final sections of this chapter. In what follows, two short vignettes are presented to highlight the ongoing battles for affordable housing, in two neighbourhoods in the megacity.

---

3. There is currently a lawsuit underway in New York in which "120 real estate companies, brokers and property owners" are being sued for discriminating against housing voucher users, and denying access to housing (Zaveri 2022). This suggests a continuation of steering and restriction based on race, ethnicity and income.

Rent control, zoning and diversity: Montclair New Jersey

Montclair is a suburban community located in Essex County, in the New Jersey part of the megacity. Some 12 miles from the urban core, it is a community that has been lauded for its efforts to promote desegregation, although it has continued to struggle to meet this aspiration.

Montclair has a long history in the realm of civil rights. Consider, for example, that in 1946 when President Truman's civil rights committee called upon communities across the United States to measure and strengthen civil rights, Montclair was one of a handful of towns to take up the call. In 1948 it published the results of its audit of "civil rights". The township explored the degree to which its black population's civil rights were being met. Among other things, the study found that the town was indeed spatially and racially divided. The causes were largely attributed to the private real estate sector. The study found that black residents were being charged higher rents and purchase prices for homes than white residents, specifically in white-dominated neighbourhoods. Realtors were also steering black populations to black communities and away from white ones. At the time, the physical dividing line between these populations was "Bloomfield Avenue" (Mitang 1948). Today that same roadway serves as the centre of the town's business district and has become ground zero for gentrification and displacement of lower-income minority populations. While in 1948 spatial segregation was the result of private housing markets and racial steering, today it is policy and planning that are at the core of both the problem and the proposed solutions.

In some regards this early civil rights audit might be viewed as an indicator of the willingness of some in this community to grapple with its history of racial division. However, that aspiration was not always shared by all. Court cases in the 1960s and a state order to desegregate schools in the 1970s reveal these challenges. While the township has endeavoured to use policy and planning to achieve integration, it has also used zoning and land use in ways that may be pushing back against efforts to maintain its racial and ethnic diversity.

Today, with a population of almost 41,000, it has a low poverty rate (6.6 per cent), and a median income of $134, 308 (US Census Bureau 2021). The township is an affluent one. The vast majority of its residents are employed in nearby Newark or Manhattan, thus the area and its population is economically tied to the core. Today, 38 per cent of Montclair residents identify as African-American, Latino, and Asian, 39 per cent of the population are renters (US Census Bureau 2021). Montclair's efforts to support diversity have long served as a magnet, attracting urban residents seeking a more diverse suburban lifestyle. However, these same pull factors have led to displacement of that diversity.

The township has been regularly subject to the pressures of gentrification, causing displacement of the less affluent residential population. This has only been exacerbated by the pandemic. Minority populations make up a large component of the renters in the area. The median income for black residents is 60 per cent less than the median income for white residents, so as costs for housing increase, these communities are the hardest hit (Rudoy 2021).

While Montclair's integration efforts have long been lauded by policymakers, a look at its recent history of land use and zoning reveals the subtle ways in which these policies may in fact be doing the exact opposite. Growth incentives were used to promote development of the central business district and increase density. As growth occurred, nearby residents experienced a parallel increase in their cost of living. New housing in the area tends to lean towards the luxury end of the spectrum. The brunt of the cost of living increases have fallen largely on the backs of the minority community, concentrated around the commercial core. The result has been a precipitous displacement. As Rudoy (2021) highlights, since 2000, 33 per cent of the area's black residents have been displaced, and those that remain are concentrated into the most densely developed parts of the area. Zoning and land use for economic growth may be increasing segregation once again.

In an effort to mitigate some of the displacement, Montclair has also incorporated MIH regulations for new development. However, these regulatory efforts have failed to generate adequate affordable housing stock. Developers have been able to negotiate with the township regarding the precise allocation of affordable housing within new developments. Although the goal is 20 per cent, researchers suggest that it is more common to find 10 per cent allocated for these purposes (Martin 2019). Not surprisingly, the demand for affordable housing in this neighbourhood is significant.

In April 2020 the township passed an ordinance to limit rent increases to 4.25 per cent and 2.5 per cent for seniors. The law was to be applied to dwellings with more than four units (Township of Montclair 2020). The goals of the legislation were to control rampant speculation and to protect older residents from displacement. Although the ordinance did get passed by the municipal government, it was subsequently challenged in the courts by the real estate interests. They argued that the law was implemented during the Covid-19 pandemic, when many residents had decamped to more distant locations, thus invalidating the law. The courts have since refused to strike down the rent control ordinance and, in April 2022, the town council prevailed and the policy is now due to go into effect (Winters 2022).

This short vignette is simply used to highlight the idea that, while often the narrative has been that the market is the best mechanism to control housing distribution, in a region where the pressures for housing are so great, policy tools may be needed to maintain ethnic, racial and economic diversity. The patterns set by a history of segregation are not easily overcome. But, as the residents of Montclair have illustrated, diversity is perceived to be a strength, one worth protecting, and the regulation of rent may well be a core mechanism to achieve this and prevent displacement. As one resident comments:

> We bought homes in Montclair in large part to join a diverse community. We love that Montclair has all different kinds of housing – single family houses, multi-family houses, apartments, condos, owner-occupied and rental houses – which enables people with a wide range of resources and income levels to all call Montclair home. But our Montclair community is changing … fighting for rent control in Montclair can help maintain the community we all know and love.
> (Hackett, Perez & Tessler, 23 August 2020: para 1)

Mandatory affordable housing as a tool to create affordable housing in East New York

As discussed above, in the core, MIH is currently being promoted as a means of generating affordable housing. However, the questions remain: Can it serve to deconcentrate poverty? Can it enable the region to become less segregated? The implementation of this programme would suggest that the answer lies in where MIH is placed. Currently, MIH is primarily being used in the inner-ring urban communities of the megacity (Montclair as a suburban supporter of MIH is somewhat unique). In the core, MIH is being applied specifically to those areas that were up-zoned in recent years. The problem, of course, is that most up-zoning in the core and inner ring is specifically in low-income African-American and Latino dominated communities. MIH, in its current iteration, allows developers to create market-rate housing in these areas, so long as it includes a small percentage of housing for those earning less than the AMI. The result is that the programme is more likely to bring affluent residents into these communities, as opposed to bringing low-income communities into the more affluent parts of the city.

Indeed, in one community in Brooklyn, East New York, developers have been buying up property in anticipation of plans for up-zoning to increase density. Thus, as the re-zoning process ensues, which makes the area eligible for MIH, displacement is already underway (Savitch-Lew 2016).

> The East New York plan … requires developers to set aside a certain percentage of units under rent thresholds amid other market-rate units.

> One of the bands requires that 20 percent of new units be created for households making up to 40 percent of Area Median Income ($31,080 for a household of three) and the second option requires 25 percent of units at 60 percent AMI (including 10 percent at 40 percent AMI). Developers will be able to choose which of the two options they prefer when building on a parcel of land. (Kurshid 2017: para 10)

Almost 200 developers put in proposals to build in this community. Now this area is made up of 78 per cent renters, it is 82 per cent African-American and Latino, and the median income is 48 per cent lower that the AMI (Shelton 2018: 2–4). The arrival of a significant number of more affluent residents will inevitably create displacement. The affordable housing that is being built is not affordable to existing residents. Thus, if the programme continues to be touted for poor minority communities it will also then be likely to "intensify racial segregation" (Shelton 2018: 6).

It would appear that, yet again, when policy is overlaid onto neighbourhoods of concentrated poverty, it is unlikely to help those most in need. MIH is as much about location as it is about investment and redevelopment. It will therefore be interesting to see what the impacts of MIH will be under the leadership of the core's new mayor, Eric Adams, given his intent to promote MIH in wealthy neighbourhoods and his interests in increasing affordable housing in neighbourhoods such as East New York. These policy choices may bring greater diversity to the more affluent largely white communities. However, the of living in these areas will continue to be a barrier to integration. Thus, as race and economics intersect, segregation is likely to continue, albeit in different parts of the megacity.

Conclusions: policy, planning and geography – understanding diversity and segregation in the megacity

Neighbourhoods have been shaped by public policy, larger political and economic forces and individual actions. The impacts of policies on neighbourhoods are now and have always been variable. History shows that:

> … there is a distinct racial hierarchy in the … [megacity] housing market, whereby whites enjoy the broadest access to high quality housing and neighborhoods, followed by Asians, and then Hispanics. Blacks, however, are at the bottom of this hierarchy… Race/ethnicity, then is a far more potent predictor of locational outcomes than are social and economic achievements "individual

and institutional acts of discrimination" are powerful reasons for these patterns.

(Rosenbaum & Friedman 2007: 184–5)

The megacity has been a place for innovation at some moments and for stagnation at others. It is a region in constant flux. As this chapter suggests, housing and land use go a long way to help one to understand how diversity and segregation can coexist. The megacity continues to attract people. At the same time, it must find ways to accommodate the diverse needs that these populations have. Change is possible but, as the region's history suggests, this may require a more activist role for the public sector and an acceptance that market forces alone will not meet the needs of all populations. When markets are left unregulated, segregation is likely to endure.

6

Globalization in the megacity

What globalization is not

Not all megacities are global. Some megacity qualities, such as having a large dominating economy, are *necessary* for a city to reach global status, although not in themselves *sufficient* to achieve that end. Global cities may sometimes overlap with megacities but they are also sharply different from them. Megacities are defined within a local context and with reference to their size, scope and complexity, whereas global cities are defined by their international stature and their communications with the rest of the world. For example, by local standards, Kinshasa (Democratic Republic of the Congo) is a megacity. Its population of 12 million covers an area of more than 3,000 square miles and it is packed with more than 20 communes. Its proper functioning depends upon a sizeable infrastructure of highways, electric grids, reservoirs and bridges. Yet Kinshasa should not be mistaken for a "global city". Outside of Africa its connection to the rest of the world is tenuous and its economic integration into the global economy is almost non-existent.[1]

Further, globalization is very different from "internationalization". Globalization is not, as Thomas Friedman wrongly put it, an act of discovering faraway continents and it certainly did not show up because Columbus crossed the ocean in 1492 (Friedman 2005). If travel outside the known world

---

1. Thus, according to one standard of globalization by Globalization and World Cities Research Network (GaWC), Kinshasa has been classified outside the first 200 cities and is not considered a global city. There are differences between the Global North (cities in advanced industrial nations, many of which were colonial powers) and the Global South (cities in undeveloped economies that were occupied by colonial powers). For the most part, our own references are to cities in the Global North. See, for example, Robinson (2015).

constituted the presence of globalization, we could go back centuries and call the movement of Neanderthals across Europe an early form of "globalization". Rather, globalization represents a qualitative change in the substance of inter-national intercourse. That qualitative difference can be measured by the rapid, if not instantaneous absorption of values, information and symbols across boundaries. Things do not just move rapidly, they are assimilated, absorbed and reacted to across boundaries in a stroke of a computer key.

Understanding globalization

Fundamentally, globalization is a *process* that is driven by *multidimensional* forces. The key words are "process" and "multidimensional". By "process" we refer to a condition that is not a permanent state of affairs but a continual flow of activity involving the cross-national integration of people, economies, business firms, social organizations and governments. We can think of this process as affecting cities with differential impacts. Some cities have been able to ride its waves exceedingly well, some have been crushed by it, while others have been barely affected. The advance of globalization is not uniform but is said to be "spiky"; highly prevalent in some areas, mildly present in others and almost entirely missing in other areas (Feiock, Moon & Park 2008). Generally speaking, the more advanced and wealthier a city, the greater the chances of it being globalized. Globalization occurs over time and will advance or regress though a series of critical events, breakthroughs and distinct patterns. Nor are the effects of globalization necessarily benevolent; globalization can certainly yield great benefits but it can also bring about severe hardships. Periods of ups and downs are therefore quite common.

Globalization is also multidimensional, meaning that the process is driven by numerous forces that are characteristic to a given locale (Van der Bly 2005; Boschken 2022). These forces include digital technology, instantaneous com-munication, standardization and serving as a gateway for international traf-fic. Digital technology is the energy that propels globalization. The speed of change is nothing short of spectacular. The late nineteenth and much of the twentieth century were defined by the "industrial era" – consisting of steel making and heavy manufacture of everything from household appliances to jet planes. Beginning with the decade of the 1970s, the advanced world went through a massive economic transformation from "industrialization" to a "digital age". Instead of "making things" the new era worked by "exchanging information". Cities proved themselves able to transition from "industrialism" to "post-industrialism", presciently brought to light by Daniel Bell (1973). Its most significant sources of employment are in FIRE. Sassen (1991) called the composite of these functions "advanced producer services" or APS, because they advertised, organized, regulated and adjudicated the new economy. They include accounting, advertising, finance, law supply chain logistics and other types of business information.

Standardization is an important feature of globalization because it facilitates the exchange of goods and services. Once goods and services look alike, they become recognizable across cultures and nations. Common currency, international standards of measurement, universal professional criteria, and interchangeable parts are ways of achieving standardization. Likewise, international news monopolies (BBC, CNN), international products (Nike) and multinational sports competition are leading vehicles for globalization. Just as the grid system of streets helped land development during the industrial era, so standardization facilitates information exchange in a global era.

Serving as a gateway for all kinds of international traffic puts a city at the centre of global commerce. Much of this turns on free trade, free flows of electronic information and, ultimately, developing a specialized niche in an interdependent world. Gateway cities take the lead in facilitating interaction with other localities across the world. Since the onset of globalization, New York, London and Tokyo have served as the world's gateway cities. Each city serves effectively as a "node of production", dividing their labour according to what each is best suited.[2] New York produces the financial instruments necessary to ensure liquidity, London acts as a 24-hour transmission belt by sorting through financial options, and Tokyo applies capital investment around the world (Sassen 1991).

Like so many complex phenomena, globalization is a mixed blessing. For a while the globalized world bloomed. The American economy surged during the 1990s and cities were a major beneficiary. As cities prospered, they gained new employment, for the first time in decades their populations grew and their neighbourhoods enjoyed a burst of new investment. Between 1990 and 2000 New York City added nearly 700,000 people, amounting to a 9 per cent growth rate. Los Angeles added 200,000 residents for a 6 per cent rate of growth. Chicago, San Francisco and Boston also grew, albeit at lesser rates (Glaeser & Shapiro 2001). Those cities that did prosper under globalization invariably held a high number of APS jobs, having succeeded in place themselves at the intersections of the international economy. Journalists, economists and politicians applauded the virtues of open trade and the North

---

2. Referred to otherwise as comparative advantage. Comparative advantage is the ability to produce services, goods or other products more cheaply, easily or efficiently than other competitors.

American Free Trade Agreement (NAFTA) was regarded as a major step into the new era. In terms of productivity, we should not sell globalization short. An estimated 1.2 billion people have been lifted out of poverty since 1990 (*Economist* 2019a).

Most telling are the changes in East and South Asia, and these gains are quite real (Kenny 2011). Much has depended upon the ability of a society to take advantage of global opportunities. Principal cities were catapulted onto the world stage by deliberate policies of powerful nations. China flexed its manufacturing muscle and captured world markets, bringing to the fore Shanghai and Beijing. Taiwan and South Korea exploited manufacturing opportunities, allowing Taipei and Seoul to become global cities. India's vast resources and size were stepping stones for the globalization of Mumbai and the rise of hitech Bangalore. The tiny island of Singapore was an exception to the powerful nation rule. It climbed into the global hierarchy by taking advantage of its strategic port at the tip of the Malay Peninsula and making the most of its proximity to the South China Sea.

Globalization's positive results impressed Washington and pundits in New York. Bill Clinton's White House celebrated his reputation as the "globalizing president". Nobel awardee and columnist, Paul Krugman, counted globalization as the era's single great achievement. But a good thing never quite stays the same and has a way of killing the very thing it seeks to promote. "Freedom" has its excesses and can create a cycle of rejection. The mass exodus of manufacture in search of cheap labour created a terrible void in rustbelt economies. Globalization overheated with speculation and bursting financial bubbles. The surges of the global process created massive wealth, but deep economic inequalities (Boschken 2021, 2022; Flaherty & Rogowski 2021). By the new millennium, the globalizers were eating their words, with Krugman admitting that "manufacturing employment fell off a cliff after 2000" and the trade deficit was more worrying than ever (Hirsch 2019).

There were other downsides. Globalization allowed disease to travel more rapidly than ever. Aids, West Nile Virus, SARS and Ebola induced serious global health alerts. It took months of hard scientific work and international cooperation to keep those diseases contained and, for a while, health officials thought they had matters under control. But the threats posed by smaller epidemics turned out to be a harbinger of something even more serious. By early 2020 Covid-19 struck, inducing a worldwide pandemic and an abrupt halt to both globalization and its freewheeling economy.

Still another dark side of globalization facilitated the spread of deadly force against civilians. Within a short time, terrorists discovered that global cities were the best targets for attack (Savitch & Ardashev 2001). The vast and commanding economic bases of global cities turned out to be more fragile than expected, their cavernous buildings all too easily vulnerable to physical attack. The concentration of media in global cities became publicity mills for terrorists seeking attention, allowing every attack to reverberate around the world. The ease of travel, the easy transfer of money and the sharing of weaponry made it possible for terrorists to do more deadly work. A Sarin gas attack in the Tokyo subway in 1995, followed by New York's 9/11, were initiating points and within a decade London and Paris became victims of random slaughter. Smaller, lesser globalized cities such as Jerusalem, Munich and Mumbai suffered tremendously. In all three cities the atrocities were broadcast around the world and witnessed at the very moment they were occurring.

The irony of globalization is that it follows the same path of "growth", "crisis" and "adaptation" that typified the evolution of other critical events in New York City. Just as boom periods in housing led to increased segregation and dangerous bubbles, so too globalization followed a similar trajectory of crisis. The rapid growth of globalization in the 1980s and 1990s was followed 20 years later by strains of economic inequity, conflicts over multiculturalism and growing frictions. Politicians, journalists and, most of all, ordinary citizens began to recoil from the thought of "globalizing". In the most sober language, they described the pain of abandoned factories and lost jobs. The loss of manufacture was especially felt in smaller industrial towns such as Bethlehem (Pennsylvania) and Gary (Indiana), which did not have the wherewithal to make the transition to post-industrialization. Even megacity New York, which possessed all the advantages for a successful transformation, showed serious pockets of decline. Brooklyn's East New York and sections of Newark began to resemble bombed-out Berlin. By the elections of 2016 political candidates and their followers were talking about rebalancing the global economy and bringing back manufacturing. Indeed, Donald Trump and Bernie Sanders made the pushback of globalization and the comeback of manufacturing central components in their campaigns of 2016 and 2020. Both themes enjoyed enormous popular support.

Identifying global cities and locating New York

The GaWC analysis is a leading indicator of global city rankings. Although hardly the last word on the subject, it does provide exacting metrics for ranking a large number of cities. Those metrics are based on a series of "connectivities", which are consistent patterns of communication between business firms in one city with those in other cities around the world. The methods used to measure connectivity focus on APS that facilitate global business flows.[3] Whereas the GaWC's rankings largely emphasize commercially related measures, it has begun to incorporate political and cultural factors into its ranking. GaWC puts as many as 300 cities into 12 possible categories. City globalization is framed along a continuum that begins with Alpha++ cities, meaning those that are the most integrated into the world economy, and goes to Alpha+ cities, whose connectivities are of somewhat lesser significance but are still strong integrators. Various levels of Beta cities maintain connectivities that are moderate and pertain to smaller economies. Still considered as "world cities", are those in the Gamma category, whose connectivities are less substantial. Finally, cities in the category of "sufficient" are considered to be important for regional economies but are not considered to be global cities (Taylor 2004; GaWC 2020). Table 6.1 displays a shortened list of GaWC cities. The list has been modified to contain no more than eight cities per category.

Table 6.1 Global Cities by GaWC (2020)

Alpha++	London, New York
Alpha+	Singapore, Hong Kong, Paris, Beijing, Tokyo, Dubai, Shanghai
Alpha	Sydney, Sao Paolo, Milan, Chicago (US), Mexico City, Mumbai, Moscow, Brussels
Alpha−	Dublin, Melbourne, Washington, DC (US), New Delhi, Bangkok, Zurich, Vienna, Boston
Beta+	Prague, Ho Chi Minh City, Boston, Copenhagen, Dusseldorf, Athens, Munich
Beta	Doha, Karachi, Nicosia, Geneva, Montevideo, Berlin, Montreal, Denver (US)
Beta−	Port Louis, Minneapolis (US), Chennai, Seattle (US), Stuttgart, Santo Domingo, Rio de Janeiro, Detroit
Gamma+	Guayaquil, Cleveland (US), Riga, Baku, Adelaide, Vilnius, Birmingham, Baltimore (US)
Gamma	Phoenix, Tegucigalpa, Austin (US), Pune, Guadalajara, Dalian, Tbilisi, Charlotte (US)
High sufficiency	Queretaro, Abuja, Port Alegre, Seville, Hartford (US), Milwaukee (US), Curitiba, Liverpool
Sufficiency	Belo Horizonte, Christchurch, Florence, Richmond (US), Seville, Bordeaux, Hamilton, Cincinnati (US)

Source: https://en.wikipedia.org/wiki/Globalization_and_World_Cities_Research_Network

---

3. These include but are not limited to accountancy, advertising, management, banking/finance and law.

GaWC tells us that globalization is spread far and wide, albeit in different ways at different places. Sitting comfortably atop the global city hierarchy are New York, London and Tokyo – all three are outposts of powerful nations. Other cities have consistently been designated in the Alpha+ category, with Singapore, Paris, Tokyo and Shanghai not far away from the top tier. In recent years Dubai has managed to become a globalized city through its strategic port and position in the oil rich Gulf. It too is an exception to the powerful state rule. Brussels and Vienna are also exceptions to the big nation requirement. They are also small cities with populations of under three million and land areas of less than 15 square miles. Despite the modest size of their populations, land area and economy, these types of cities are well ensconced in the global network of cities through political influence (Brussels is the seat of the EU) or by historic repute (Vienna was the seat of the Austro-Hungarian Empire).

We see multiple paths to global status. Politics, culture or quality-of-life factors may be sufficient to attract corporations or corporate headquarters to settle within a city, thereby enhancing its global status. Sydney and Stockholm are known for their excellent quality of life and, no doubt, this has contributed to their overall attraction. We should not, however, discount the differences between top- and lower-tier cities. Top-tier cities are qualitatively different in that they compound a multiplicity of assets and project them in altogether different and unique ways. As we shall see, there are many reasons why New York holds that status.

We also point out that GaWC has not come up with a list that is unexpected. There is, indeed, a considerable overlap between GaWC and other rankings, particularly at upper levels. Organizations may use different criteria, but New York, London, Paris, Tokyo and Singapore invariably appear at the top of any scale. *Foreign Policy* magazine uses political and cultural factors. The Mori Memorial Foundation relies on amenities, quality of life, the "magnetism" of a city, environmental conditions and ease of transportation. Finally, AT Kearney uses factors related to human capital, information exchange and political engagement.

All of these evaluations show global rankings to be remarkably consistent (*Foreign Policy* 2010; Mastercard 2019; AT Kearney 2020; GaWC 2020; Mori Memorial Foundation 2020). The Kearney listings are particularly interesting because they go back six years to reveal the positions of cities from 2015 to 2020. Table 6.2 provides a glimpse of this movement. New York, London, Paris and Tokyo have not budged. This should tell us something about the forces that keep cities in relative equilibrium with one another. That steadiness may be due to the dynamics of growth begetting still more growth. The dynamic produces a virtuous circle of investment, where simply "being there" is enough to catalyze exponential growth.

Table 6.2 AT Kearney ranking of six top global cities, 2015–20

City	2020 rank	2019 rank	2018 rank	2017 rank	2016 rank	2015 rank	2019–2020
New York	1	1	1	1	2	1	—
London	2	2	2	2	1	2	—
Paris	3	3	3	3	3	3	—
Tokyo	4	4	4	4	4	4	—
Beijing	5	9	9	9	9	9	+4
Hong Kong	6	5	5	5	5	5	−1

Source: Airports Council International, 2020.

New York's catalysts of globalization

All this understood, global cities have much more varied levels of autonomy than most rankings would suggest. Some are capable of enormous independence of action (Lever 2008). This will vary by national practice. France, Japan and strong, centralized nations exert a strong pull on their principal cities. Great Britain and Germany are less commandeering. By comparison, federalist, decentralized America has a long tradition of local autonomy. "Home rule", freewheeling private enterprise and open markets typify local government. Business was so "free" in nineteenth and early twentieth-century America that it often dominated city politics or acted in coalition with local politicians (Warner 1987; Stone 1989). Even "leftist" New York has been highly pro-business and given a free hand to build and develop as it sees fit. Driving New York's globalization are the multiple attributes of economic might, business innovation, a strong international profile, its world media and its cultural magnetism.

We should put the trajectory of New York's globalization in context. Globalization and economic prosperity reached high points in the 1990s. Employment, income and living standards were on the rise, complemented by high productivity and low inflation The resuscitating effects of the new digital economy carried far and wide. Cities were well on their way to a dramatic comeback from the gloomy 1970s and "gentrification" regarded as a positive force for once struggling neighbourhoods (Ley 1996; Grogan & Proscio 2001). New York was a major beneficiary of Clinton-era prosperity and its well-known sector in FIRE was never in better shape. Property speculation was always a leading industry in New York and office markets a key indicator for how well the region was doing. By the mid-1990s rental occupancy for office space reached an unprecedented 87 per cent and the costs per foot of space were among the highest in the world (Savitch & Kantor 2002: 64–6).

The trend came to a stunning halt in the early days of the new millennium. A high-tech bubble burst in March 2000 and sent the NASDAQ into a tailspin, shaking up the economy and setting off a recession. New York's precarious economy was grist for the attack on 9/11 and, once the buildings collapsed, so too did the once robust job market. Within 24 hours of the attack, the stock market suffered its worst one-day point loss and biggest one-week losses in its history. Suffice it to point out that the economic shock of 9/11 generally lasted for roughly a decade. The message here is that statistical trends for the current decade will perforce start at low levels for the beginning of the millennium.

Keeping this lens on the issue, we turn to the megacity's GMP. At its 2019 level of $1.4 trillion, the New York megacity is quite impressive, but as we trace the line graph back two decades, we can also spot the wobbliness of the process. Figure 6.1 shows GMP movement as it bumped along the bottom in the early years of the new millennium. Not until the fading of economic crisis after 2008 did it spike with consistency.

The larger picture is that of prosperity, mainly couched in the Clinton and Bush 43 era policies that furthered globalization. Propelling globalization in New York are the catalytic effects of particular economic and social features. The first of these catalysts was the enormous growth in the employment sectors that composed the core of Sassen's APS – shown in Figures 6.2 and 6.3 as "finance" and "professional and business services". These display the trajectory of employment for each of these sectors from 2000 up through 2019.

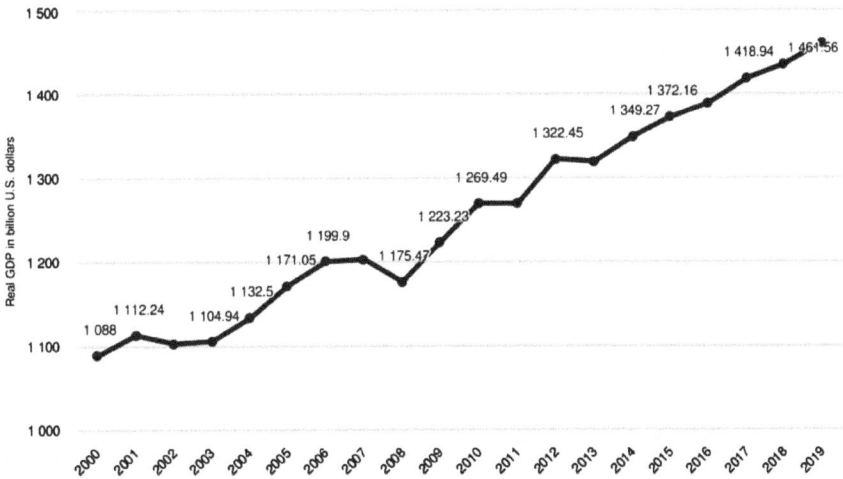

Figure 6.1 Gross metropolitan product in the New York megacity.
Source: One NYC, New York, NY.

While both sectors were more volatile than GMP, they did track along its upward path after the 2008 economic crisis. Observing Figure 6.2 we see that from 2013 onwards the financial sector recovered its earlier strength. Looking at Figure 6.3 we see that professional and business services did even better,

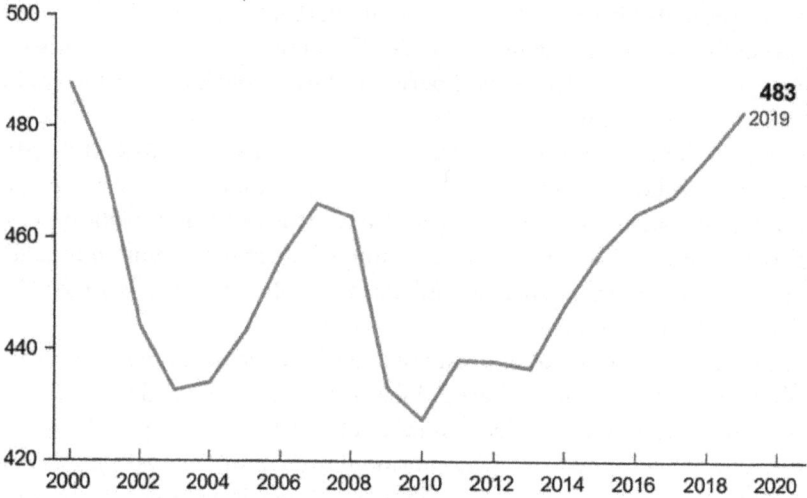

Figure 6.2 Megacity employment in finance, 2000–19.
Source: U.S Bureau of Labor Statistics; Moody's Economy.com.

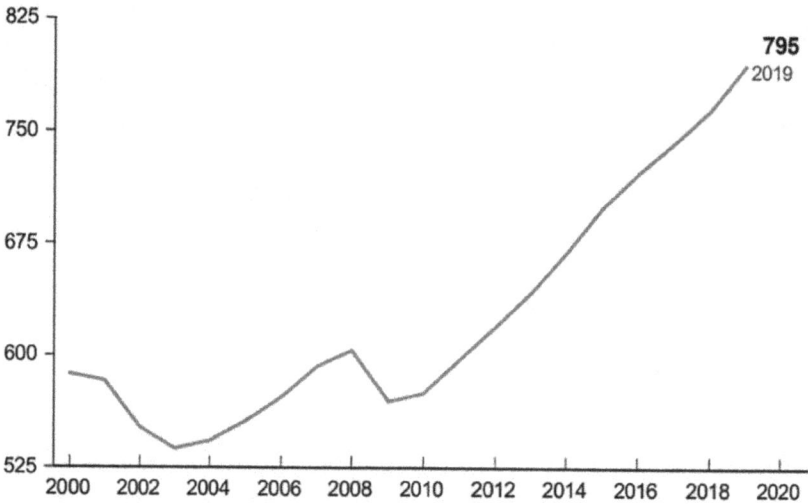

Figure 6.3 Megacity employment in professional and business services, 2000–19.
Source: U.S Bureau of Labor Statistics; Moody's Economy.com.

with job gains of 40 per cent within just a decade. These were no mere gains of ordinary employment. Wall Street accounted for 5 per cent of the city's private sector jobs and 17 per cent of the state's tax revenue. A fifth of the city's total wages are earned in these sectors, whose average salaries come to nearly $400,000 per year (DiNapoli & Bleiwas 2019). More significantly, these sources of employment are tied to international commerce, trade and business relations. Almost every international financial transaction is processed by specialists in some aspect of finance and they resonate throughout the globe. The effects of a transaction can run into billions of dollars and have a profound impact on industry, people and products. "Wall Street" is one of the world's largest globalization mills.

We have then a strong base of economic might, which has been amplified by other attributes of the megacity. A city's capacity for research and development (R&D) is another catalyst having a direct impact on the economy. While R&D may not have the most scintillating ring, it is the very stuff that energizes an economy. Global cities often vie for a competitive edge in R&D. The most vigorous competitors are New York, London, Tokyo, Paris, Shanghai and Singapore – plus, for specialized areas, Boston, San Francisco and Seoul. According to the Mori Memorial Foundation (2020: 13), New York came out first in both number of researchers and expenditure towards R&D. It also took a leading place among the top prize winners in science and technology as well as the number of start-ups. In the category of utility patents, the New York megacity came in second, just behind Silicone Valley (US Patent and Trademark Office 2016).

The third of our catalysts focuses on workforce quality and captures a city's ability to attract and hold talent. Labour talent is also a chief source of a megacity's creativity, enabling it to renew itself. Should that creativity be compromised, the megacity's economy would wilt and the rest of it begin to stagnate. Educational attainment has something to do with workforce quality, and the megacity's 13 counties boast that nearly 39 per cent of residents hold a bachelor's degree or higher. That percentage has consistently increased over the past two decades and was up by 10.5 per cent within a decade (US Census Bureau 2018a). Immigrant labour has actually enhanced the workforce skills, with more than 30 per cent of immigrants holding a college degree and an equal proportion serving as business owners (American Immigration Council 2020). Immigrants, most especially from South Asia, have boosted labour talent in the megacity's critical hi-tech industry. These workers hold more than one-third of the jobs in computer systems design, software publishing and data processing. Highly qualified immigrants have brought new sites to life in downtown Brooklyn, Long Island City and a new joint university centre on Roosevelt Island (DiNapoli & Bleiwas 2014).

The quality of the megacity's workforce is matched by the relative attractiveness of their workplaces. Again the New York megacity scores highest on the criterion of "workforce options", with Hong Kong, Singapore, London and Los Angeles, respectively, occupying the remaining positions. However, by the standard of "workplace flexibility", New York slips to seventh place, preceded by Shanghai (#1) Dubai (#2) Zurich (#3) Boston (#4) and others. Most telling are the responses from workforce participants themselves. Asked about a city's environment concerning "risk-taking" and "taking on challenges", corporate executives chose London first and New York second (followed by Singapore, Amsterdam and Paris). The Mori Memorial Foundation (2020) evaluation of highly skilled workers turned on the direct question of worker capacity to "act across the world stage regardless of borders or nationality". On this criterion London came in first, New York second and Paris in third place. An important factor for London has been its ability to facilitate workers travelling across national borders and its popularity as a place where "skilled professionals from across the world gather to study". New York (#2) and Paris (#3) were both evaluated highly for special characteristics related to the city's ability to afford opportunities for new workers (Mori Memorial Foundation 2000: 18).

The last, but hardly the least important catalysts are those that amplify existing, high-profile assets. We turn to our third catalyst, internationalism (cosmopolitanism) and fourth catalyst magnetism (charisma). To start with cosmopolitanism, the New York megacity has been America's leading destination for immigrants and it is among the most international cities in the world. If we go by the numbers, the impact of immigrants on globalization is enormous. Nearly five million foreign-born residents live in the megacity, making up one-third of its population and over 40 per cent of its workforce. Immigrants are the megacity's human globalizers. The digital world has allowed for "transnational space", where immigrants often stay in contact with their brethren abroad. Whole communities in Flushing, Queens and Hudson County, New Jersey maintain contacts across the seas through family remittances, frequent visits and social networks. The digital flow enables people and ideas to circulate throughout urban society. Even foreign language newspapers help link cultures together. Today some 95 foreign newspapers, with a total circulation of 2.9 million, thrive in various shops and newsstands throughout the megacity (*New York Magazine* 2014).

If none of this is sufficient for establishing a dominating global voice, there is always the United Nations (UN), which sits in Manhattan's Upper East Side (Turtle Bay). New York is home to 93 permanent missions, 114 consulates and thousands of supporting staff. This includes international civil servants working for the UN and diplomats connected to a country mission. The UN is both a source of great pride to the megacity and problem. Prestige-wise the

Table 6.3 Fifteen busiest cities in the world, airline passengers, 2019

1	London	United Kingdom	180,957,374
2	New York	United States	143,797,000
3	Tokyo	Japan	128,706,040
4	Shanghai	China	121,791,337
5	Los Angeles	United States	113,876,671
6	Paris	France	112,004,890
7	Atlanta	United States	110,531,300
8	Beijing	China	108,209,128
9	Bangkok	Thailand	106,796,098
10	Chicago	United States	105,743,975
11	Istanbul	Turkey	103,682,634
12	Moscow	Russia	103,012,403
13	Dubai	United Arab Emirates	101,645,868,
14	Seoul	South Korea	96,618,138
15	Dallas	United States	91,847,114

Source: CAPA Centre for Aviation based on data from Airports Council International; also found at https://en.wikipedia.org/wiki/List_of_busiest_city_airport_systems_by_passenger_traffic

existence of an international headquarters in New York brings a concentration of important international actors into the very sinews of the city (hotels, cafés, newsrooms). Its problems, however, occur daily, ranging from a squeeze UN personnel put on housing and consumer prices, to the abuse of immunity-related and parking privileges.

Immigration and the presence of the world's most notable international organization creates busy airports. Besides, air travel brings people together and personalizes globalization. Table 6.3 displays the total passenger numbers at leading cities for the year 2019, just one year before Covid-19 put a near halt to air travel. As the figures show, New York stands very high as a "gateway city", although not at the very top. London occupies the distinction of being first on this criterion, with New York second. Tokyo and Shanghai are further down.[4] The ability to travel and reach foreign destinations is very much tied to

---

4. If we take the immediate Covid-19 year of 2020, when total airport travel fell and travel was severely restricted, the figures do change radically. New York falls off the charts, while Atlanta rises to the top along with Guangzhou, China. During these unusual years, total passengers fell to less than half of the pre-Covid-19 years. See Airports Council International (2021).

levels of globalization. Obviously, more travel produces a greater mix of foreign tourists, business personnel, professionals, customers, journalists, professors, students and the like. Travellers from different countries may not mix in great numbers but they do share a wealth of common experience. Airports are not just terminals from which people depart and arrive, but places where people dine, purchase goods, watch television and simply stroll around.

Moreover, global media is concentrated in the New York megacity and many agencies are in the business of instant messaging. Conducting that business moment to moment are CNN, the Hearst Corporation, NBC Universal, the New York Times Company, the Fox Corporation, Thomson Reuters Corporation, WarnerMedia and ViacomCBS (Tampa Bay Outlets 2006). New York City is a centre for independent films, has the largest concentration of documentary film producers in the United States (BCG 2015), and is second "only to Los Angeles in the number of films and television programs produced" (NYC Media and Entertainment 2021). More than 200 newspapers and 350 consumer magazines have an office in the city and the book publishing industry employs about 25,000 people. Even in ordinary times, this is an enormously busy centre of communication and, some would say, globalization's megaphone.

The last of our catalysts, magnetism or charisma, is the least tangible. Charisma is an elusive quality. Most everyone can feel its presence but struggle to precisely identify it. The noted sociologist Max Weber (1968) emphasized its magical appeal and ability to generate mass enthusiasm, admiration or reverence. Charisma also carries with it the notion of reputation and image. Just as important as charisma itself is the power to project a city's image to the rest of the world through media, films and politics.

Whatever we might say about New York, it is a place of multiple images. No other city is quite like it because it has so many dimensions and all of them are quintessentially "New Yorkish". From a business perspective it is a fast-track, competitive city where everyone seems to be in a hurry and lots of people make lots of money. Ambitious artists, entrepreneurs and swindlers are drawn to it because it offers a bundle of opportunities. From the perspective of *haute culture*, New York is rich in theatre, museums, symphony orchestras, opera and dance performers, poetry readings and off-Broadway drama. The ultra-rich and intellectuals are attracted to it because it suits their tastes and they can choose from a plethora of Michelin 3-star restaurants. For most others, New York glows with street life, lights and an endless array of spectacles. Well-deserved is its reputation as a city that "never sleeps". For ordinary people seeking relief from the routines of small-town life, it is the perfect venue to celebrate a special occasion. The more adventurous are not likely to be disappointed.

New York's geography and scale make all this possible. The megacity is profusely filled with transportation corridors, easily accessible to many points of the world. Its scale fills the megacity with a huge reservoir of human talent. It is as if someone took its most essential qualities and rolled it into a ball of "charisma". Only London matches (and sometimes exceeds) New York for originality, robustness, multidimensionality and distinctness of image. This is why, on most global scales, New York and London shift and trade places. No other two cities consistently hold the top two rankings. And no others combine economic/demographic weight with the catalytic power of charisma. Thus, Paris holds its own "magical charisma", but its economy and population are not weighty enough. Tokyo and Beijing have the economic and demographic weight but lack the charismatic power of projection.

Indeed, it is that search for a charismatic edge that brought New York and London to consult with management firms for ways to project it. Each time one of these two great global cities moved ahead of the other in the rating charts, its political leaders scurried to regain its former place.

Comparing New York's globalization via the 3Cs

What matters most for New York's globalization can be summarized as the 3Cs, namely *capital, cosmopolitanism* and *charisma*. We reiterate that capital puts New York on the global stage. While hardly the last of the megacity's industrial sectors (health services and construction also carry immense value), producer services are essential to its globalism. The catalysts for economic power can be found in the megacity's cosmopolitanism (internationalism) and charisma (magnetism), both of which are unusually robust and uniquely suited to the megacity. The 3Cs are a handy way of exploring New York's strengths relative to other great cities. As we seek to explain its global appeal, Emile Durkheim's dictum comes to mind, that "knowledge begins with comparison". While comparable cross-national data for cities is not available, we can reliably compare New York with other great American cities. Chicago and Los Angeles come closest to New York's status – at least by global standards. Both Chicago and Los Angeles are ranked by GaWC as Alpha cities and are considered to be major world cities. They also offer the advantage of being located in very different parts of the continent from New York – allowing for a contrast between the coastal east, the Midwest and the coastal west of the country. Content-wise all three megacities are quite different from each another – allowing for a contrast between modestly sized Chicago, sprawling Los Angeles and densely packed, gargantuan, New York.

Table 6.4 features the 3Cs and displays how New York, Chicago and Los Angeles fare on specific measures. Also displayed is their standing relative to other cities in the United States. Between five and six measures have been chosen for each of the three categories. The measures differ from those discussed earlier and broaden our picture of New York's global status.[5] The table also offers an opportunity to understand some of the variables that go into the making of each 3C category. Accordingly, our expanded measures of capital include total employment, number of Fortune 500 companies, top hi-tech companies and the like. Cosmopolitanism expands to include foreign tourists, foreign consulates and other factors. The concept of charisma is expanded to include Google hits, a creativity index, an internet movie base and other factors.

Turning to the table we see that megacities with high capital not only do well on GMP but enjoy the largest number of producer service jobs, per capita income, top hi-tech firms and the like. New York captures the top slot on all of these variables and stays ahead of Chicago and Los Angeles, although it is not always highest relative to other American cities. Thus, with a per capita income of $79,477, the New York megacity is higher than Chicago ($63,500) and Los Angeles ($31,563). But when compared to the rest of the country, New York finds itself down the line at 4/25.

Of course, these large areas vary a great deal internally. Manhattan would be one of the richest cities in the nation if it were separately incorporated, while the Bronx would be one of the poorest. Interestingly, when it comes to "top" hi-tech companies, New York, Los Angeles and Chicago are quite close to one another, with similar numbers in the mid-50s. The Mori Memorial Foundation (2020: 13) does list a lower category of hi-tech firms for 2019 and on this criterion the numerical gaps are greater for two of our cities. New York, with 850 lower-end "start-ups", had more than twice that of Los Angeles, whose lower-end "start-ups" stand at just 400. New York's cheaper loft and once empty factory buildings provided ample opportunities for new businesses to incubate. New York's loft experiments began in the SoHo neighbourhood of Manhattan during the 1970s and moved elsewhere in Lower Manhattan (Zukin 2014). As that experiment succeeded and available space became scarce, additional space was found in Brooklyn (Williamsburg and Greenpoint) and Queens (Astoria, Long Island City). New York's availability of incubation space is more elastic than its counterparts and it has been able to maintain new "start-ups" at a healthy pace. More recently, as Brooklyn and Queens have filled up, Jersey City and Newark have become new incubators.

---

5. The actual numbers for some variables may differ from those found elsewhere in the text because of different time periods and, in some cases, small variations in territorial scales.

Table 6.4 A 3Cs comparison of New York, Chicago and Los Angeles

	New York	US rank	Chicago	US rank	Los Angeles	US rank
Capital						
GMP (US$ billion) 2018	1876.6	1/25	737.3	3/25	1152.4	2/25
Employment total, 2017	4,417,362	1/25	1,458,473	3/25	2,126,063	2/25
Fortune 500, 2019	46	1/23	12	3/23	3	14/23
Per capital income, 2019	$79,844	10/25	$63,500	12/25	$66,684	13/25
Top 50 high-tech cities, 2018	55	2/25	53	5/25	55	2/25
US utility patent (2000–2015)	92,577	2/25	46,991	6/25	74,381	4/25
Cosmopolitanism						
Immigrants, 2017	3,180,098	1/25	563,879	4/25	1,484,731	2/25
Foreign tourists, 2016	9,800,000	1/12	1,466,000	6/12	4,977,000	2/12
Airline passengers international, 2018	14,411,700	1/24	3,622,639	4/24	9,626,144	2/24
Embassy and foreign consular offices, 2019	139	2/21	47	4/21	57	1/7
Global connectivities, 2018	Alpha++	1/23	Alpha	2/23 *tied	Alpha	2/23 *tied
Gross connectivities, 2010	95,838	1/21	55,324	2/21	44,637	3/21
Charisma						
Google hits (millions), 2017	1100	1/25	447	2/25	361	4/25
Creativity index ranking, 2011	0.871	11/24	0.829	14/24	0.901	9/24
Most fun, 2019	55.29	1/25	51.38	2/25	47.88	7/25
Internet movie database, 2019	7,968	1/25	1,554	4/25	3,618	2/25
Best cities to live, 2019	6.3	19/24	6.1	22/24	6.1	23/24

Source: CAPA Centre for Aviation based on data from https://en.wikipedia.org/wiki/Airports_Council_International, also found at https://en.wikipedia.org/wiki/List_of_busiest_city_airport_systems_by_passenger_traffic

As we proceed to cosmopolitanism ("internationalism") we see New York with higher numbers of immigrants and foreign tourists, a large amount of international travel, a surfeit of consulates and tens of thousands of global connections. We would expect that the attractions of Los Angles (Hollywood, Disneyland, dramatic coastline) would make it more competitive with New York for tourism, but even here New York counts twice as many tourists at nearly ten million, while Los Angeles remains at approximately five million. Any number of reasons might explain this, including New York's proximity to Europe, its more numerous international communities and its "city-like" concentrations of activity that make it easier to get around.

The last attribute, charisma, illustrates New York's dominance, but also reveals some surprises. By far New York has the largest number of Google hits and does well on its Bohemian ranking, but Los Angeles stays ahead of New York on the "creativity index". On this count Los Angeles shows real strength and is put ahead by writers, film makers and editors who are tied to Hollywood. Los Angeles also profits from a class of Silicon Valley "hi-techs" that have migrated southward. Despite Los Angeles' advantage as the home of the film industry, New York also scores at the top of film mentions. This is part of New York popularity as a site for film making. Its big-city atmosphere and exciting street life have proven to be an ideal location for "situation comedies" (*When Harry Met Sally*) and police films (*The French Connection*). As expected, New York scores highest as a "fun city". The list for what constitutes "fun" is very long, but the index captures dining at fine restaurants, going to bars and clubs, playing outdoor sports and attending concerts or music bashes. Other forms of "fun" include a thrilling ride on a roller-coaster, going to the movies or theatre, or playing video games. New York poses a surfeit of pleasures, so much so that it would make a good run for the world's capital of hedonism.

Last, as a place to live New York comes out ahead of its counterparts, but that is not saying much. New York is not for everybody, and for some it does fall short on "quality of life" issues. Cleanliness, long commutes, the rush of daily life, the rough vernacular of New Yorkers, and high residential rentals weigh heavier against New York (Mori Memorial Foundation 2020: 16). New York, however, has made some progress by providing amenities for its citizens. Parks, running tracks and the conversion of old infrastructure have gone a long way in making life more palatable. Mayor Michael Bloomberg served an extraordinary three terms as mayor between 2002 and 2013, and took a special interest in creating amenities. One of his most notable accomplishments was his work (with citizen groups) in creating the "Hi Line", converting an old, elevated railway line into a linear park. Bloomberg was also keen on environmental preservation and undertook to successfully plant a million trees throughout the city.[6]

Is New York deglobalizing?

A triple whammy, Black Swan crisis

For the New York megacity the Covid-19 pandemic and global decline were a perfect storm. The intersection of two disasters created a near breakdown in 2020 – a momentous, economic, border year where the line is sharply drawn between prosperity and distress. Just two years later Russia invaded Ukraine, making for a triple whammy of disasters in just a few years. Economists refer to extraordinary shocks like this as Black Swan events. Black Swans are totally unpredictable, high-impact events that have unexpected negative consequences. In the course of their encroachment, Black Swans severely damage, destroy or permanently alter the societies they strike. The question is whether New York's Black Swan has transformed the megacity or whether a normal recovery will prevail. The Black Swan period put New York back on its heels and created a rhetorical flurry towards "deglobalization".

New York's global economy is intensively decentralized and relies on extensive cross-national ties. The massive but delicate economy faced a serious threat by the election of Donald Trump in 2016 and, most decidedly, by his embrace of an "America First" policy. Trump's effort to renegotiate trading agreements brought a trade war with China and the outbreak of tensions between once friendly trading partners (Canada, Mexico, the EU). What might have been reasonable modifications to poorly constructed trade pacts were soon overdone. The very frameworks that inaugurated globalization were undermined. Under

---

6. A word should be said about Chicago's invariable second- or third-place standings. Chicago has come to embrace the accolade of America's "second city" and doing so does provide some advantage. The city has found its identity as the big city that is not New York – more manageable, cleaner and more affordable, with a hominess of its own. If the song "New York, New York" echoes lyrics such as "If you can make it there you can make it anywhere", the "second city's" rejoinder is a much warmer, "Chicago … the kinda town that won't let you down". Chicago is also filled with opportunities and sophistication. Its magnificent architecture, its sports teams and its celebration in story have enabled the city to fill the promise of a world city. Corporations move their headquarters to Chicago because its image now allows for a prestigious location and its geography provides the advantage of easy access to anywhere in the world. For some, Chicago makes the word "second" sound like the best, but its place in the charts will always reflects its position down the line.

Trump, rules and norms of commerce were rewritten to accommodate "America First". This meant that investors and firms were no longer to be treated equally. Rules of privacy, data security and espionage began to splinter; anti-trust laws and accounting principles came to be compromised and tax systems were bent for nationalistic ends. New tariffs hindered free trade. For the first time in the history of a dollar-dominant world, the United States began to weaponize its power over the global payment system (*Economist* 2019b).

The earliest components of the global economy to unravel were the supply lines that fed every advanced nation in the world. Globalization's supply lines were always very robust, because they had to be, but they were also fragile. The economy was not only ripe for a Covid-19 pandemic that paralyzed employment, but the Russia–Ukraine war significantly aggravated the situation. Economics is about perception, and once the signals flashed, the elaborate labyrinth of free trade began to cave. Beef, agricultural products, paper supplies and manufactured goods went into semi-paralysis. As the early 2020s passed, both supplies and supply lines became even more tenuous, particularly in the manufacture of microchips for electronic components, automobiles and aircraft. Both the country and the megacity were beset by runaway inflation, reaching more than 8 per cent and said to be the highest in 40 years.

Once the crisis broke, decades of building international markets and foreign investments were reversed before Wall Street's very eyes. The word "deglobalization" came to dominate the economic discourse. Headlines from the ardently free trade *Economist* (2019b) screamed, "Globalisation is dead and we need to invent a new world order". The lead in the *Wall Street Journal* proclaimed, "globalization in retreat" and gloomily suggested "it may shrink even more in the years ahead" (Irwin 2020). Somewhat belatedly, the *New York Times* joined the pessimists with an editorial warning that "the city will face an extended financial crisis, the likes of which has not been seen since the 1970s" (Rubinstein 2020).

Globalization was severely faulted for causing social inequality. Global sceptics had long claimed that globalization widened income gaps between social classes. Boschken's use of path analysis pretty much established that the "centrality of global cities" had a "significant impact on economic inequality" (Boschken 2022: 9). The more intense the competition at the top of the global pyramid, the more severe the economic inequality. Having occupied the number one or two spots on that pyramid, New York also held the title of having one of the largest income gaps in the nation.[7]

---

7. There is a difference between relative income as measured by "income inequality" and absolute income as measure by real total income. Despite the gap, the New York megacity's population is still among the richest in the world.

The empirics are borne out by a train of neighbourhood in-migration and out-migration, where more prosperous and better educated households replace former residents, drive up prices and make the neighbourhood less affordable for moderate- and low-income groups. The reasoning directly touches on the gentrification of neighbourhoods, where real estate purchases by affluent buyers and speculators have resulted in the displacement of the poorer population. More amenities and fancy boutiques also mean higher prices and a steeper cost of living for residents. To be sure, gentrification has brought on reinvestment, renewal of worn-down neighbourhoods and reductions in crime, but there was a price to be paid.

The pain has been particularly acute in the area of housing. Opportunities have been severely limited for those seeking to buy property. Within New York City the average price for a modest apartment stood at more than $800,000 in 2022. Between pre-crisis 2019 and post-crisis 2022, housing prices rose by 21 per cent since the pre-crisis year of 2019. Prices are somewhat lower in the rest of the region, but that too varies by township or city. Rental costs in New York City are even steeper. In Manhattan, parts of Brooklyn and northwest Queens, rents skyrocketed by 40 per cent during the course of just three recent years. At $4,000 per month for a two-bedroom apartment, most residents find themselves out of range (Reyes 2022).

Adaptation

New York has always been a "liberal" left of centre city and prone to intervene in crises when that seemed necessary. The year 2020 and its aftermath was no different, except for the rise of a distinct flank in the Democratic Party, which, at least rhetorically, was further "left". This segment of "progressive Democrats" was prone to tax the affluent in the interests of promoting wider social benefits or ease up on criminal penalties in the interest of being "antiracist". While he held office, Bill de Blasio led the progressives under the banner of "tax the hell out of the rich".

Other progressives backed full-time day care, increased funding for assisted housing and "no cash bail" for some criminal defendants. On the increasingly prevalent issue of crime, the move towards the left was offset by the election of Eric Adams, who campaigned for tougher policies on crime and fiscal support for the city's police.

Economic issues were, however, another matter and a host of actors have stepped in to support higher taxes and increased intervention. The Black Swan crisis of 2020 would not be a repeat of the crises of 1975, when Republican President Gerald Ford turned down fiscal assistance for the city, and state officials enforced fiscal discipline on the city. Nor was the effort at adaptation similar to the fiscal crisis of 2008, when the Obama administration kept a distance from the New York's fiscal business. In both of these earlier crises the city was obliged to go through considerable "belt tightening" with layoffs and budget cutting.[8] But 2020 was quite different and the city was flush with federal money, shrugging off any real cuts. Out of a city workforce of approximately 325,000, the city lost just 12,000 positions, absorbed by normal attrition and retirements (Glazer & Gillers 2021).

The policies came from the top downward. By midyear the Biden White House was fully engaged. More than $22 billion in Covid-19 funding alone poured into New York City. While it will be distributed over several years, the very weighty federal money is equivalent to nearly a quarter of the city's budget. Additional federal money brought the totals into trillions. Federal funds were mostly borrowed or, as the term came to be known, "financialized" – that is, central banks pumped money into the economy by buying assets or equities and using other financial instruments to increase the monetary supply. Public borrowing soared and became one of the few motors of the economy. Overall, the gross public debt to gross domestic product ratio rose from approximately 105 per cent in 2019 to 132 per cent by 2021 (*Economist* 2019b). State and city budgets also swung into action. New York State proved itself to be just as progressive as the city, as it levied new taxes on the wealthy and on business. State income tax rates on those earning a million dollars or more per year rose precipitously to one of the highest levels in the nation, reaching nearly 11 per cent in 2021. Corporations were also subject to the highest taxes in the nation, increasing from 6.5 per cent to 7.25 per cent over the course of two years. Under de Blasio, the city's budgets had steadily increased, with the mayor calling it a "radical investment in working families" (De Blasio 2015; Mayor's Office 2021).

The takeaway of these policies is that crisis has brought heavier government to the megacity's future. The political-economic cost of these measures is yet to be determined. One such cost is runaway inflation and that has begun to show very ill effects, both on the city and the region. Another possible cost is that the megacity's billionaires may go elsewhere. Florida recently appealed to New York's financial industry to move southward. Florida's governor and Miami's mayor openly courted New York's commercial classes by pointing to

---

8. The 1975 crisis devastated the city's workforce and severely restricted its budget. As mentioned in Chapter 2, the city was put into virtual receivership and run by state-appointed boards. During the 2008 recession, the number of full-time equivalent personnel decreased from a previous high of 311,018 in fiscal year 2008 to 293,550 in fiscal year 2012– a reduction of 17,468 or 5.6 per cent (Citizens Budget Commission 2020, 8 May).

Florida's "low tax" and "freedom loving" culture. In past decades, New Jersey also tried to pirate industry from Wall Street, but that state has also taken the high tax/high interventionist route, with its governor commenting, "If taxes are your issue, then New Jersey's probably not your state" (Stilton 2021). This leaves the entire megacity open for a policy test on whether government is the proper vehicle to guide its global economy.

Last, we return to the question of whether New York is "deglobalizing"? Under the circumstances, deglobalization is very doubtful and the long-term evidence for it has not materialized. In fact, the current thinking now centres around the notion of "reimaging of global capitalism". In the wake of the Black Swan, the idea is to substitute the old "efficiency" of globalization with measures of "resilience" and "security" regarding suppliers. The advice is to stay away from aggressive autocracies (Russia, China) in favour of reliable democracies (EU, NAFTA). Also to be sought is "vertical integration", where the production process is controlled from nickel mining to chip design. The idea is to adapt by the warding off the crises of war, disease and economic convulsion (*Economist* 2022).

There are other structural reasons why "deglobalization" is not likely to occur and this also pertains to why there is not likely to be a mass exodus of billionaires. The sunk costs of a globalized, corporate-laden megacity are simply too massive, too great and too successful to abandon. The critics may complain and the treatises may bemoan the inequalities, but they ignore the sources of the megacity's wealth and its accomplishments.

Conclusions

Globalization is a continuous process of information flows. It is not linearly progressive, evenly distributed or always beneficial. Rather, globalization is "spiky", affecting many cities in the advanced world, but barely touching others. One remarkably consistent feature of globalization is that a handful of cities have become "nodal points" in a complex, decentralized world economy. The New York megacity stands at the very pinnacle of globalized cities. Only London competes with New York and both possess similar attributes of abundant capital accumulation, a unique cosmopolitanism and a compelling charisma. New York's standing as a global city is a reflection of its dominance in APS. Other factors contributing to the megacity's status lie in its special profusion of media and publications that project its extraordinary features and charisma to the rest of the world.

Like so many other critical experiences of the city, globalization has gone through a cycle of growth, crises and an adaptation. That experience was encapsulated in the confluence of the Covid-19 pandemic, an accelerated global economic decline (deglobalization) during the critical year 2020 and, more recently, the Russian invasion of Ukraine. The experience is also known as a Black Swan because of its high-impact, unpredictable negative effects. What makes the Black Swan so extraordinary are the policies employed to recover from its ill-effects. In a rather usual display of political unity, New York City, New York State and Washington DC have adopted market interventionist policies, pouring billions of dollars onto the fires of crisis. The policies emphasize high budgets, high borrowing and high taxes. How and when the megacity exits from this crisis is anybody's guess. We live in an era of uncharted passage and whatever the outcome, it is likely to be marked by trauma.

7

Conclusions

Megacity change

During the course of editing this manuscript, our editor, Alison Howson, questioned whether New York crises were "inevitable". The question penetrated all that we had written and touches on a key finding of our work – the centrality of crisis. Our model of change at the beginning of this volume, locates *crises/ tensions* between *growth* on one hand and *adaptation* on the other hand. While tensions refer to "pressures" emanating from groups, "crises" are transition points that can morph into system-wide breakdown.[1] As such they are pivotal to transformation. Crises can also generate innovation, as evidenced by the flood-resistant redesign of Lower Manhattan put into motion after superstorm Sandy. While "inevitable" is not the word we would use, crises have been a major part of the New York's history and some authors have treated it as an inevitability.[2]

Crises have a certain tenacity and seem to always lurk in the background of any serious event. Such was evident across the cases and themes documented throughout this volume. Hence, tensions in the system are seen as having the potential for leading to crises, and ultimately regime change. The most recent incidents of protests/riots in the summer of 2020 and subsequent rising crime rates in 2021–22 were serious enough to disrupt political and social order.

---

1. See for example Hall (2002), who highlights the idea that crisis, although "disruptive", can also be generative. It is the shaking up of the system that can lead to new opportunities for reorganization and systemic change.
2. Notable work on the subject does picture crises as inevitable. "Crisis" is central to a neo-Marxist approach and has had an enduring effect over generations of scholarship. See, O'Conner's *The Fiscal Crisis of the State* (1977), Hackworth's *The Neo Liberal City* (2007) and Holtzman's *The Long Crisis* (2021).

Given enough duration and severity the electorate might have turned towards extremes of left or right. While voters did not take to the extremes, instances of sequential disorder tell us something about the fragility of change.

The protests/riots of 2020 had ample precedent and like most critical events they had both distant and proximate causes. The distant cause revolved around police abuse all too common in encounters with African-American neighbourhoods. The proximate cause or immediate "trigger" for rioting usually entailed an incident between citizens and the police or between different social classes that resulted in injury or death.

During the 1960s protests/riots erupted throughout the megacity. In Harlem riots burst onto the streets in 1964, due to the shooting of a black youth by a white off-duty police officer, and again in 1968 following the assassination of Martin Luther King. Harlem's 1964 rioting lasted for six nights and spread into Bedford Stuyvesant. Newark's 1967 riot began when a black cab driver was beaten by two police officers. That particular riot was the worst to hit the metropolitan area in more than a century. For a week, gunfire, gasoline bombs and fires enveloped the city. Stores were looted and set ablaze, whole buildings collapsed and more than 7,000 police officers, state troopers and national guardsmen were summoned to stop the conflagration (National Advisory Commission of Civil Disorders 1968).

Little more than two decades later, in 1991, protests/riots burst onto the Brooklyn neighbourhood of Crown Heights. Crown Heights is a prominent Jewish, Hassidic neighbourhood, marked by tree-lined streets and porched houses. It is, however, one neighbourhood sitting alongside a collection of diversity. The surrounding vicinities are mostly mixed income and predominantly black, ranging from upper-middle-class gentrifiers in Bedford Stuyvesant to Caribbean entrepreneurs in East Flatbush, to deep poverty in Ocean Hill/ Brownsville. The actual rioting occurred when a car, providing security for a Hassidic motorcade, accidentally struck two Guyanese children, killing one and seriously injuring another. Within hours roving bands of youths took to the streets, throwing rocks and setting fire to buildings and automobiles. As the riot flared they shouted anti-Semitic slurs, accompanied by the roar of "Heil Hitler" and "Death to the Jews" (Goldman 2011: 4).[3] During the tumult a religiously garbed young Jewish man was attacked and subsequently died from stab wounds. Numerous civilians and police were wounded during the

---

3. Rev. Al Sharpton came to the scene, stoking the flames of anti-Semitism by accusing the Hassidic community of apartheid and drawing links between that community and international diamond dealers. Sharpton, who was found culpable of liable in another case, has gone on to become a political celebrity and a "go-between" for presidential aspirants and Harlem voters. He also hosts a news programme on a major television network.

rampage (State Director of Criminal Justice 1993). Much to the consternation of the public, the police were conspicuously absent during the early hours of the Crown Heights riot. At the time, Mayor David Dinkins feared that a police presence would provoke still more violence and held off a critical "nip in the bud" police deployment.

What is past is prologue. There are similarities between past protests/riots and what occurred in the spring of 2020. First, a distant cause lay in distressed black neighbourhoods, whose residents experienced day-to-day police surveillance and stoppage. The proximate cause for protests/riots of 2020 was the killing of George Floyd by a police officer in Minneapolis. It made little difference that "proximity" was 1,200 miles from New York. Millions of television viewers watched the gruesome sight of a black man lying on the ground, while a white police officer ground his leg into the victim's neck – it was a painful reminder of similar problems closer to home (of Anthony Baez in 1994, Abner Louima in 1997, Amadu Diallo in 1999, Sean Bell in 2006 and Eric Garner in 2014).

Within a day of the George Floyd killing, protestors flocked onto the streets of New York. Unlike previous protests the crowds were racially mixed and marched into commercial areas, public spaces or integrated neighbourhoods. Most of the participants were young men and women, carrying signs, clapping and intoning slogans. The locations of the demonstrations were concentrated in Manhattan and Brooklyn. In Manhattan protestors gravitated towards Times Square, Union Square, Greenwich Village and SoHo. In Brooklyn protestors favoured its downtown at the Barclay's Center, Cadman Plaza behind Brooklyn Borough Hall, and parts of Flatbush.

While the overwhelming majority of protests were peaceful, some marchers were not. As nightfall descended the demonstrations spewed into arson and wanton assault. Buildings were set on fire in commercial districts, stores were looted, firebombs thrown at the scene, police cars were vandalized, journalists covering the bedlam ran for their safety and some bystanders were assaulted. Looters gravitated towards high-end shops along Fifth and Madison Avenues. Others moved into SoHo carrying laundry bags to be filled with merchandise. Sometimes cars pulled up to store fronts in order to carry away the spoils, and one vehicle was found with $17,000 in stolen goods (CNBC 2020).

By the end of the rampage, commercial establishments of every type had been ransacked. The targets ranged from an upscale Macy's department store, to middle-level Target and CVS outlets, to small privately owned shops. The city did impose curfews and deployed police, but duty officers claimed the rioting was too fluid to control. Others saw the police as having been paralyzed by informal orders from upper-level police brass or by politicians (Gurri 2020). As the crisis deepened, Governor Andrew Cuomo took to the airways declaring, "The NYPD and the mayor did not do their job last night." He described the city as "shocked to its very core". Cuomo threatened that, should the violence continue, he could (in principle) "displace" the mayor and put the city under a different rulership (CNBC 2020). Herein lay a risk to New York's governance.

Early summer brought more sharply defined political objectives, and another warning to the existing political order. In New York City demonstrators coupled their demands to potential violence – brandishing clenched fists to the slogan of "no justice, no peace". Others swarmed police cars, deployed temporary gates and hurled traffic cones to block the imposition of order. Police stations began barricading the streets surrounding their facilities as they became the subject and object of protest. By July the slogans had already reached City Hall in demands for "defunding" the police. Protestors saw their actions as a way to transform society, demanding that at least $1 billion designated for the police be reassigned to housing, education and social services. Protestors camped behind City Hall and blocked entrances. As police tried to unblock entry points, they were forcibly resisted and had to ward off bottles and other objects hurled at them. The episode ended with what might be called policy adaptations. City Hall allocated $1 billion, nearly one-sixth of the operating budget, from the police department to other agencies.

From a broadly analytic perspective, the riots/protests of 2020 and the aftermath signalled enormous tensions over the question of "law and order". The questions were especially poignant because, in both past and present disorders, the police were unprepared for what was to come and inconsistent in their use of force (NYC Department of Investigation 2020). Political tension grew between those who wanted to "defund the police" and devote money to social justice programmes versus people who called for "law and order" and wanted to allow police a freer hand to ensure public safety. The splits and controversy of 2020 were soon compounded by a surge in crime. Rightly or wrongly, politicians, journalists and policy analysts linked the rise in crime to the riots, citing the "broken windows" syndrome (minor disorder leads to crime) or alluding to the "Ferguson effect" (collective violence and reduced police activity lead to crime).[4]

The concerns were not without cause. Within the critical years of 2020 and 2022 the city was beset by an alarming increase in crime rates. The overall crime index jumped by 36.5 per cent. The index was driven by a 59.4 per cent escalation in auto theft, a 48.4 per cent increase in robbery and a

---

4. The Ferguson effect was coined by a St Louis police chief, who claimed that, after the protests in connection with the shooting of a black youth in Ferguson, Missouri, officers became hesitant to enforce the law, due to fears of criminal prosecution. The term became popular after Heather MacDonald used it in a *Wall Street Journal* article (29 May 2015) to explain the rise in crime rates in some US cities, as due to "agitation" against police forces.

40.5 per cent increase in grand larceny. Citywide burglaries also increased by 40 per cent and citywide shootings rose by 16 per cent (NYPD 2022). Public safety is a hot-button issue in New York. It is heavily publicized by the press and readily understood by the citizenry and business. Politicians are frequently elected or unelected on the issue of crime and safety, and everybody seemed on edge about where New York was heading. Crime was the major issue in the 2022 race for New York state's governor. The question was would the public turn staunchly right or radically left?

In the midst of a mayoral campaign and local elections the language became more strident. Those who stood against crime were charged with being "racist", while those who advocated for social justice were labelled as being "soft on crime". There were times when the sides seemed irreconcilable – the "Woke" on one side and "Trumpers" on another. New York, it seemed, had been rubbed raw with controversy. As it turned out, the voters elected a mayor, Eric Adams, whose background, at least in principle, allowed him to bridge the gaps. Adams was both an African-American and a former police captain, who supported firm measures to combat crime, but also promoted social equity. The sheer circumstance of Adams' election blunted any threats to the existing order. How Mayor Adams will implement moderate politics is another question. Nevertheless, the higher lesson is that the system absorbed the shock and held its ground. Through it all New York held together. We conclude that crisis is a type of stress test to determine the resilience of a system and, for a variety of reasons, the New York megacity appears to have weathered the storm.

Megacity resilience

Resilience is the ability to absorb, accommodate, bounce back, recover from and adapt to a severe disturbance (Gross 2009). Resilience requires a governmental capacity to ensure external shocks and effectively buffer against their possible damage (Wolman *et al.* 2017). Governance and the act of politics are the means by which a fragmented system is pulled together in order to bring about collective action. It is needed for everything ranging from superstorms, pandemics, riots, crime waves and the like.

Our findings show that, while the New York megacity lacks a uniform governance system, its parts are drawn together as urgencies become apparent. The process is not always neat and often works incrementally – piece by piece over instance upon instance. The megacity does this through a combination of public benefit corporations, special districts, interlocal agreements among municipalities and joint action by the governors of New York and New Jersey. This kind of megacity governance has expanded over the course of time.

Indeed, there is a growing body of research that highlights the dependencies and asymmetries within the megacity and how this leads actors to engage strategically and often competitively in regard to the management of growth and development (Kantor *et al.* 2012; Gross & Nelles 2018).

One feature is clear: policy and planning ideas seem to transfer quite regularly (in part or in whole) among the municipalities, townships and neighbourhoods that make up the megacity. Here, "policies are not simply transiting intact between jurisdictions, but evolve through mobility, while at the same time (re)making relational connections between policymaking sites" (Peck & Theodore 2010: 170). In some ways, therefore, these transfers have also generated the appearance of some degree of institutional coherence in regard to policy, planning and governance.

Decisions about how streets are laid out, housing is built, crises are managed and how the needs of the residents are met are often emulated by political actors across the region. This also speaks to the benefits of megacity agglomeration, not only from the perspective of growth and development, but also by a process of policy innovation. Proximity can allow networks to form, ideas to flow and innovations to be shared (Hambleton 2014).

Our findings also point out that, while the megacity has been very effective at adaptation in some areas, it is also shaped by significant path dependencies. This was especially evident in regard to the ongoing dynamics of spatial segregation. As we saw, the past is often prologue, and when institutionalized through regulation or zoning, some features seem to endure. This is especially the case when powerful private sector interests (real estate and finance) see change as a threat to livelihood. At the same time, we have seen that new groups and new leaders can avoid policy "lock-ins" and circumvent path dependency (Hanger-Kopp *et al.* 2022). As newcomers become permanent residents, they can force change and push back against business as usual. This was illustrated in the case of the failed Amazon HQ2 bid.

We also show that, despite worthy criticism of globalization, it has been a net positive for the New York megacity. The megacity's ability to absorb global processes and pressures helped it to manage a robust economic transition into a post-industrial economy, it helped diversity in its economy and, not the least, it added significant household income to its demographic base, which spilled into neighbourhoods and suburbs. In total, New York's global reach has given it the economic strength to be resilient.

Certainly, geography and natural characteristics allowed the megacity to grow into a global powerhouse. However, geography alone was not enough, and it also required political leadership, effective planning, incentives, regulation, responsiveness and governance capacity. This combination of features channelled and targeted resources in ways that would attract development and growth, support investments in infrastructure and care for the diverse needs of its equally diverse population. That too contributed to megacity resilience.

A megacity such as New York must inevitably contend with regional asymmetries that manifest in socio-economic inequities and produce tensions among stakeholders. Those who "have", seek to hold on to their resources and maximize them. Those who "have not", seek access to resources and politically leverage them. The greater the disparity, the more likely that unrest will ensue. Our findings show that wealth and income disparities have persisted and even grown in the megacity.

The obvious fact is that wealth does not always trickle down in the ways that some economists suggest and public intervention has not been particularly effective. Despite the rhetoric, former Mayor de Blasio's initiatives had fallen egregiously short. Neither have the governors of New York and New Jersey been able to whittle down income differences between social classes. One might argue that the move from voluntary to mandatory affordable housing in New York City and the Mount Laurel decision in New Jersey requiring balanced land use for housing were steps in the right direction, but they were insignificant relative to the problem. It may be that even giant megacities possess neither the will nor the capacity to tackle the issue of wealth distribution. Then again, as the saying goes, we ought not to sacrifice the "good for the perfect". Warts and all the megacity has proven to be remarkably resilient.

Five concluding axioms

We offer five axioms that may shed light on why the New York megacity has survived and often thrived in the face of crises, change and challenge.

Axiom 1: It is hard to "kill the city" because it epitomizes the human craving to rebuild and adapt

Disaster is the mother of adaptation. The Great Chicago Fire of 1871 gave way to the invention of steel-framed skyscrapers and served as a model for other cities such as New York, whose first skyscraper was completed in 1899, at 11 storeys. Today there are more than 300 skyscrapers in the urban core alone, averaging 45 storeys or more. And these same structures have spilled over into the wider region. For example, there are an estimated 122 skyscrapers in Jersey City, 60 in Brooklyn, 36 in Queens, 30 in Newark and 20 in Hoboken. These range in size from 11 storeys to 94 storeys. The Freedom Tower in Lower

Manhattan is 94 storeys, but just across the Hudson in Jersey City there is a 79-storey tower, and in Brooklyn a 93-storey tower was completed in 2022. The megacity is not only growing horizontally, it is also growing vertically.

As cities saw their manufacturing collapse in the 1970s in the face of economic restructuring, they took old uses and transformed them through planning and policy to suit a contemporary service-based economy. Witness how changes to the zoning codes across the megacity allowed industrial land to be converted to mixed use. With this, private sector developers converted factories into loft spaces, and new mixed-used communities emerged across the region. DUMBO, Industry City and Domino Park in Brooklyn, the Gold Coast, Hoboken and Jersey City in New Jersey, and Long Island City in Queens are examples.

Non-profit and private sector partners have also been central, transforming the megacity. The High Line offers a case in point. Here local residents and businesses banded together and formed a non-profit to protect, develop and now manage this highly successful urban park, built from the bones of the region's industrial past. New public park spaces can be found on both sides of the Hudson River waterfront. Jaume Plensa's 80-foot sculpture, "Water's Soul", in Jersey City, opened to the public in 2021, symbolically designed to "unite the city of Jersey City and New York City" (Lungariello 2021), while highlighting the environmental challenges of rising sea levels. And on the New York side, a two-acre garden and concert space, "Little Island", opened its doors to the public in 2021. Urban transformation continues from industrial ports into public parks, obsolete docks into marinas and unused rail tracks into bike trails.

Even theatres and movies houses have remade themselves and successfully compete with televised and video recordings. Hotel spaces have been used to house front-line workers during the pandemic, and today underutilized office spaces are being repurposed to accommodate changes in the way people work and live.

Axiom 2: Crises force cities to become politically resilient

The fiscal calamity that besieged New York in 1975 initially gave way to governance via state-controlled boards and later to a series of "conservative coalitions" under mayors Koch (1978–89), Giuliani (1994–2001), Bloomberg (2002–13) and most recently Adams (2022–), who has convened a business leadership council. Whatever else one might say about each of these mayors, they met their most major challenges head on. In different ways and in different proportions, they respectively fostered investor confidence in New York's fiscal condition, made it feel safer for most residents to live in their neighbourhoods and filled the city with a reinvigorated built environment that attracted creative and professional workers.

The pandemic brought coordinated responses between New York, New Jersey and Connecticut, revealing a political resiliency in the face of massive loss of life and the need for collaboration around the shared health of the entire region. New York once again faces a calamitous economic situation as a result of the pandemic. If history reveals anything, it seems likely that New York will go through a seemingly endless crisis and re-emerge through sheer political adjustment.

Axiom 3: Most crises involve the paralysis of city life; in New York, crises have tended to generate new synergies

The New York megacity is a huge bundle of high energy, housing smaller bundles of high energy. All of this is to be found in its diverse population and equally diverse neighbourhoods. Stopping its movement debilitates the megacity and saps its vitality. But in New York, one is more likely to see forces in play that keep that energy alive, innovative and regenerative.

The attack on the World Trade Center, a global symbol of capitalism, tried to fill New Yorkers (and indeed the American public writ large) with fear and social paralysis. But in many ways it did exactly the opposite. The objective of terrorism is to create fear, intimidate people and halt normal activities. In this instance megacity residents came together to support one another and spur a return to normality.

Superstorm Sandy operated in the same way, by wreaking catastrophe on the infrastructure and built environment, rendering them unable to facilitate movement. Clogged streets, electric outages and flooded buildings allowed Sandy to incapacitate the region for a time. Again, a crisis had its positive side as the megacity focused on the need for climate resiliency.

The arrival of Covid-19 also put much of the region into jeopardy – keeping people indoors, closing businesses, preventing recreation, choking off the transmission of culture and smothering education. Despite the stifling nature of the disease, New Yorkers found ways to circumvent and mitigate its effects. New York managed to channel its energy via the internet, social distancing, face covering and innumerable tactics and more efficient communication. Indeed, the nightly sound of banging pots, beating drums and applause could be heard on both sides of the Hudson River at 7pm, as populations came together to support front-line workers and first responders. The fact that this went on for three months or more was evidence of this phenomenon.

Axiom 4: Hard times and shutdowns bring out the innate, indispensable value of cities as places of human gathering

There is a reason why cities emerge from crises and eventually thrive. Humans have an intrinsic need for social interaction. As the previous discussion has shown, loneliness and feeling cut off can make one quite ill. One study suggests that lack of human contact is comparable to smoking 15 cigarettes a day (Bregman 2020). At an opportunistic level, there is also an edge one gets from serendipitous encounters and personal knowledge.

Cities and most particularly megacities are necessary for civil, commercial and social interaction. Should they be physically attacked, they will bounce back simply because there is no alternative to them. We should remember that in the dark days of the 1970s New York City lost more than 800,000 residents. Less than two decades later it had regained nearly twice that number. 9/11 also wreaked havoc on New York, but within a decade it had recovered. Even in the case of the pandemic, new reports reveal that the out-migration from many neighbourhoods has already reversed (Holder 2022). This has not yet made up for the losses overall at the height of the pandemic, but the signs suggest that, yet again, the megacity has a powerful lure. The incessant bombing of Dresden and Tokyo during the Second World War did not stop them from rising again (Davis & Weinstein 2002). Nor do natural calamities prevent cities from coming back, often more strongly than before. San Francisco rose to grand heights after the earthquake of 1906 and New Orleans largely came back after the devastation of Hurricane Katrina in 2005. New York seems poised for a similar trend.

Axiom 5: Sooner or later the bad times pass; they do, however, leave a residue

New York's fiscal crises frightened nearly everybody: from the banks to the unions to the political class and most citizens. The political institutions that were created to deal with fiscal default may be dormant but are capable of coming alive. Fifty years later Governor Andrew Cuomo decided to reappoint members of the Financial Control Board and publicly entertained the idea of what it might do (Fink 2020). As for 9/11 and crime waves, their remnants can still be seen in the surveillance networks established by local and federal authorities two decades ago. Cameras, barriers, special plain-clothes squads and CompStat were employed to deal with crime and terror more than a decade ago, and they are still very much available.

One challenging residue of the fiscal crisis has been its impact on neighbourhoods. Planning, policy and private covenants left us with a diverse but segregated city. The megacity is left with spaces of extreme wealth that coexist alongside extreme poverty. This enduring legacy of spatial segregation is not easy to overcome. But another aspect of the region's resilience has been the willingness of leaders to promote policies designed to respond to these problems. Rather than bury their heads in the sand, leaders have regularly aspired to achieve the goal of building a more balanced region – albeit it in different ways.

Is the Covid-19 crisis different? Will this be the crisis that finally brings the city to breakdown? Like earlier crises, the pandemic has produced its doomsayers. The enemy is density and, more particularly, crowds. Retail stores are said to be on their way out, supplanted by online shopping and home deliveries. The death of the department store is now predicted, as consumers seek to avoid other consumers. Remote work and learning are thought to eliminate the need for office towers and university campuses. The list of coming catastrophes is long and entails destroying the very foundations of urban life – the end of mass transit, the demise of theatres and the obsolescence of public forums.

Viewed from the immediacy of disaster, these limitations seem convincing. In the broader vision they are far less persuasive. For one, cities have been through pandemics before. We mentioned the city's experience with plagues earlier in this book, but they bear some elaboration. The worst of all medieval epidemics struck Florence in 1348 during the "decade of disaster". The Bubonic Plague killed 30–70 per cent of Europeans. Florence itself suffered a death rate of about 60 per cent. Soon after that deadly sweep, Florence began to recover. New commerce emerged, schools and universities blossomed and a reformed legal system opened up the city to a new class of citizen. Florence flourished as never before. What had been the crater of the Black Death became the heart of the Renaissance. The Florentine lesson does not suggest that plagues are a good thing, but that cities have survived the worst of them and have come back from them with gusto.

Second, the reasons behind city revival are as important as the comebacks themselves. Cities are the natural product of human civilization. Adaptation, rebuilding, political resilience, individual energy, ingenuity and social gathering are the most natural of human activities. The Covid-19 pandemic will be dealt with by a combination of those attributes. The capacity of humans to adapt, adjust and bypass the worst outcomes is limitless. Crises cause misery but they also engender opportunity and rebirth.

Last but hardly least, New York's viability will overtake shutdowns, restrictions and other hardships. It very well may be that recovery is slow, arduous and even subject to short-term reversals. But it will endure. The doors will open, people will greet one another on the streets and stare at one another in the subway. We will again hear the cheering at City Field and Yankee Stadium, the clapping at Carnegie Hall and the scraping of elevated trains. The rush of humanity has already reappeared on Broadway. There will come a time when we look back at the bad years and rejoice at the good ones.

References

Abel, J., J. Bram & R. Deitz 2020. "New York Fed Surveys: business activity in the region sees historic plunge in April". *Liberty Street Economics*. 16 April. New York Federal Reserve. https://libertystreeteconomics.newyorkfed.org/2020/04/new-york-fed-surveys-business-activity-in-the-region-sees-historic-plunge-in-april.html

Adams, E. 2021. "Housing – create and preserve affordable housing, for all who need it". Gotham Gazette. www.gothamgazette.com/city/11096-adams-2021-affordable-housing

Airports Council International 2021. *Annual World Traffic Report*. https://aci.aero/?s=Annual+World+Traffic+Report

Alba, R., J. Logan & K. Crowder 1997. "White ethnic neighborhoods and assimilation: the greater New York region, 1980–1990". *Social Forces* 75(3): 883–912.

Alexander, L. 2011. "Hip-hop and housing: revisiting culture, urban space, power, and law". *Hastings Law Journal* 63: 803.

American Factfinder 2018. "U.S Bureau of the Census". Washington DC.

American Immigration Council 2020. "Immigrants in New York". www.americanimmigration council.org/research/immigrants-in-new-york

Apmann, S. 2012. "The birth of the tenement fire escape". Off the Grid, Village Preservation Blog. www.villagepreservation.org/2021/02/02/the-birth-of-the-tenement-fire-escape/

Apmann, S. 2016. "Tenement Housing Act of 1901". Off the Grid, Village Preservation Blog. www.villagepreservation.org/2016/04/11/tenement-house-act-of-1901/

Apollo Technical 2022. "Statistics on remote workers". www.apollotechnical.com/statistics-on-remote-workers/#:~:text=During%20COVID%2D19%20close%20to,to%20work%20from%20home%20permanently

Arian, A. *et al.* 1991. *Changing New York City Politics*. Abingdon: Routledge.

AT Kearney 2020. *Global Cities Index: New Priorities for a New World*. www.kearney.com/global-cities/2020

Austin American Statesman Fact-Check 2020. "Did Fauci say coronavirus was 'nothing to worry about?" April 29. www.statesman.com/story/news/politics/elections/2020/04/29/fact-check-did-fauci-say-coronavirus-was-nothing-to-worry-about/984113007/

Baics, G. & L. Meisterlin 2016. "Zoning before zoning: land-use and density in mid-nineteenth-century New York City". *Annals of the American Association of Geographers* 106(5): 1152–75.

Bailey, R. 1984. *The Crisis Regime*. Albany, NY: SUNY Press.

Barkan, R. 2021. "As soon as Covid hit, Cuomo downplayed the danger". *Daily Beast*, April 29. www.thedailybeast.com/as-soon-as-covid-19-hit-cuomo-downplayed-the-danger

Ballon, H. (ed.) 2011. The Greatest Grid: The Master plan of Manhattan 1811–2011. Museum of the City of New York.

Beeson, E. & T. De Poto 2012. "Price tag of Sandy's damage to N.J. businesses could reach $30B". The Star-Ledger. 1 November. www.nj.com/news/2012/11/price_tag_of_sandys_damage_to.html

Bell, D. 1973. *The Coming of Post-Industrial Society*. New York: Basic Books.

Berg, B. 2007. *New York City Politics: Governing Gotham*. Brunswick, NJ: Rutgers University Press.

Bernstein, I. 1990. *The New York City Draft Riots: Their Significance for American Society and Politics in the Age of the Civil War*. New York: Oxford University Press.

Bertaud, A. & S. Malpezzi 2003. "The spatial distribution of population in 35 world cities: the role of markets, planning, and topography". Wisconsin-Madison CULER Working Papers 01–03, University of Wisconsin Center for Urban Land Economic Research.

Billy, C. & M. Gewolb. 2019. "Reflections of the 2018 Charter Revision Process". *CITYLAND, New York Law School, Center for New York City Law*, 10 October, para. 1. www.citylandnyc.org/reflections-on-the-2018-charter-revision-process/

Biondi, M. 2007. "How New York changes the story of the civil rights movement". *Afro-Americans in New York Life and History* 31(2): 15–31.

Blake, A. & J. Rieger 2020. "New York Mayor Bill de Blasio's repeated comments downplaying the coronavirus". Washington Post, 1 April.

Block, L. 2022. "New York's pandemic rent crisis". Association for Neighborhood Housing and Development. https://anhd.org/report/new-yorks-pandemic-rent-crisis

Bloom, N.& M. Lasner (eds) 2016. *Affordable Housing in New York: The People, Places, and Policies that Transformed a City*. Princeton, NJ: Princeton University Press.

Boschken, H. 2021. "Income inequality and the imprint of globalization on US metropolitan areas". *Cities*. https://doi.org/10.1016/j.cities.2021.103503

Boschken, H. 2022. "Economic inequality in US global cities". *Journal of Urban Affairs*. DOI:10.1080/07352166.2021.2018934

Boston Consulting Group 2015. *The Media and Entertainment Industry in NYC: Trends and Recommendations for the Future*. Boston, MA: BSG.

Bregman, R. 2020. *A Positive History of Humankind*. London: Bloomsbury.

Brown University 2010. *Residential Segregation*. https://s4.ad.brown.edu/projects/diversity/segregation2010/Default.aspx

Burrows, E. & M. Wallace 1998. *Gotham: A History of New York City to 1898*. Oxford: Oxford University Press.

Bush, G. 2001. "Bullhorn moment at World Trade Center". *US News*. www.usnews.com/news/blogs/ken-walshs-washington/2013/04/25/george-w-bushs-bullhorn-moment

Caro, R. 1975. *The Power Broker: Robert Moses and the Fall of New York*. New York: Random House.

Catsmaditis, J. 2020. Cats Roundtable. https://soundcloud.com/john-catsimatidis/dr-anthony-fauci-1-26-20

Centers for Disease Control 2020. "Public attitudes, behaviors, and beliefs related to COVID-19, stay-at-home orders, nonessential business closures, and public health guidance – United States, New York City, and Los Angeles". *Morbidity and Mental Health Weekly* 69(24): 751–58.

Charleston, D. & M. Randall 2019. "Are megadeals a bad idea? Lessons from Amazon's cancelled plans in New York". *Urban Wire: Neighborhoods, Cities and Metros*. The Urban Institute. 20 February.

Chernick, H. 2005. "Introduction", In H. Chernick (ed.), *Resilient City*. New York: Russell Sage.

Citizens Budget Commission 2020. *The Growth of NYC Employee Headcount*. https://cbcny.org/research/growth-nyc-employee-headcount

City Observatory 2022. "America's least (and most) segregated metro areas: 2020". https://cityobservatory.org/most_segregated2020/#:~:text=The%20median%20Black%2DWhite%20dissimilarity,past%20half%20century%20or%20more

City of Newark 1983. *A Development Plan for the Newark Passaic Riverfront*. 21 February. Office of Planning and Grantmanship.

City of New York 2011. *PlaNYC: A Greener, Greater New York*. New York.

City of New York 2019. *One New York*, 1. New York.

Climate Central 2014. "New York and the Surging Sea: A Vulnerability Assessment with Projections for Sea Level Rise and Coastal Flood Risk". Princeton, New Jersey.

CNBC 2020. "Cuomo urges de Blasio to use more cops against looters after night of intense protests in NYC". CNBC. www.cnbc.com/2020/06/02/cuomo-urges-de-blasio-to-use-more-cops-against-looters-after-nyc-protests.html

CNBC News 2021. "Mayor De Blasio accuses Gov. Cuomo and MTA of 'fear mongering' insists subways are safe". 17 May. www.cbsnews.com/newyork/news/de-blasio-says-cuomo-is-fear-mongering-about-subway-crime/

Costin, A. 2019. "New Jersey's zoning amendment". *New Jersey Studies: An Interdisciplinary Journal* 5(2): 28–56.

Danielson, M. & J. Doig 1982. *New York: The Politics of Urban Regional Development*. Berkeley, CA: University of California Press.

Dantzler, P. 2016. "Exclusionary zoning: state and local reactions to the Mount Laurel doctrine". *Urban Law* 48: 653.

Davis, J. 2018. "NYC's industrial business zone program: examining the intersection between economic development and land use policy". American Planning Association Economic Development Division News & Views. www.planning.org/divisions/economic/scholarships/?mc_cid=857c1a2688&mc_eid=c9ba39113f

Davis, J. & H. Renski 2020. "Do industrial preservation policies protect and promote urban industrial activity? Examining the impact of New York City's industrial business zone program". *Journal of the American Planning Association* 86(4): 1–12.

Davis, W. & D. Weinstein 2002. "Bones, bombs, and break points: the geography of economic activity". *American Economic Review* 92 (Dec): 1269–89.

De Blasio, W. 2015. *One New York: The Plan for a Strong and Just City*. City of New York.

De Blasio, W. 2020. *Mayors Management Report*: Preliminary Fiscal 2020, January. City of New York.

De Forest, R. 1914. "A brief history of the housing movement in America". *Annals of the American Academy of Political and Social Science* 51(1): 8–16.

De La Roca, J. & D. Puga 2017. "Learning by working in big cities". *Review of Economic Studies* 84(1): 106–142.

DiNapoli, T. 2018. *Annual Report on Local Governments*. Albany, New York: New York State Comptroller.

DiNapoli, T. & K. Bleiwas. 2014. "New York City's growing high-tech industry". New York State Comptroller Deputy Comptroller Report, April.

DiNapoli, T. & K. Bleiwas 2019. "The securities industry in New York City". New York State Deputy Comptroller Report, October. www.osc.state.ny.us/files/reports/osdc/pdf/report-9-2020.pdf

Drennan, M. 1991. "The decline and rise of the New York economy". In J. Mollenkopf & M. Castells (eds), *Dual City: Restructuring New York*, 25–42. Russell Sage Foundation.

Economist 2019a. "Slowbalisation: the steam has gone out of globalisation": *The Economist*, 24 January.

Economist 2019b. "Globalisation is dead and we need to invent a new world order". *The Economist*, 28 June.

Economist 2020a. "Even as traditional globalisation has slowed, a new kind has sped up". *The Economist*, 7 November.

Economist 2020b. "The destiny of density". *The Economist*, 13 June.

Economist 2022. "The tricky restructuring of global supply chains". *The Economist*, 17 June.

Eide, S. 2015. "New York's campaign finance delusions". *City Journal*. Winter. www.city-journal.org/html/new-york's-campaign-finance-delusion-13698.html

Elstein, A. 2018. "Urban suburbia: more local businesses are catering to suburban tastes". *Crain's New York Business*, 15 January. www.crainsnewyork.com/article/20180116/FEATURES/180119957/suburbanites-flocking-to-the-city-are-looking-for-some-of-the-lifestyle-they-left-behind-increasingly-they-re-fin

Enright, T. 2014. "The great wager: crisis and mega-project reform in 21st-century Paris". *Cambridge Journal of Regions, Economy and Society* 7(1): 155–70.

Epstein, J. 1977. "The last days of New York". In R. Alcaly & D. Mermelstein (eds), *The Fiscal Crisis of American Cities*, 59–77. New York: Vintage.

Fainstein, S. 2001. *The City Builders: Property Development in New York and London, 1980–2000*. Lawrence, KS: University Press of Kansas.

Falcon, J. 2020. "New York City apartment vacancy rates reach record highs". *Housingwire*, 9 July. www.housingwire.com/articles/new-york-city-apartment-vacancy-rates-reach-record-highs/

Faust, J., L. Zhenqiu & C. Del Rio 2020. "Comparison of estimated excess deaths in New York City during the COVID-19 and 1918 Influenza pandemics". JAMA Network. https://jamanetwork.com/journals/jamanetworkopen/fullarticle/2769236

Federal Emergency Management Agency (FEMA) 2013. *Hurricane Sandy FEMA After-Action Report*. www.fema.gov/media-library-data/20130726-13-25045-7442/sandy_fema_aar.pdf

Feiock, R., M. Moon & H. Park. 2008. "Is the world 'flat' or 'spiky'? Rethinking the governance implications of globalization for economic development". Public Administration Review. https://onlinelibrary.wiley.com/doi/epdf/10.1111/j.1540-6210.2007.00832_2.x

Feron, J. 1978. "Suburban poll: Ties that bind". *New York Times*. 19 November.

Ferré-Sadurní, L. 2018. "The rise and fall of New York public housing: an oral history". *New York Times*, 9 July.

Ferretti, F. 1976. *The Year the Big Apple Went Bust*. New York: Putnam.

Fink, Z. 2020. "Cuomo looking to bring back financial control board to steer New York finances". *Spectrum News*, NYC1, 8 October.

Fischler, R. 1998. "The metropolitan dimension of early zoning: revisiting the 1916 New York City ordinance". *Journal of the American Planning Association*, 64(2): 170–88.

Fitzsimmons, E. 2020. "Progressives killed Amazon's deal in New York. Is Industry City next?". *New York Times*, 12 August.

Flaherty, T. & R. Rogowski 2021. "International challenges to the liberal international order". *International Organization* 75(2): 495–523. https://doi.org/10.1017/S0020818321000163

Flusty, S. 1997. "Building paranoia". In N. Elin (ed.), *The Architecture of Fear*. New York: Princeton Architectural Press.

Fogelson, R. 2013. *The Great Rent Wars: New York, 1917–1929*. New Haven, CT: Yale University Press.

Foreign Policy 2010. "The global cities index". *Foreign Policy*, 11 August. https://foreignpolicy.com/2010/08/11/the-global-cities-index-2010/

Frazier, E. 1935. "The negro in Harlem: a report on social and economic conditions responsible for the outbreak of March 19, 1935". La Guardia Papers, New York City Archive.

Freudenberg, N. *et al.* 2006. "The impact of New York City's 1975 fiscal crisis on the tuberculosis, HIV, and homicide March". *American Journal of Public Health* 96(3): 424–34. https://pubmed.ncbi.nlm.nih.gov/16449588/

Friedman, T. 2005. *The World is Flat*. New York: Farrar, Straus & Giroux.

Fuerst, F. 2005. "The impact of 9/11 on the Manhattan office market". In H. Chernick (ed.), *Resilient City*. New York: Russell Sage.

Furman Center for Real Estate and Urban Policy 2006. "Housing policy in New York City: a brief history". Working Paper 06–01.

Gale, D. 2006. *Greater New Jersey: Living in the shadow of Gotham*. Philadelphia: PA University of Pennsylvania Press.

Gallup Poll 2019. "Terrorism". https://news.gallup.com/poll/4909/terrorism-united-states.aspx

Galster, G. *et al.* 2010. "Wrestling sprawl to the ground: defining and measuring an elusive concept". *Housing Policy Debate* 12(4): 681–717.

Garbarine, R. 1988. "A home-building upturn for Newark". *New York Times*, 7 August.

GaWC 2020. "The world according to GaWC 2020". GaWC Research Network, 26 August.

Gelinas, N. 2020. "NYC's urban model faces existential crisis in post-pandemic world". *New York Post*, 26 May.

Geringer-Sameth, E. 2022. "An unprecedented job program: Adams promises overhaul of workforce development in New York City". *Gotham Gazette*, 14 January.

Gershman, B. & E. Haub 2017. "No end to Westchester's racially-polarized housing games". *Huffington Post*, 15 July. www.huffpost.com/entry/no-end-to-westchesters-ra_b_10948214

Glaeser, E. 2011. *Triumph of the City*. London: Penguin.

Glaeser, E. 2022. "Urban resilience". *Urban Studies* 59(1): 3–35.

Glaeser, E. & J. Shapiro 2001. "City growth and the 2000 census: which places grew and why". Washington, DC: Brookings Institution. www2.lawrence.edu/fast/finklerm/whygrowth.pdf

Glazer, M. & E. Gillers 2021. "New York City's wealthy will pay highest tax rate, how will that help the rebound?" *Wall Street Journal*, 8 April.

Goldman, A. 2011. "Telling it like it wasn't". *The Jewish Week*, 9 August.

Gonzalez, E. 2007. *The Bronx*. New York: Columbia University Press.

Goodman, D. 2019. "Amazon's New York charm offensive includes a veiled threat". *New York Times*, 30 January.

Goodman, D. & E. Fitzsimmons 2018. "What Amazon may mean for Queens: gentrification and (more) packed trains". *New York Times*, 6 November.

Goodman, D. & K. Weise 2019. "Why the Amazon deal collapsed: a tech giant stumbles in N.Y.'s raucous political arena". *New York Times*, 15 February.

Gottlieb, D. 2019. "Hoboken is burning: yuppies, arson, and displacement in the postindustrial city". *Journal of American History* 106(2): 390–416.

Greenberg, J. 2020. "In context: as Trump criticizes, a look back at Fauci's early coronavirus statements". PolitiFact.com, 14 July. www.politifact.com/article/2020/jul/14/context-trump-criticizes-look-back-faucis-early-co/

Grogan, P. & T. Proscio 2001. *Comeback Cities: A Blueprint for Urban Neighborhood Revival.* Boulder, CO: Westview.

Gross, J. 2009. "Sustainability versus resilience what is the global urban future and can we plan for change?" *Community Resilience: A Cross-Cultural Study Revitalizing Community within and across Bboundaries.* Washington DC: Woodrow Wilson International Center for Scholars.

Gross, J. 2017, "Hybridization and urban governance: Malleability, modality, or mindset?" Urban Affairs Review 53(3): 559–577.

Gross, J. 2018. "The governance of superdiversity: a tale of two North American cities". In T. Caponio, S. Schilten & R. Zapata-Barrero (eds), *Routledge Handbook of the Governance of Migration and Diversity in Cities*, 231–40. Abingdon: Routledge.

Gross, J. & J. Nelles 2014. "The route more traveled: unpacking policy coordination in the New York City Metro region". City Futures Conference, Cité Descartes, Marne-la-Vallée, France, 19 June.

Gross, J. & J. Nelles 2018. "Contesting the region: transportation and the politics of scale in New York". In J. Gross, E. Guliani & L. Ye (eds), *Constructing Metropolitan Space: Actors, Policies and Processes of Rescaling in World Metropolises*. New York: Routledge.

Group of 35 Task Force 2001. "Preparing for the future: a commercial development strategy for New York City". 11 June.

Gurri, M. 2020. "Everything magnified". *City Journal*, Summer: 23–25.

Hackett, L., L. Perez & T. Tessler 2020. "Rent control critical to keeping Montclair affordable". Letter to the Editor. Baristanet, 23 August. https://baristanet.com/2020/08/letter-to-the-edi tor-rent-control-critical-to-keeping-montclair-affordable/

Hackworth, J. 2007. *The Neo Liberal City*. Ithaca, NY: Cornell University Press.

Hall, S. 2002. "Gramsci and us". In *Antonio Gramsci: Critical Assessments of Leading Political Philosophers*, 227–38. Abingdon: Routledge.

Halverson, J. & T. Rabenhorst 2013. "Hurricane Sandy: the science and impacts of a superstorm". *Weatherwise* 66(2): 14–23.

Hambleton, R. 2014. *Leading the Inclusive City: Place-based Innovation for a Bounded Planet*. Bristol: Policy Press.

Hanger-Kopp, S. *et al.* 2022. "Defining and operationalizing path dependency for the development and monitoring of adaptation pathways". *Global Environmental Change* 72: 1024–25.

Hanley, R. 1986. "The political campaign: Bergen, after 271 years, to elect first executive". *New York Times*, 30 October.

Henning-Santiago, A. 2021. "How Covid-19 has highlighted housing issues". *City & State*, 11 February. www.cityandstateny.com/politics/2021/02/how-covid-19-has-highlighted-housing-issues/175191/

Henry, D. 1982. "A midtown developer in Queens". *New York Times*, 21 April.

Hill, E. & I. Lendell 2005. "Did 9/11 change Manhattan and the New York region as a place to conduct business?" In H. Chernick (ed.), *Resilient City*. New York: Russell Sage.

Hirsch, M. 2019. "Economics on the run". *Foreign Policy*, 22 October.

Holder, S. 2022. "More people are moving to Manhattan than before the pandemic". *Bloomberg CityLab*, 9 June. www.bloomberg.com/graphics/2022-manhattan-real-estate-moving-data/

Holtzman, B. 2021. *The Long Crisis*. Oxford: Oxford University Press.

Honan, K. & G. David 2022. "Eric Adams says yes to city real estate development – if only the council could agree". *The City*, 1 June. www.thecity.nyc/2022/6/1/23151011/eric-adams-real-estate-development-council.

Hughes, C. 2022. "Keeping an eye on the middle". *New York Times*, 11 February.

Institute on Race and Poverty 2002. "Racism and the opportunity divide on Long Island". www.eraseracismny.org/storage/documents/education/IRP_Full_Report_with_Maps.pdf

Irwin, D. 2020. "Globalization in retreat". *Wall Street Journal*, 16 December.

Jacobs, J. 1961. *The Death and Life of Great American Cities*. London: Vintage.

Jensen, M. 1975. "Bankers, in key role shun spotlight". *New York Times*, 8 September.

Jensen, N. 2019. "Five economic development takeaways from the Amazon HQ2 bids". Brookings Institute. www.brookings.edu/research/five-economic-development-takeaways-from-the-amazon-hq2-bids/

Johnson, C. 2019. "Does the Amazon deal deliver for New York City residents? A preliminary equitable growth evaluation". New York City Council Finance Division, Speakers Office, 30 January.

Kantor, P., H. Savitch & S. Haddock 2002. "Do cities choose their economic future? A comparative bargaining perspective". Annual Meeting of the European Research Association, Turin, Italy.

Kantor, P. *et al.* 2012. *Struggling Giants: City-Region Governance in London, New York, Paris, and Tokyo*. Minneapolis, MN: University of Minnesota Press.

Kenny, C. 2011. *Getting Better: Why Global Development Is Succeeding–And How We Can Improve the World Even More*. New York: Basic Books.

Kerr, A. 2021. "A historical timeline of Covid 19 in New York City". Investopedia. www.investope dia.com/historical-timeline-of-covid-19-in-new-york-city-5071986

Kilborn, P. 1985. "New York home prices surge". *New York Times*, 24 May.

Kilgannon, C. & S. Piccoli 2019. "'Wrong side of history': in Queens, Amazon deal's demise reveals deep divisions". *New York Times*, 14 February.

King, K. 2020. "Immigration to New York City declines, amplifying economic concerns". *Wall Street Journal*, 7 September.

Kober, E. 2019. "Long Island City, without Amazon". *City Journal*, Autumn. www.city-journal. org/long-island-city-without-amazon

Koch, E. 1984a. "Excerpts from the Text of the State of the City Address Given by Mayor Koch". *New York Times*, 10 January.

Koch, E. 1984b. "Text of Koch's Statement on his Financial Plan for the Fiscal Years 1984-88". *New York Times*, 17 January.

Kofsky, J. 2018. "What's inside Jersey City's unsuccessful Amazon HQ2 proposal?" Jersey Digs. https://jerseydigs.com/jersey-city-amazon-hq2-proposal/

Kolbert, E. 1991. "Region around New York sees ties to city faltering". *New York Times*. December 1

Kolomatsky, M. 2021. "Did the suburbs kill the city real estate market? Maybe Not". *New York Times*, 6 May.

Koning, K. & D. Redlawsk 2016. *Polling Post Hurricane Sandy*. New Brunswick: Rutgers University Press.

Kucsera, J. & G. Orfield 2014. "New York State's extreme school segregation: inequality, inaction and a damaged future". The Civil Rights Project, UCLA.

Kully, S. 2020. "Six down, one to go: where de Blasio's rezonings stand". *CityLimits*, 10 September. https://citylimits.org/2020/09/10/six-down-one-to-go-where-de-blasios-rezonings-stand/

Kunstler, J. & N. Saligeros 2001. "The end of tall buildings". *Planetizen*, 17 September.

Kurshid, S. 2017. "The East New York rezoning, one year later". *Gotham Gazette*, 23 March. www. gothamgazette.com/city/6825-the-east-new-york-rezoning-one-year-later

Leibbrand, C. *et al.* 2020. "The great migration and residential segregation in American cities during the twentieth century". *Social Science History* 44(1): 19–55.

Lever, W. 2008. "Delinking urban economies: the European experience". *Journal of Urban Affairs* 19(2): 227–38.

Lewis, K. & S. Burd-Sharps 2018. "A portrait of New York City 2018: well-being in the five boroughs and the Greater Metro area". New York: Measure of America, Social Science Research Council.

Ley, D. 1996. *The New Middle Class and the Remaking of the Central City*. Oxford: Oxford University Press.

Lincoln Institute of Land Policy 2022a. "New Jersey: state-by-state property tax at a glance". www. lincolninst.edu/sites/default/files/nj_january_2022_0.pdf

Lincoln Institute of Land Policy 2022b. "New York: state-by-state property tax at a glance". www. lincolninst.edu/sites/default/files/ny_january_2022_0.pdf

Logan, J. H. Molotch 2007. *Urban Fortunes: The Political Economy of Place*. Los Angeles, CA: University of California Press.

Long Island City Partnership 2019. LIC Neighborhood Quickfacts. https://longislandcityque ens.com/media/filer_public/bd/7a/bd7a312a-09e8-439e-b280-5d558abcf617/1q2019_lic_ quickfacts.pdf

Long Island City Partnership n.d. Planning & Development. www.longislandcityqueens.com/ do-business/planning-and-development/

Lueck, T. 1989. "Transforming downtown Brooklyn". *New York Times*, 22 January.

Lungariello, M. 2021. "Massive Jersey City art installation appears to tell NYC to quit down". *New York Post*, 14 October.

Marcuse, P. 1980. "Housing in early city planning". *Journal of Urban History* 6(2): 153–76.

Marcuse, P. 1987. "Neighborhood policy and the distribution of power: New York City's community boards". *Policy Studies Journal* 16(2): 277.

Martens, B. 2009. "A political history of affordable housing". *Journal of Housing and Community*. January: 6–12.

Martin, J. 2019. "What's down the road for 'affordable housing' in Montclair?" *Northjersey.com*, 10 June. www.northjersey.com/story/news/essex/montclair/2019/06/10/affordable-housing-montclair-nj-what-does-it-mean/1289955001

Mastercard 2019. *Global Destination Cities Index 2019*. https://foreignpolicy.com/2010/08/11/the-global-cities-index-2010/

Mastro, R. 2013. "On the voter's terms: amending New York City's charter to protect voter-imposed term limits". *New York Law School Law Review* 58:139.

Mayor's Office 2021. "June 2021 adopted budget, fiscal year 2022". Office of the Mayor, New York City.

McCann, P. & F. Van Oort 2019. "Theories of agglomeration and regional economic growth: a historical review". In R. Capello & P. Nijkamp (eds), *Handbook of Regional Growth and Development Theories*. Cheltenham: Elgar.

McDonald, C. 2019. "Could Bayonne be the future home of Amazon's HQ2?" *The Jersey Journal*, 16 January. www.nj.com/hudson/2017/09/could_the_former_military_ocean_terminal_in_bayonn.html

McQuiston, J. 1993. "Long Island judge rules Nassau board of supervisors is unconstitutional. Weighted voting is a 'mathematical quagmire'". *New York Times*, 14 April.

Miller, D. & R. Cox 2014. *Governing the Metropolitan Region*. Abingdon: Routledge.

Miller, S. 2016. "Is tri-state transportation too big to plan?" *The Village Voice*, 6 September. www.villagevoice.com/2016/09/06/is-tri-state-transportation-too-big-to-plan/

Mironova, O., S. Stein & G. Baiocchi 2022. "Racial justice and the right to remain". Policy Brief, Community Service Society. www.cssny.org/publications/entry/racial-justice-right-to-remain-good-cause-eviction

MIT Technology Review 2022. "New map of NYC's cameras shows more surveillance in black and brown areas". www.technologyreview.com/2022/02/14/1045333/map-nyc-cameras-surveillance-bias-facial-recognition/

Mitang, H. 1948. "Created equal? Montclair, NJ, sets an example for other communities by its 'audit' of civil rights". *New York Times*, 13 June. www.nytimes.com/1948/06/13/archives/created-equal-montclair-n-j-sets-an-example-for-other-communities.html

Mitchell, B. & J. Franco 2018. "HOLC 'redlining' maps: the persistent structure of segregation and economic inequality". Washington DC, National Community Reinvestment Coalition.

Mollenkopf, J. 1994. *A Phoenix in the Ashes: The Rise and Fall of the Koch Coalition*. Princeton, NJ: Princeton University Press.

Mollenkopf, J. 2017. "The evolution of New York City's black neighborhoods". Metropolitics. https://metropolitics.org/The-Evolution-of-New-York-City-s-Black-Neighborhoods.html

Mollenkopf, J. & M. Castells 1991. *Dual City: Restructuring New York*. New York: Russell Sage Foundation.

Morel, D. 2018. *Takeover: Race, Education, and American Democracy*. Oxford: Oxford University Press.

Mori Memorial Foundation 2020. *Global Power Index 2020*. GlobalCityPowerIndex (2020) summ.pdf.

Morris, C. 1980. *The Cost of Good Intentions*. New York: McGraw Hill.

MTA Info 2018. New York City Subway and Bus Ridership. https://new.mta.info/agency/new-york-city-transit/subway-bus-ridership-2019

MTA Network 2019. Public Transportation for the New York Region. http://web.mta.info/mta/network.html

Municipal Art Society of New York 2019. "Amazon withdraws plan for HQ2 in Long Island City". www.mas.org/news/amazon-withdraws-plan-for-hq2-in-long-island-city/

Murphy, J. 2021. "He's a bit of an enigma: what Eric Adams' development record and housing plan tells us". *City Limits*, 20 April. https://citylimits.org/2021/04/20/hes-a-bit-of-an-enigma-what-eric-adams-development-record-housing-plan-tell-us/

Mutter, J. 2016. "Who really benefits from post-disaster rebuilding efforts". Foreign Affairs, 18 April. www.foreignaffairs.com/articles/2016-04-18/opportunity-crisis

Myers, S. 1993. "The 1993 campaign: The Referendum; A measure to limit terms draws incumbents' fire". *New York Times*, 31 October.

National Oceanic and Atmospheric Administration (NOAA) 2020. Water Levels: Tides & Currents. 10 September. https://oceanservice.noaa.gov/navigation/tidesandcurrents

New Jersey Association of Counties 2020. *County government works – New Jersey's efficient regional form of government.* https://njac.org/county-government-works-new-jerseys-regio nal-form-of-government/

Newark, City of, 1983. *Final Report of the Charter Commission of the City of Newark.* 3 September.

Newman, K. 2004. "Newark, decline and avoidance, renaissance and desire: from disinvestment to reinvestment". *Annals of the American Academy of Political and Social Science* 594(1): 174–76.

Newman, K. 2018. "Urban governance and inclusionary housing in New York City". In M. Davidson & D. Ward (eds), *Cities Under Austerity: Restructuring the US Megacity*, 127–43. Albany, NY: SUNY Press.

New York City Campaign Finance Board. n.d. Ballot Issue 98. www.nyccfb.info/public/voter-guide/ballot_98/stadium.htm?sm=public

New York City Council 2019a. Oversight – Amazon HQ2 – Stage 2: does the Amazon deal deliver for New York City residents? Committee on Finance Report, 30 January.

New York City Council 2019b. Transcript of the Minutes of the Committee on Finance, 30 January.

New York City Council n.d. About Participatory Budgeting. https://council.nyc.gov/pb/

New York Magazine 2014. "*The rise of foreign language newspapers*". https://nymag.com/intelligen cer/2014/10/rise-of-new-yorks-foreign-language-newspapers.html

New York State 2018. *Division of Local Government Services Local Government Handbook.* March.

New York State 2020. Labor Statistics in the New York City Region. www.labor.ny.gov/stats/nyc/index.shtm

New York State Association of Counties 2015. County Government Organization in New York State. February.

New York Times 1975. "Union county Democrats act to restore ethics to politics". *New York Times*, 10 August.

New York Times 1998. "The 1998 campaign referendum; Mayor's campaign finance plan challenges the council's". *New York Times*, 2 November.

New York Times 2012. "Mapping Hurricane Sandy's death toll". *New York Times*, 17 November.

Nussbaum, J. 2015. "The night New York saved itself from bankruptcy". *The New Yorker* 16. www.newyorker.com/news/news-desk/the-night-new-york-saved-itself-from-bankruptcy.

NYC Board of Health 2020. Covid-19 Data. https://coronavirus.health.ny.gov/positive-tests-over-time-region-and-county

NYC Data 2021. "New York City (NYC) tourism". Weissman Center for International Business, Baruch College, CUNY. www.baruch.cuny.edu/nycdata/tourism/index.html

NYC Department of Investigation 2020. Investigation into NYPD Response to the George Floyd Protest. 18 December. www1.nyc.gov/assets/doi/reports/pdf/2020/DOIRpt.NYPD%20 Reponse.%20GeorgeFloyd%20Protests.12.18.2020.pdf

NYC Department of Transportation 2016. *New York City Mobility Report.* October. www1.nyc.gov/html/dot/html/about/mobilityreport.shtml

NYC Health 2020. Covid 19 data: trends & totals & vaccines. www1.nyc.gov/site/doh/covid/covid-19-data-totals.page.

NYC Mayor's Office of Climate Resiliency 2020. FIDI and Seaport Climate Resilience Plan.

NYC Mayors Office of Immigrant Affairs 2021a. NYC's Asian and Pacific Islander (API) immigrant population. June. www1.nyc.gov/assets/immigrants/downloads/pdf/Fact-Sheet-NYCs-API-Immigrant-Population.pdf

NYC Mayor's Office of Immigrant Affairs 2021b. A demographic snapshot: NYC's Latinx immigrant population. October. www1.nyc.gov/assets/immigrants/downloads/pdf/Hispanic-Immigrant-Fact-Sheet.pdf

NYC Media & Entertainment 2021. *New York City Film & Television Industry Economic Impact Study 2021*. New York.

NYC Planning 2017. "NYC's foreign born, 2000–2015". March. www1.nyc.gov/assets/planning/download/pdf/about/dcp-priorities/data-expertise/nyc-foreign-born-info-brief.pdf?r=1

NYC Planning 2020. "New York City population by Borough 1950–2040". https://data.cityofnewyork.us/City-Government/New-York-City-Population-by-Borough-1950-2040/xywu-7bv9

NYC Planning n.d. "Rezoning affecting manufacturing districts: 2002 to 2012: Queens, map and timeline". www1.nyc.gov/assets/planning/download/pdf/zoning/districts-tools/mfg/qn.pdf

NYC Votes n.d. "2022 Ballot Proposals". www.nycvotes.org/meet-the-candidates/2022-general-election/2022-ballot-proposals/

NYPD 2022. "Police department announces citywide crime statistics for March 2022".6 April. www1.nyc.gov/site/nypd/news/p00041/nypd-citywide-crime-statistics-march-2022

O'Conner, J. 1977. *The Fiscal Crisis of the State*. New York: St Martin's Press.

Ostrom, E. 1990. *Governing the Commons: The Evolution of Institutions for Collective Action*. Cambridge: Cambridge University Press.

Palermo, V. et al. 2020. "Assessment of climate change mitigation policies in 315 cities". *Sustainable Cities and Society*. 60: 1–14.

Parks, R. & R. Oakerson. 1989. "Metropolitan organization and governance: A local public economy approach". *Urban Affairs Review* 25(1): 18–29.

Peck, J. & N. Theodore 2010. "Mobilizing policy: models, methods, and mutations". *Geoforum* 41(2): 169–74.

Pew Research Center 2002. "One year later New Yorkers more troubled, Washingtonians more on edge, the personal toll persists, policy opinions change". 5 September. http://people-press.org/reports/print.php

Phillips-Fein, K. 2017. *Fear City: New York's Fiscal Crisis and the Rise of Austerity Politics*. New York: Metropolitan Books.

Podair, J. 2002. *The Strike That Changed New York*. New Haven, CT: Yale University Press.

Pratt, E. 1911. *Industrial Causes of Congestion of Population in New York City* (109). Columbia University, Longmans, Green & Co.

Reagan, M. 2017. "Capital city: New York in fiscal crisis, 1966–1978". University of Washington: 2017 Reading Committee.

Reock, E. Jr. 1985. "The changing structure of New Jersey municipal government". State of New Jersey: County and Municipal Government Study Commission.

Reock, E. Jr. 2015. "Municipal charter revision in New Jersey: an inventory of change 1950–2015". Center for Government Services, Rutgers University. https://celg.rutgers.edu/sites/celg.rutgers.edu/files/documents/muni_charter_reock.pdf

Reyes, R. 2022. "The rent is too damn high!" *Daily Mail*. November 5.

Rivlin-Nadler, M. 2018. "Everything you need to know about NYC's dueling charter commissions". *Gothamist*, 10 October. https://gothamist.com/news/everything-you-need-to-know-about-nycs-dueling-charter-commissions

Research Gate 2019. Discussion Posting on Gini Index. 24 February. www.researchgate.net/post/What_does_the_value_of_the_Gini_coefficient_02876_mean

Riis, J. 2011. *How the Other Half Lives*. London: Macmillan.

Roberts, S. 2010. "Listening to (and saving) the world's languages". *New York Times*, 29 April.

Robinson, J. 2015. "Debate on global urbanisms and the nature of urban theory". International Journal of Urban and Regional Research, 21 December.

Rodriguez, C. 2013. "As Bloomberg built affordable housing, city became less affordable". *WNYC News*, 9 July.

Rose-Redwood, R. 2011. "Mythologies of the grid in the Empire City, 1811–2011". *Geographical Review* 101(3): 396–413.

Rosenbaum, E. & S. Friedman 2007. *The Housing Divide: How Generations of Immigrants Fare in New York's Housing Market*. New York: NYU Press.

Rossiter, C. 1948. *Constitutional Dictatorship*. Princeton, NJ: Princeton University Press.

Rothstein, R. 2017. *The Color of Law: A Forgotten History of How Our Government Segregated America*. New York: Liveright Publishing.

Routley, N. 2020. "Charting the last 20 years of supertall skyscrapers". *Visual Capitalist*, 13 June. www.visualcapitalist.com/charting-the-last-20-years-of-supertall-skyscrapers/

Roy, A. 2018. "Intersectional ecologies: positioning intersectionality in settings-level research". *New Directions for Child and Adolescent Development* 161: 57–74.

Rubinstein, D. 2020. "We're at war, New York faces a financial abyss". *New York Times*, 28 September.

Rudoy, C. 2021. "The inclusion of control: the diminishing diversity of Montclair, New Jersey's renters and rent control's potential to relieve pressure of longtime tenants". Unpublished Capstone Project, Hunter College, CUNY.

Rutgers University 2013. The Impact of Superstorm Sandy on New Jersey Towns Households, School of Public Affairs and Administration. Rutgers-Newark. http://spaa.newark.rutgers.edu

Salmore, B. & S. Salmore 2008. *New Jersey Politics and Government: The Suburbs Come of Age*. New Brunswick, NJ: Rutgers University Press.

Samaha, A. 2013. "Mayors Bloomberg and Giuliani oversaw NYC's segregation increase". The Village Voice, 19 August. www.villagevoice.com/2013/08/19/mayors-bloomberg-and-giuliani-oversaw-nycs-segregation-increase/

Sassen, S. 1991. *The Global City: New York, London Tokyo*. Princeton, NJ: Princeton University Press.

Sassen, S. 2007. "The global city". In D. Nugent & J. Vincent (eds), *A Companion to the Anthropology of Politics*. Oxford: Blackwell-Wiley.

Savitch, H. 1985. "Boom and bust in the New York region: Implications for government policy". Economic Prospects for the Northeast, 164.

Savitch, H. 2008. *Cities in a Time of Terror*. Armonk, NY: Sharpe.

Savitch, H. & G. Ardashev 2001. "Does terror have an urban future?" *Urban Studies* 38 (13 December): 2515–33.

Savitch, H. & C. Brown 2017. "Storms, flooding and resilience on the Jersey Shore". Woodrow Wilson Center for International Scholars.

Savitch H. & P. Kantor 2002. *Cities in the International Marketplace*. Princeton, NJ: Princeton University Press.

Savitch, H., P. Kantor & S. Vicari 2002. *Cities in the International Marketplace: The Political Economy of Urban Development in North America and Western Europe*. Princeton, NJ: Princeton University Press.

Savitch, H. & C. Perez 2016. "Regional resilience and policy transfer". Woodrow Wilson Center for International Scholars.

Savitch, H., J. Sawislak & J. Renne 2020. *Protecting South Florida*. Florida Atlantic University.

Savitch-Lew, A. 2016. "Some suspect East New York rezoning has triggered speculation". *City Limits*, 10 March. https://citylimits.org/2016/03/10/some-suspect-east-new-york-rezoning-has-triggered-speculation/

Sayles, M. 1902. "Housing conditions in Jersey City". *Annals of the American Academy of Political and Social Science* 20(1): 139–49.

Schaller, B. 2010. "New York City's congestion pricing experience and implications for road pricing acceptance in the United States". *Transport Policy* 17(4): 266–73.

Schwartz, R. *et al.* 2016a. "Study design and results of a population-based study on perceived stress following Hurricane Sandy". *Disaster Medicine and Public Health Preparedness*, 10(3): 325–32.

Schwartz, R. *et al.* 2016b. "The lasting mental health effects of Hurricane Sandy on residents of the Rockaways". *Journal of Emergency Management* 14(4): 269–79.

Schwartz, S. *et al.* 2008. "A comprehensive transportation policy for the 21st Century: a case study of congestion pricing in New York City". *NYU Environmental Law Journal* 17: 580.

Shefter, M. 1992. *Political Crisis/Fiscal Crisis: The Collapse and Revival of New York City.* New York: Columbia University Press.

Shelton, J. 2018. "The cost of affordability: Inclusionary zoning and displacement in, East New York" *Metropolitics*, 20 March: 1–6.

Sites, W. 1997. "The limits of urban regime theory: New York City under Koch, Dinkins, and Giuliani". *Urban Affairs Review* 32(4): 536–57.

Sites, W. 2003. *Remaking New York: Primitive Globalization and the Politics of Urban Community.* Minneapolis, MN: University of Minnesota Press.

Soffer, J. 2010. *Ed Koch and the Rebuilding of New York City.* New York: Columbia University Press.

State Director of Criminal Justice 1993. A Report to the Governor on the Disturbances in Crown Heights. Albany, New York.

Statista 2019. GDP of New York Metropolitan Area: 2001 to 2018 (chained to 2012 dollars). www.statista.com/statistics/183815/gdp-of-the-new-york-metro-area/#:~:text=In%202 018%2C%20the%20GDP%20of,trillion%20chained%202012%20U.S.%20dollars.&text= New%20York%20metro%20area's%20

Statista 2020. Bureau of Economic Analysis, Real Domestic Product of New York, 2000–2019.

Statista 2022. Covid Cases State by State. www.statista.com/statistics/1102807/coronavirus-covid19-cases-number-us-americans-by-state/

Stein, R. 1976. "The New York City budget: anatomy of the fiscal crisis". *FRBNY*, Winter 1975–76: 1–12.

Stein, S. 2019. *Capital City: Gentrification and the Real Estate State.* London: Verso.

Sternlieb, G. & J. Hughes 1977. "Metropolitan decline and inter regional job shifts". In R. Alcaly & D. Mermelstein (eds), *The Fiscal Crisis of American Cities*, 145–64. New York: Vintage.

Stewart, E. 2019. "Why Bill de Blasio is so hated, explained". *Vox*, 31 July. www.vox.com/policy-and-politics/2019/7/16/20694916/bill-de-blasio-2020-polls-eric-garner

Stetson, D. 1975. "Charter change would be city's 5th". *New York Times*, 6 August.

Stilton, P. 2021. "If taxes are your issue…". *New Jersey News*, 17 October. www.shorenewsnetwork. com/2021/10/17/if-taxes-are-your-issue-njs-not-for-you-murphy-says-comment-taken-out-of-context/

Stone, C. 1989. *Regime Politics: Governing Atlanta 1946–1988.* Lawrence, KS: University of Kansas Press.

Stringer, S. 2019. Affordability Index. New York City Comptroller, New York, NY. comptroller. nyc.gov/reports/affordability-index /

Stringer, S. 2020. "New York by the numbers weekly economic and fiscal outlook". New York City Comptroller, 3 August. https://comptroller.nyc.gov/newsroom/new-york-by-the-numb ers-weekly-economic-and-fiscal-outlook-no-12-august-3-2020/

Susskind, R. 2006. *The One Percent Doctrine.* New York: Simon & Schuster.

Sutton, S. 2020. "How Covid-19 made New Jersey's Phil Murphy the most powerful governor in America". *Politico*, 8 September. www.politico.com/news/2020/09/08/phil-murphy-power ful-governor-america-409522

Tampa Bay 2006. "12th largest media market now". https://web.archive.org/web/20070808072 027/http:/tampabay.org/press.asp?rls_id=991&.

Taylor, P. 2004. *World City Network: A Global Urban Analysis.* Abingdon: Routledge.

Taylor, P. *et al.* 2014. "Advanced producer service firms as strategic networks, global cities as strategic places". *Economic Geography* 90(3): 267–91.

The City 2022. https://projects.thecity.nyc/2020_03_covid-19-tracker/

Thompson, P. 1999. "Public housing in New York City". In *Housing and Community Development in New York City: Facing the Future*, 119–42.

Torres, E. 2020. "A timeline of Cuomo's and Trump's responses to coronavirus outbreak". *ABC News*, 3 April. https://abcnews.go.com/US/timeline-cuomos-trumps-responses-corona virus-outbreak/story?id=69914641

Township of Montclair 2020. Ordinance Establishing Rent Control in the Township of Montclair. 10 March. www.montclairnjusa.org/UserFiles/Servers/Server_5276204/File/Gov ernment/Mayor%20&%20Township%20Council/2020%20Meeting%20Agendas/04-07-20/ O-20-05.pdf

Union of Concerned Scientists 2018. *Underwater, Rising Seas, Chronic Floods, and the Implications for US Coastal Real Estate*. https://sealevel.climatecentral.org/research/reports/new-york-and-the-surging-sea

US Bureau of Labor Statistics. n.d. Quarterly Census of Employment and Wages, www.bls.gov/cew/about-data/data-availability.htm

US Bureau of Labor Statistics 2017. CPI Inflation Calculator. https://data.bls.gov/cgi-bin/cpicalc.pl

US Census Bureau 1864. 1860 Census: Population of the United States. Washington DC: Government Printing Office.

US Census Bureau 1895. 1890 Census: Population of the United States. Washington DC: Government Printing Office.

US Census Bureau 1902. Twelfth Census of the United States – 1900 Census Reports Volume VIII – Manufactures Part II, States and Territories. Washington DC: Government Printing Office.

US Census Bureau 1950. Census of Population and Housing, Decennial.

US Census Bureau 1960. Census of Population and Housing, Decennial.

US Census Bureau 1970. Census of Population and Housing, Decennial.

US Census Bureau 1980. Census of Population and Housing, Decennial.

US Census Bureau 1990. Census of Population and Housing, Decennial.

US Census Bureau 2018a. ACS Selected Social Characteristics, 5-Year, Table DP02.

US Census Bureau 2018b. ACS Selected Housing Characteristics, 5-Year, Table DP04.

US Census Bureau 2019a. ACS Selected Social Characteristics, 5-Year, Table DP02.

US Census Bureau 2020a. ACS Selected Social Characteristics, 5-Year, Table DP02.

US Census Bureau 2020b. Census of Population and Housing, Decennial.

US Census Bureau 2021. Population and Housing Unit Estimates, QuickFacts. County Level.

US Patent and Trademark Office 2016. Patenting in technology classes breakout by origin, US metropolitan and micropolitan areas count of 2000–2015 utility patent grants.

Van der Bly, M. 2005. "Globalization: the triumph of ambiguity". *Current Sociology* 53(6): 875–93.

Van Riper, F. 1975. "Ford to city: drop dead". *Daily News* 57(109): 1.

Varadarajan, T. 2022. "Can America's cities make a comeback?" *Wall Street Journal*, 28 May.

Viteritti, J. 1989. "The tradition of municipal reform: charter revision in historical context". *Proceedings of the Academy of Political Science* 37(3): 16–30.

Viteritti, J. 1995. "Municipal home rule and the conditions of justifiable secession". *Fordham Urban Law Journal* 23: 1.

Viteritti, J. 2014. *Summer in the City: John Lindsay, New York, and the American Dream*. Baltimore, MD: Johns Hopkins University Press.

Vogel, R. & B. Swanson. 1989. "The growth machine versus the antigrowth coalition: the battle for our communities". *Urban Affairs Quarterly* 25(1): 63–85.

Walters, C. 2021. *Not All Housing Units are Created Equal: A Report on the Relationship between Rezonings, Affordable Housing and Racial Equity*. Association for Neighborhood Housing Development.

Ward, S. 1994. "Trends in the location of corporate headquarters, 1969–1989". *Urban Affairs Quarterly* 29(3): 468–78.

Ware, L. 2021. "Plessy's legacy: the government's role in the development and perpetuation of segregated neighborhoods". *Russell Sage Foundation Journal of the Social Sciences* 7(1): 92–109.

Warner, S. 1987. *The Private City*. Philadelphia, PA: University of Pennsylvania Press.

Waters, M. & P. Kasinitz 2014. "Nativism, racism, and immigration in New York City". In N. Forner *et al.* (eds), *Immigration in New York and Amsterdam*, 143–69. New York: NYU Press.

Weber, M. 1968. *On Charisma and Institution Building*. Chicago, IL: University of Chicago Press.

Weikart, L. 2009. Follow the Money: Who Controls New York City Mayors? Albany, NY: SUNY Press.

Wiese, A. 1995. "Racial cleansing in the suburbs: suburban government, urban renewal, and segregation on Long Island, New York, 1945–1960". *Contributions in Political Science* 352: 61–70.

Wilson, J. 1967. "The bureaucracy problem". *The Public Interest* 6(3).

Winters, J. 2022. "Rent control is coming to Montclair May 9: how it'll work". *Montclair Local*, 3 May. https://montclairlocal.news/rent-control-is-coming-to-montclair-may-9-how-itll-work/

Wolf-Powers, L. 2005. "Up-zoning New York City's mixed-use neighborhoods: property-led economic development and the anatomy of a planning dilemma". *Journal of Planning Education and Research* 24(4): 379–93.

Wolman, H. *et al.* 2017. *Coping with Adversity: Regional Economic Resilience and Public*. Ithaca, NY: Cornell University Press.

Wood, R. 1961. *1400 Governments: The Political Economy of the New York Metropolitan Region*. Cambridge, MA: Harvard University Press.

Yates, D. 1977. *The Ungovernable City*. Boston, MA: MIT Press.

Zaveri, M. 2022. "Rents are roaring back in New York City". *New York Times*, 7 March.

Zukin, S. 2014. *Loft Living: Culture and Capital in Urban Change*. Brunswick, NJ: Rutgers University Press.

Index